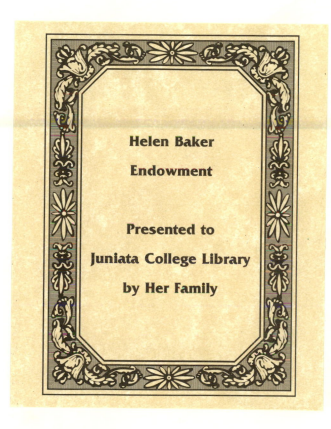

AN
OPPORTUNITY
LOST

AN OPPORTUNITY LOST

The Truman Administration
and the
Farm Policy Debate

VIRGIL W. DEAN

University of Missouri Press
Columbia and London

Library of Congress Cataloging-in-Publication Data

Dean, Virgil W.
  An opporunity lost: the Truman administration and the farm
policy debate / Virgil W. Dean.
      p.   cm.
  Summary: "Examines Charles Brannan's agricultural plan, the
farm policy debate, and Harry S. Truman's quest for a long-range
agricultural program. Assesses Truman's relationships with farmers
and with politicians and the search for a workable peacetime
program, especially as it related to the parity price foundation and
price supports"—Provided by publisher.
  Includes bibliographical references and index.
  ISBN-13: 978-0-8262-1650-2 (hard cover : alk. paper)
  ISBN-10: 0-8262-1650-1 (hard cover : alk. paper)
  1. Agriculture and state—United States—History—20th century.
I. Title.
  HD1761.D366   2006
  338.1'87309044—dc22   2005033406

Designer: Stephanie Foley
Typesetter: Phoenix Type, Inc.
Printer and binder: The Maple-Vail Book Manufacturing Group
Typefaces: Simoncini Garamond, Goudy Handtooled

*The University of Missouri Press offers its grateful acknowledgment to
an anonymous donor whose generous grant in support of the publication of outstanding dissertations has assisted us with this volume.*

For Jan

CONTENTS

Preface

On Thursday afternoon, April 12, 1945, "a load of hay" fell on an ex-farmer from Missouri, Harry S. Truman. Vice president for only three months before the death of President Franklin D. Roosevelt on this fateful spring day, Truman took the oath of office at 7:09 p.m. and became the thirty-third president of the United States. Within a month, the war in Europe was over, but the new president's problems had only just begun. The defeat of Japan, the organization of the United Nations, and the postwar reconstruction in Europe were just a few of the challenges that lay ahead. On the home front, the overriding issue was reconversion to a peacetime economy. The avoidance of sky-rocketing inflation and massive unemployment were objectives for which there were no easy policy choices. The difficult task of winning the peace, or confronting the perplexing problems of a vastly altered postwar America and world, had fallen on a man about whom most people knew very little.

The Truman administration ultimately could claim considerable success in the area of foreign policy. Under Truman's leadership, America took on the unprecedented role of world leader, accepting a global responsibility that the country had rejected in 1919. The United Nations was launched successfully only weeks after Truman's ascension and soon massive aid programs were approved by a traditionally penny-pinching Congress. Aid to Greece and Turkey, the Marshall plan, and the North Atlantic Treaty Organization for which Truman built a bipartisan coalition received hearty support. There emerged a cold war consensus that would dominate American thinking and policy in world affairs for decades to come. Obviously, there were problems and some considerable opposition, but most agreed with the president's basic assumptions and accepted the idea that America must be a bulwark of democracy against the spread of communism around the world.

On the domestic front, politics as usual was the rule of the day. Truman, who had been among President Roosevelt's most faithful supporters during the 1930s and early 1940s, sought to strengthen and extend many New Deal measures including social security, minimum wage, and farm price supports. He realized, however, that some of these programs had been none to successful before the war and that they would need significant modification to handle postwar economic realities. President Truman also had his own domestic policy agenda and, especially after his 1948 election, launched a Fair Deal program that promised to guide America into a new age of peace and prosperity.

The president's objectives for America were ambitious, and he faced weighty political obstacles. As the first chief executive to follow in the "shadow of FDR," Truman was challenged on the political left by some who could not accept the leadership of anyone other than Roosevelt, especially not that of this quintessential Missouri politico. More important, though, was the opposition from the political right, represented by a coalition of Republicans and southern Democrats who opposed Truman at almost every turn in the domestic policy area. Whether they resisted the administration because of philosophical objections to big government and excessive federal spending or because of deeply ingrained racial attitudes, this coalition was a formidable obstacle that successfully blocked most of Truman's Fair Deal initiatives.

Within the scope of this domestic program, which sought abundance and looked toward an ever-expanding American economy, agricultural policy was an indispensable component. Many still believed that general prosperity began on the farm and that the nation had an important stake in a healthy and vibrant farm economy. Thus, it is no surprise that the administration made farm policy a focal point of its domestic program along with various types of labor legislation, housing, national health care, aid to education, and civil rights. In 1949 the Brannan plan for agriculture became a cornerstone of Truman's Fair Deal agenda.

Because of this central position and its resilience as an issue of importance to many twentieth-century Americans, the farm policy dilemma deserves far more scholarly attention than it has thus far received. This is especially true with regard to the immediate postwar search for a long-range agriculture program. With its initiative—the Brannan farm plan—the Truman administration took the offensive in the effort to devise a rational policy to confront effectively the problems of an industry in the midst of a technological revolution. The effort failed and the nation missed a golden opportunity to effect a major and much needed change in U.S. agricultural policy, but the issues raised and the concepts debated remained at the heart of the farm policy debate for most of the next half century.

In addition, a study of the Brannan plan's defeat casts considerable light on the fate of the Fair Deal in general. Americans who supported the Brannan plan did so because they considered the old approach wholly inadequate and saw the administration's plan as a step toward greater social and economic equity. Those who opposed it did so because they feared excessive government spending, creeping socialism, and the regimentation of the nation's agricultural industry. Most opposed the Truman administration's initiatives in other domestic areas for similar reasons. Despite the monumental change of the past few decades, these same philosophical differences, whether rational or not, continue to frustrate efforts to come to terms with the nation's age-old social ills.

ACKNOWLEDGMENTS

If *An Opportunity Lost* succeeds in making a scholarly contribution to the vast literature on the administration of Harry S. Truman, it will do so in large part because of the support and encouragement I have received over the last two decades from many valued friends and colleagues—certainly, many more than can be mentioned here. In addition, scholars such as Alonzo L. Hamby, Allen J. Matusow, and Willard W. Cochrane, among many others, have been laboring in this field and contributing to our understanding of the Truman era for many years. I have simply tried to learn from, build on, and perhaps add to what they have already accomplished. I am certainly aware of the benefits I have derived from the comments of several anonymous readers and the editors of both of the book manuscript and the articles that preceded it in *Agricultural History, The Historian,* and the *Great Plains Quarterly.*

I also have benefited greatly from a wealth of good research material pertaining to the Truman presidency and agriculture in a number of wonderful repositories. The Records of the Office of the Secretary of Agriculture at the National Archives and Records Administration provided an abundance of information, as did the Records of the Bureau of the Budget. Various collections at the Harry S. Truman Library in Independence, Missouri, also were invaluable, as were the Clifford R. Hope Papers in the collections of the Kansas State Historical Society, my employer for most of the past two decades, and the George D. Aiken Papers in the Bailey/Howe Library at the University of Vermont.

Special thanks are due the above-mentioned institutions, as well as the libraries of the University of Kansas, and to the many helpful professionals who provided much valuable assistance. Dennis Bilger and Randy Sowell, archivists at the Truman Library, and James Rush of the civil reference branch of the National Archives were especially helpful. My friends and colleagues in the Library and Archives Division of the Kansas State Historical Society, past and present, are too numerous to mention by name, but they deserve and have my respect and gratitude.

Since this project began during my graduate school days, I also would like to acknowledge the support and encouragement I received from many people in the Department of History at the University of Kansas: the office staff, the faculty, and my fellow graduate students. First among these cherished friends and colleagues was my graduate adviser and true mentor, the late Donald R. McCoy, a distinguished professor and well-known scholar of the American presidency and the Truman era. Don provided invaluable guidance, encouragement, and occasional friendly prodding during those early days and was principally responsible for my acquiring gainful, if not lucrative, employment in the field of history and for my completion of the degree program in a relatively timely fashion. I will always count it a high honor and distinct privilege to have had the opportunity to work and to study under his direction.

Finally it is a pleasure to have this opportunity to acknowledge and thank an equally great scholar and fine gentleman, Professor Robert H. Ferrell, who took an interest in my nearly dormant book manuscript and in me and introduced us both to Beverly Jarrett, director and editor-in-chief of the University of Missouri Press. It has certainly been a delightful experience working with Bev and her wonderful staff at the press these past months.

Over the last few years I have had the opportunity to publish four related articles in three fine scholarly journals: *Agricultural History, The Historian,* and *Great Plains Quarterly.* I would like to thank the publishers of these journals for allowing me to use portions of the following articles here: "Why Not the Brannan Plan?" *Agricultural History* 70 (Spring 1996): 268–82 (chapter 6), and "Charles F. Brannan and the Rise and Fall of Truman's 'Fair Deal' for Farmers," *Agricultural History* 69 (Winter 1995): 28–53 (chapter 5), by permission of the University of California Press; "The Farm Policy Debate of 1949–1950: Plains State Reaction to the Brannan Plan," *Great Plains Quar-*

terly 13 (Winter 1993): 33–46 (chapters 5 and 6), by permission of the Center for Great Plains Studies; and "Farm Policy and Truman's Campaign of 1948," *The Historian* 55 (Spring 1993): 501–16 (chapters 4 and 5), by permission of Blackwell Publishing. Blackwell also kindly authorized my use of quotations in chapter 9 from Willard W. Cochrane's important article, "The Need to Rethink Agricultural Policy in General and to Perform Some Radical Surgery on Commodity Programs in Particular," *American Journal of Agricultural Economics* 67 (December 1985): 1002–1009.

AN
OPPORTUNITY
LOST

1

INTRODUCTION

Agriculture was a prominent item on the agenda of President Harry S. Truman when he addressed the nation in his second State of the Union message on January 6, 1947. Truman, a former Missouri farmer and merchant, had faced firsthand the economic recession that followed the Great War, and he reminded the country of that era's farm crisis. For Truman, it was vital that America meet "the problems which we failed to meet after the first World War."[1] Three and a half months later, the United States Senate and House of Representatives began an exhaustive investigation of the farm situation to determine the proper course for American agricultural policy in the post–World War II era. The problems facing those concerned about the welfare of the American farm were complex. Their search for a workable peacetime program, especially as it related to price supports for agricultural commodities, and the failure to come to terms with the issues while standing on the threshold of this new age is the focal point of this inquiry.

More than a half-century later, we know that agriculture persists as a perplexing problem that continually defies solution and remains among the country's major political, economic, and social issues. This was most definitely the case in the late 1940s as farm leaders initiated a long-range policy search. It was uppermost in the mind of President Truman's secretary of agriculture, Charles F. Brannan, when he

1. Truman, *Public Papers of the Presidents of the United States: Harry S. Truman, 1945–1950,* 8. See also Richard S. Kirkendall, "Harry S. Truman: A Missouri Farmer in the Golden Age," 467.

introduced the so-called Brannan plan for agriculture—a plan the administration hoped would prove politically, socially, and economically palatable. For a host of reasons, the Truman-Brannan quest for a solution to the farm problem ended in failure, rejected by a Congress that encompassed a myriad of notions about how best to resolve this old bugaboo.

A partial explanation for the muddle lies in the very nature of the issue. The farm problem was and is an enigma—a complex puzzle of many pieces. As Congressman Clifford R. Hope (R-KS) observed in 1949, it was, more accurately, "thirty-five or forty farm problems."[2] The problem is different not only for farmers from one commodity to another, but also for farmers within one commodity from region to region. Wheat growers and cotton producers, for example, often find that their interests are not equally served by a given policy or program because of disparate circumstances. Livestock producers and feed-grain farmers may conflict because the former will often benefit from low market prices for feed grain. These and other differences, as well as the often discordant interests and opinions of processors and consumers, compound the problem and complicate the solution.

From the beginning of what became a long and frequently intense and controversial search for a policy that everyone hoped would provide permanent prosperity for American agriculture, President Truman's administration was deeply and continuously involved. Before looking at the players, and turning to this particular phase of the contest, however, it is important to understand the game. It is instructive to look briefly at the origin of the problem or problems. What obstacles confronted the American farmer in the decades following the First World War? How were they different than the problems of earlier periods? Why were so many, well-intentioned executive officials, members of Congress, and farm leaders unable to find a solution to the industry's afflictions? And, even more to the point, what was the nature of America's post-World War II farm problem, and why, at a time of

2. Hope to John Davenport, June 3, 1949, Finder file, Clifford Hope Papers, collection 50, Library and Archives Division, Kansas State Historical Society (hereafter cited as FF, Hope Papers). My understanding of the issues and of the role played by the Kansas congressman during his thirty-year stint in the U.S. Congress benefited greatly from conversations with Clifford Hope Jr. and from the reading of his *Quiet Courage: Kansas Congressman Clifford R. Hope.*

general agricultural prosperity, were so many farm protagonists beginning to search for a new remedy?

Like President Truman, most historians and economists agree that World War I was a pivotal point in the history of American agriculture. It must be remembered, however, that the nation's farmers had experienced some dramatic changes before the war as a result of what has been called the "first agricultural revolution." Characterized by the mid-nineteenth-century "change from manpower to animal power" and the application of mechanical farm implements, this revolution resulted in a rapid increase in individual productivity and, in its later stages, the precipitous decline in the percentage of the population engaged in farming.[3] By 1920, the total rural population had slipped just below the 50 percent mark, and the percentage of the population working in agriculture had dropped to twenty-seven (13.4 million). The actual number of farmers began to decline as well, and the trend toward fewer but larger farms cultivated by fewer farmers commenced. In 1940 employment stood at 17 percent of the total on 5.8 million farms.[4]

Despite their numerical decline, farmers continued to wield political and emotional influence far in excess of their actual strength. The explanation for this agricultural ascendancy is at least twofold: first, the tradition of agrarianism was, and to an extent still is, pervasive in the American psyche; and, second, rural America enjoyed a disproportionate amount of political power before the U.S. Supreme Court's "one man, one vote" rulings of the 1960s.[5] The former issue will be discussed later, and the latter is relatively self-explanatory. Suffice it to say that by the 1940s, nearly twenty years before the high court mandated the equalization of legislative and congressional districts, policy makers had recognized the disparity. Farm leaders knew that

3. Wayne D. Rasmussen, "The Impact of Technological Change on American Agriculture, 1862–1962," 578.

4. Walter W. Wilcox, Willard W. Cochrane, and Robert W. Herdt, *Economics of American Agriculture*, 5.

5. Grant McConnell, *The Decline of Agrarian Democracy*, 12. McConnell defined the agrarian tradition as the belief that agriculture was the only truly productive endeavor. The philosophy dates back at least to Thomas Jefferson and had a significant impact on late nineteenth-century Populism as well as on twentieth-century developments (*Baker v. Carr*, 369 U.S. 186 [1962] and *Wesberry v. Sanders*, 376 U.S. 1 [1964]). See also Joseph G. LaPalombara, "Pressure, Propaganda, and Political Action in the Election of 1950," 300.

an urban revolt had to be avoided and that consumer concerns must be considered in the formulation of long-range agricultural policy.[6]

Meanwhile, in the face of this overall farm population decline, production continued its steady climb as farm labor productivity rose sharply during the decades following the First World War. As was the case throughout the economy during the 1920s, American farms experienced dramatic gains in their efficiency of production, reducing the number of people needed in agricultural employment and greatly increasing the out-migration of the rural population and the size of the average farm unit.[7]

These general trends would seem to indicate that those people who remained active in the industry stood to gain financially from its transformation. Instead, "the general drift of income in farming relative to income in industry was down" during the two decades after 1919.[8] The unfavorable per capita income position of the farm population and the disparity in farm purchasing power was the result of three main factors: (1) a large natural increase in the farm population that nearly offset the net migration off the farm; (2) an increased supply of farm products resulting from the application of advanced technology; and (3) a loss of many overseas markets that was not offset by significant increases in domestic demand. During the interwar period, the average net income of individuals engaged in farming remained consistently below (less than half) the wage incomes of nonagricultural workers. Farm incomes rose dramatically as a result of the Second World War but continued to lag well behind those of the nonfarm sector: $1,735 compared to $2,900 by the end of the decade. The disparity continued into the 1950s, with the question of parity price (and income) remaining the focus of the farm policy debate.[9]

6. Charles M. Hardin, "The Politics of Agriculture in the United States," 576.

7. Theodore W. Schultz, *Agriculture in an Unstable Economy,* 86; Wilcox, Cochrane, and Herdt, *Economics of American Agriculture,* 5, 293; Gladys L. Baker, Wayne D. Rasmussen, Vivian Wiser, and Jane M. Porter, *Century of Service: The First 100 Years of the United States Department of Agriculture,* 371; Ingolf Vogeler, *The Myth of the Family Farm: Agribusiness Dominance of U.S. Agriculture,* 4.

8. Schultz, *Agriculture in an Unstable Economy,* 102, 30.

9. Walter W. Wilcox and Willard W. Cochrane, *Economics of American Agriculture,* 361.

The statistics and trends on the agricultural landscape during the decades following the First World War only begin to tell the story of what became known in the 1920s as the farm problem. In 1947 President Truman expressed a widely held view of the earlier farm crisis. According to his interpretation, the problem was essentially one of markets. "In the early twenties," the president explained, "the Nation failed to maintain outlets for the new productive capacity of our agricultural plant. It failed to provide means to protect the farmer while he adjusted his acreage to peacetime demands. . . . Farm production stayed up while demand and prices fell, in contrast with industry where prices stayed up and output declined. Farm surpluses piled up, and disaster followed."[10]

This presidential explanation of the post-World War I problem in agriculture is rather brief and simplistic, but without question the farm situation in the early 1920s was disastrous. Efforts to deal with the crisis revealed a dramatic change in the nature of farm problems and ultimately led to a fundamental change in the role of the government in agriculture.[11] The government, which heretofore had dealt almost exclusively with helping and encouraging farmers to increase their production, now confronted the issues of overproduction and surplus that were to emerge as recurring factors in the troubled farm situation; this was the new era's bugbear.[12]

10. Truman, *Public Papers of the President, 1947,* 7; Murray R. Benedict, *Farm Policies of the United States, 1790–1950: A Study of Their Origins and Developments,* 165; Henry C. Wallace, *Our Debt and Duty to the Farmer,* 127.

11. James H. Shideler, *Farm Crisis, 1919–1923;* Theodore Saloutos, *The American Farmer and the New Deal,* 3; George Soule, *Prosperity Decade: From War to Depression: 1917–1929,* 78–87, 121.

12. America's shift from a debtor to a creditor nation, the structural change in the nation's economy that created an "inelastic demand" in relation to price for most farm commodities, and changing dietary habits partly in response to wartime propaganda also must be considered (see Saloutos, *American Farmer and the New Deal,* 4, 9; Soule, *Prosperity Decade,* 234; Earl O. Heady, *A Primer on Food, Agriculture, and Public Policy,* 38). The U.S., according to Heady, reached its "mature stage" of economic growth about 1920, and producers began to experience a "farm price squeeze." Demand for food in the U.S. came to depend primarily on population increases, while demand for nonfarm products increased with per capita income. By bidding up the "prices for nonfarm goods and services, the consumer also bids or keeps up the cost of steel, labor, petroleum, and other materials that produce luxury goods. Consequently, the cost of tractors, lumber, fuel, fertilizer, and other cost items of the farm is kept up." For

Throughout this decade of general prosperity and farm depression, spokespeople for farmers searched for a solution to a perplexing dilemma. Since the notion that farmers should produce at something less than their full capacity was sacrilege to many, policy efforts usually focused on marketing. Farm leaders became increasingly aware that the application of new technology and steady increases in production were providing benefits to the consumer but not equally providing benefits to the producer. Recognizing that their problems were marketwide, farmers looked to the federal government.[13]

Although a change in the nature of federal farm policy would not come overnight, increased concern about the problem inspired considerable debate on the nature of American agriculture and attracted the attention of economists, farm leaders, and politicians throughout the country. The Republican administrations of the 1920s emphasized the traditional issues and solutions that finally had gained currency in many farm circles: cooperative marketing, improvements in government credit assistance to farmers, effective tariff protection, and freight rate adjustment.[14] Nevertheless, both Secretary of Agriculture Henry C. Wallace and Henry C. Taylor, head of the newly created Bureau of Agricultural Economics (BAE), concerned themselves with more radical efforts to assist farmers in gaining their fair share of the national income. Wallace and Taylor launched an agricultural adjustment program that was an informational effort to encourage farmers to make their own adjustments to bring production into line with the market demand; but congressional efforts remained focused on the cooperative solution.[15]

government programs to increase production, see Luther Tweeten, *Foundations of Farm Policy,* 343.

13. Willard W. Cochrane, *The Development of American Agriculture: A Historical Analysis,* 277.

14. Donald R. McCoy, *Coming of Age: The United States during the 1920s and 1930s,* 77; Chester C. Davis, "The Development of Agricultural Policy since the End of the World War," 297; Wayne C. Rohrer and Louis H. Douglas, *The Agrarian Transition in America: Dualism and Change,* 91; Arthur Capper, *The Agricultural Bloc,* 10, 56, 64–81.

15. Harry C. McDean, "Professionalism, Policy, and Farm Economists in the Early Bureau of Agricultural Economics," 64; Shideler, *Farm Crisis, 1919–1923,* 135; "Capper-Volstead Cooperative Marketing Act of 1922," in Wayne D. Rasmussen, ed., *Agriculture in the United States: A Documentary History,* 3:

Agriculture's legislative victories during the 1920s were in large part the responsibility of the newly organized congressional farm bloc, a relatively conservative alliance of southern and western senators who had as their unifying philosophy a strong commitment to agrarianism. According to Kansas senator Arthur Capper, one of the bloc's principal leaders, the group believed that "if you help the farmer the farmer will take care of the Nation."[16] Capper further explained that farm bloc congressmen recognized that "American welfare depends upon the land and upon a permanent and prosperous agriculture"; "that national prosperity is dependent primarily upon agricultural prosperity and that unless that third of our population who live upon the farms prospers the Nation cannot have a continued growth and development."[17]

Farmers did not sit idly by during this period of hardship, waiting on others to come to their rescue. As the farm crisis deepened, agricultural interest groups and lobbies arose to assert their influence for particular policies. Early in this century, the Patrons of Husbandry (National Grange), the oldest and most conservative of the farm organizations, was joined on the national level by the National Farmers Educational and Cooperative Union (NFU), the heir of the old alliance movement. In contrast to the Grange and in keeping with its derivation, the Farmers Union soon became identified as the most radical of the farm organizations despite its adherence to the philosophy of agrarianism and early emphasis on self-help.[18] Championing the same basic solutions, a third farm organization, destined to become the largest and most powerful, emerged from the Great War. The American Farm Bureau Federation (AFBF), organized nationally in 1919, sought to give farmers a collective voice. Its national convention adopted a traditional program that included a call for effective cooperative

2153; Capper, *Agricultural Bloc,* 94; Wilcox and Cochrane, *Economics of American Agriculture,* 467.

16. Homer E. Socolofsky, *Arthur Capper: Publisher, Politician, and Philanthropist,* 153; John D. Black, *Parity, Parity, Parity,* 11.

17. Capper, *Agricultural Bloc,* 3–4. See also George W. Norris, "The Farmers' Situation, A National Danger," 9.

18. John A. Crampton, *The National Farmers Union: Ideology of a Pressure Group,* 4; Theodore Saloutos and John D. Hicks, *Agricultural Discontent in the Middle West, 1900–1939,* 219–21; William P. Tucker, "Populism Up-to-Date," 198; Shideler, *Farm Crisis, 1919–1923,* 10.

marketing and government regulation, but not ownership, of inter-state corporations.[19] Although these organizations and others, includ-ing a number for single commodities, had little new to offer in the way of ideas for a constructive and innovative approach to farm policy, their emergence and the creation of the nonpartisan farm bloc in Congress would be extremely important for the future of farm poli-tics. "Agriculture's voice in political affairs," wrote James H. Shideler, "acquired a new clarity and power as farmers developed a group sen-sitivity and gave hints of voting solidarity."[20]

The most important legislative effort of the 1920s was embodied in the Peek-Johnson plan, later to become the core of the famous McNary-Haugen bill. The objective was equality for agriculture; the underlying philosophy was parity—popularized for the first time dur-ing a decade-long debate. In essence, acceptance of this all-important concept signaled a general recognition of the disparity that existed between the prices farmers paid for goods and those they received for the goods they sold. As Murray R. Benedict concluded, "the McNary-Haugen crusade laid the foundation for a changed attitude toward agriculture," particularly with regard to the role of the fed-eral government. Parity was "equated with justice and fairness," and it became a permanent feature of the agriculture debate.[21]

19. Christiana McFadyen Campbell, *The Farm Bureau and the New Deal: A Study of the Making of National Farm Policy, 1933–1940,* 3–9. From its inception as a support organization for county agents, the farm bureau movement, and later the AFBF, enjoyed a quasi-governmental connection with the USDA and state agricultural colleges—a relationship that was understandably resented by the other farm organizations.

20. Shideler, *Farm Crisis, 1919–1923,* 3; Hardin, "Politics of Agriculture," 575. Not everyone has been positive about the rise of the AFBF. According to Milo Reno, president of the Iowa Farmers Union, the AFBF was "born a bastard of the Railroads and the Chamber of Commerce. No farmer had anything to do with organizing [it]" (quoted in Crampton, *National Farmers Union,* 13. See also McConnell, *Decline of Agrarian Democracy,* 31–56). For an excellent analysis of the evolution of the NFU's philosophy of agrarian liberalism, its contribution to the "transformation of liberalism" during the 1930s, and the widening gulf be-tween NFU and AFBF positions, see Michael W. Flamm, "The National Farmers Union and the Evolution of Agrarian Liberalism, 1937–1946," 54, 55.

21. Shideler, *Farm Crisis, 1919–1923,* 202, 272; Benedict, *Farm Policies of the United States,* 212, 226, 238; Gilbert C. Fite, *George N. Peek and the Fight for Farm Parity,* 38; Soule, *Prosperity Decade,* 229; Cochrane, *Development of* Coy, *Calvin Coolidge: The Quiet President,* 276, 308–10, 325–27; Darwin N. Kelley,

Presidential vetoes—executed by Calvin Coolidge in 1927 and 1928—prevented the codification of McNary-Haugenism; nevertheless, when Franklin D. Roosevelt succeeded to the presidency in 1933, the stage was set for a radical policy departure. Although the New Deal borrowed most of its farm policy ideas and many of its spokesmen from the earlier period, the national depression had reached a critical point by March 1933, and many believed that action of any kind was necessary if the country was to survive. For agriculture this meant the passage of the Agricultural Adjustment Act of 1933 and the creation of the Agricultural Adjustment Administration.[22]

Although the AAA did not represent a sharp philosophical break even with the previous administration of Herbert Hoover, it emphasized acreage reduction as the best solution to the price problems of the producers of basic commodities: wheat, corn, hogs, cotton, tobacco, rice, and milk. Some administration programs continued to promote production and marketing solutions, but the AAA, "more than any other" New Deal agency, "focused on restriction of output for the sake of driving up prices."[23] Benefits from the program were only paid to producers who signed acreage restriction contracts and thereby, in theory, agreed to reduce production. As agricultural historian Gilbert C. Fite explained, "Benefit payments, raised by processing taxes, were to be the rewards for farmer co-operation in reducing plantings." Provisions for direct payments of this type were "the most revolutionary principles incorporated in the AAA," and many were

---

"The McNary-Haugen Bills, 1924–1928: An Attempt to Make the Tariff Effective for Farm Products," 170; Kenneth Finegold, "From Agrarianism to Adjustment: The Political Origins of New Deal Agricultural Policy," 1; David E. Hamilton, *From New Day to New Deal: American Farm Policy from Hoover to Roosevelt, 1928–1933,* 19–25.

22. Benedict, *Farm Policies of the United States,* 284; Van L. Perkins, "The AAA and the Politics of Agriculture: Agricultural Policy Formulation in the Fall of 1933," 220; Arthur M. Schlesinger Jr., *The Age of Roosevelt: The Coming of the New Deal;* Gertrude Almy Slichter, "Franklin D. Roosevelt and the Farm Problem, 1929–1932," 238; Wayne D. Rasmussen, Gladys L. Baker, and James G. Ward, *A Short History of Agricultural Adjustment, 1933–1975,* 2–3.

23. Broadus Mitchell, *Depression Decade: From New Era through New Deal, 1929–1941,* 185–86. See also Schultz, *Agriculture in an Unstable Economy,* 136–40; Benedict, *Farm Policies of the United States,* 284; Edward L. Schapsmeier and Frederick H. Schapsmeier, *Henry A. Wallace of Iowa: The Agrarian Years, 1910–1940,* 166.

not ready to accept "acreage curtailment, except perhaps as a temporary expedient."[24]

Those economists who resisted, or only reluctantly accepted, the administration's policy of production control as the solution to the farm depression espoused an underconsumption theory. In his influential 1945 study, *Agriculture in an Unstable Economy,* Theodore W. Schultz was critical of the general trend in policy and theory that emphasized cutting agricultural production as business and industry declined. The answer, he concluded, was for both sectors to "produce more and not less, for to do otherwise is to curtail the wealth of the nation." The problems of agriculture were caused not by overproduction but by underconsumption of agricultural commodities. Agricultural production should be kept steady during periods of economic downturn, and, rather than a price support program, government would be advised to provide a system of "compensatory payments to farmers to sustain farm income," thus allowing commodities to "move readily into internal and external trade."[25]

Benefiting from the experience of the depression and war years, Schultz was espousing a permanent and integrated approach. In 1933 the administration was reacting to the emergency.[26] The major policy goal of its first Agricultural Adjustment Act was to help producers of the basic commodities to realize parity, understood as the restoration of purchasing power equivalent to that which the farmer had enjoyed during the base period of 1909–1914. The formula used to determine the level of support was a complex one; but, in its simplest terms, parity was the ratio of equality between the prices received by farmers for the commodities sold and the prices farmers paid for the goods and services they purchased. The arbitrary base period was used in tabulating the parity ratio so that it could be determined in light of

24. Gilbert C. Fite, "Farmer Opinion and the Agricultural Adjustment Act, 1933," 658–65.

25. Schultz, *Agriculture in an Unstable Economy,* 136–37. Schultz's ideas (e.g., the theory of abundance and full employment), which would have much influence on the thinking of Charles F. Brannan and other USDA economists, also were reflected in the new liberalism of the postwar decades.

26. According to Mitchell, administration proposals were sold to Congress and the nation as emergency measures, but "there is abundant evidence that all along they intended it to be the basis of long-time policy" (*Depression Decade,* 187).

the constant fluctuation of prices. Prices for eligible commodities were supported at a given percentage of parity (generally, 52 to 75 percent) using acreage allotments, marketing agreements, government purchases, and price-sustaining loans on stored commodities.[27]

To accomplish its main goal and to provide some measure of relief to the needy in rural America, the New Deal administration launched numerous programs that were to establish the underpinnings to the farm debate for years to come. These programs included soil conservation, rural electrification, and crop insurance, in addition to measures for farm credit adjustment. Also crucial to long-range policy was the activity of the Commodity Credit Corporation (CCC), established by executive order on October 17, 1933, to administer the government's crop loan and storage programs. Adopting the widely accepted philosophy of the cooperative movement, but adding the power and financial resources of the national government on an unprecedented scale, the CCC attempted to raise farm prices on storable commodities by removing the surplus from the market when prices fell below certain levels. Producers who chose to take advantage of this program could receive nonrecourse loans from the corporation to permit them to hold crops off the market at times of low prices. The loans used the commodities as collateral, giving the farmer a certain percentage of the current market value. If the borrower chose not to reclaim the crop, presumably because prices did not increase to a level to make this profitable, the government's corporation was obligated to keep the stored commodity in full satisfaction of the loan.[28]

27. Edward L. Schapsmeier and Frederick H. Schapsmeier, *Encyclopedia of American Agricultural History,* 261; *Congressional Digest* 29 (March 1950): 73; Lauren Soth, *Farm Troubles,* 29; John L. Shover, "Populism in the Nineteen-Thirties: The Battle for the AAA," 18; Theodore Saloutos, "The New Deal and Farm Policy in the Great Plains," 346; Saloutos, *American Farmer and the New Deal,* 255; Saloutos, "New Deal Agriculture Policy: An Evaluation," 397; Fite, "Farmer Opinion," 669; Theodore Rosenof, "The Economic Ideas of Heny A. Wallace, 1933–1948," 145; Edward L. Schapsmeier and Frederick H. Schapsmeier, "Farm Policy from FDR to Eisenhower: Southern Democrats and the Politics of Agriculture," 354.

28. Rasmussen, ed., *Agriculture in the United States,* 3:2263; Rasmussen, Baker, and Ward, *Short History of Agricultural Adjustment,* 3; Mitchell, *Depression Decade,* 193. The remarkable continuity in the debate and the policy instruments that have marked the long history of U.S. farm policy can be observed in Bruce L. Gardner, *The Economics of Agricultural Policies,* 55–56.

In this way, CCC loans, tied to the parity price formula, established minimum prices for many farm products. Serious problems and prohibitive costs obviously would result from these procedures if methods for controlling production were unsuccessful—a development that did in fact plague the administration on numerous occasions before the war. In no small way, overindulgent lawmakers, inclined toward inordinate legislative tinkering, exacerbated the situation.

The secretary of agriculture initially had wide discretionary authority in the setting of loan rates; in other words, support levels were flexible. He determined and announced the specific level (between 52 and 75 percent of parity) for any given commodity in light of current supplies and anticipated demand. But Congress began to mandate levels of support in 1938, thus eliminating much of the secretary's discretionary power, and in 1941 lawmakers fixed rates for all supported commodities at 85 percent of parity. With loans mandatory at high rates and efforts at production control generally ineffective, explained Schultz, "the CCC had accumulated excessively large stocks as loan collateral and was in a critical position at the time the war started. . . . The war rescued the CCC, by converting into valuable assets (except for cotton) the huge inventories that the CCC was instrumental in accumulating."[29]

Despite its many shortcomings—administrators, for example, found it impossible to take land out of cultivation fast enough to keep pace with production increasing technological improvements and farmers' natural propensity to raise more—the New Deal legacy with respect to American agriculture is immeasurable. Perhaps most significant was the gospel of parity prices that emerged in the 1920s and became a foundation stone in the Roosevelt farm program. In addition to high mandatory supports that threatened to bankrupt the system, the most important part of the legacy is that it made the federal government an indispensable and accepted part of American farm life. It also initiated a policy of government price tampering that would be at the heart of farm policy from that point on; and, as economist

29. Schultz, *Agriculture in an Unstable Economy,* 175–76. See also Michael W. Schuyler, *The Dread of Plenty: Agricultural Relief Activities of the Federal Government in the Middle West, 1933–1939;* Walter W. Wilcox, *The Farmer and the Second World War,* 12.

Willard W. Cochrane explained in 1979, the Agricultural Adjustment Act of 1938 (second AAA) "remains the organic legislation, amended from time to time, under which many farm programs of price and income support are administered to this day."[30]

When FDR replaced "Dr. New Deal" with "Dr. Win-the-War," the American farmer's condition was altered drastically, and the farm problem went into remission. Demand for farm products was greatly increased, and, to ensure an adequate supply, the government turned to relatively high, guaranteed price supports on basic commodities to encourage production. In May 1941 Congress decided, in light of the price-freezing efforts of the recently created Office of Price Administration (OPA), that legislation also was needed to guarantee farmers some benefit from increased demand and wartime spending. Thus, support levels were raised and made rigid (mandatory or fixed), and coverage was expanded to encourage the production of certain crops thought vital to the war effort.

Initially, the only affected commodities were wheat, corn, cotton, rice, and tobacco that were to be supported at 85 percent of parity. In a matter of weeks, however, thanks to Congressman Henry B. Steagall of Alabama, the list began to grow. The Steagall Amendment, attached to a bill extending the charter of the CCC, expanded the system of government supports to include nonbasic commodities (the so-called Steagall commodities): milk, butterfat, chickens, eggs, turkeys, hogs, dry peas, soybeans for oil, flaxseed for oil, peanuts for oil, American-Egyptian cotton, sweet potatoes, and potatoes. On October 2, 1942, subsequent legislation increased the loan rate to 90 percent on basics (which now included peanuts) and nonbasics. Anticipating a need for protection during the period of postwar reconversion, Congress made provision for these guarantees to extend two years beyond the end of the war.[31]

---

30. Cochrane, *Development of American Agriculture,* 142; Rasmussen, ed., *Agriculture in the United States,* 3:2245–2323, 2369–2427. The Soil Conservation and Domestic Allotment Act of 1936 should also be considered as part of this New Deal foundation.

31. Rasmussen, Baker, and Ward, *Short History of Agricultural Adjustment,* 7–8; Schapsmeier and Schapsmeier, "Farm Policy from FDR to Eisenhower," 361–62.

The wartime situation and immediate postwar demand made it relatively easy for the government to maintain this program of price supports. More important, the popularity of the price support guarantees during the war changed the nature of the farm debate. "Government guarantees of minimum prices," explained economists Walter W. Wilcox and Cochrane, "became increasingly popular with farmers and opposition to the government's assuming this role declined." The postwar debate focused on levels of price supports and not on "*the question of whether price guarantees to farmers was an appropriate governmental function.*" The latter question had, for the most part, "*ceased to be an issue*"; and "we entered the postwar period with government price supports as the central part of the farm program."[32] Having settled the viability issue, antagonists concentrated almost exclusively on appropriate levels of support. A few advocates called for government support at 100 percent parity, but the most common point of contention occurred between proponents of a fixed 90 percent of parity and those who favored a flexible support system.

This change in policy focus did not go unobserved by experts. Theodore Schultz attempted to attract attention to the potential problems that could result from a farm policy based on an historical parity price formula. Schultz's proposals for an alternate farm policy approach, including compensatory payments, were unquestionably influential in the formulation of the Brannan plan and will be discussed in more detail later. Schultz insisted there was a need to channel resources out of agriculture because of the basic changes that had taken place in the industry. Government programs designed to address the underemployment problem in agriculture, for example, could be of great significance. But, Schultz insisted,

> To stabilize farm income by a system of price supports, or to endeavor to do so, interferes with internal and external trade and disregards the basic function of relative prices in guiding production and in directing products into consumption channels. Nevertheless, Federal statutes now in effect give it impor-

32. Wilcox and Cochrane, *Economics of American Agriculture,* 543 (emphasis theirs); Tom G. Hall, "The Aiken Bill, Price Supports and the Wheat Farmer in 1948," 14; Allen J. Matusow, *Farm Policies and Politics in the Truman Years,* 120. "By 1945," explained Matusow, "defense of the old program had become a new conservatism."

tant weight, and it may easily come to dominate Federal farm programs during the early postwar period.[33]

Schultz of course was correct, and the difficulties that arose because
of this new focus were compounded by a revolution in the application of knowledge and technology that exacerbated the old bugbear—
price-depressing farm surpluses. The second major effort of the century to redirect U.S. farm policies followed the Second World War
and took place during the early years of what Wayne D. Rasmussen
aptly characterized as the second agricultural revolution—"the change
from animal power to mechanical power and the adaptation of chem-
istry to agricultural production." The implications of this transformation were only beginning to be realized as farm leaders and legislators
began to formulate a policy for the postwar era; a change in policy
"recognizing the impact of the technological revolution" was critical.[34]
The executive leadership for this postwar policy search was to be
provided by the administration of Harry S. Truman. During that turbulent period in the wake of the Allied victory, agriculture was only
one segment of the economy that demanded the administration's attention, but it was a vital one. For many Americans, including the
president, who still held to the old philosophy that if this basic industry did not prosper all would suffer, prosperity on the farm was key
to the overall economic health of the nation. The New Deal's broad
programs for elevating the "social and economic position of farmers
rather than simply [striving to] attain stated price objectives" were important, and many were continued.[35] Truman believed these policies
were "sound," and that a firm foundation had been laid, but there
was a need for government action to expand and to extend the base
of the programs.[36] The new president continually emphasized soil

33. Schultz, *Agriculture in an Unstable Economy,* 221.
34. Rasmussen, "Impact of Technological Change," 578, 591. See also Dennis S. Nordin and Roy V. Scott, *From Prairie Farmer to Entrepreneur: The Transformation of Midwestern Agriculture,* 64–68.
35. Saloutos, "New Deal Agricultural Policy," 394; Saloutos, "New Deal and
Farm Policy," 354.
36. Truman, *Memoirs by Harry S. Truman: Years of Trial and Hope,* vol. 2,
262–63. Truman was aware that some rural residents had not benefited from
recent prosperity. For them, the government had to act to improve such things
as rural medical care, schools, roads, and electrical service.

conservation, rural electrification, and aid to America's poorest farmers; but government price support policy was the main focus of attention and point of controversy.

Concern with the nature of that postwar agriculture policy emerged early in 1945. Southern Democrats and many Republicans launched an assault against the authority of the OPA to ensure farmers some benefit from increased demand. When these efforts proved fruitless, Congressman Stephen Pace (D-GA) tried to force a modernization of the parity formula to include labor costs on the farm. This effort also failed, in large part because then Secretary of Agriculture Clinton P. Anderson, who believed wartime demand would soon end and result in damaging surpluses, opposed any action at this time that was likely to increase production incentives.[37]

The Democrat controlled Congress did, however, muster bipartisan support for a bill introduced by the chairman of the House Committee on Agriculture, John W. Flannagan (D-VA), establishing a federal school lunch program. In addition to its obvious social function, it promised to provide an outlet for surplus farm commodities.[38] Congress also turned its attention to changes in the Rural Electrification Administration (REA), the Reciprocal Trade Agreement program, the farm credit system, and future price support programs.

In June 1945, Congressman Hope, the ranking Republican on the House agricultural committee, outlined some of his concerns: these misgivings would crop up repeatedly when the debate intensified a few years later. Hope was "not entirely satisfied" with the parity formula, which he considered quite "arbitrary," because it was based on a price relationship that existed in a past period when it was assumed that farm and nonfarm prices were in proper balance. Hope thought it "difficult to make out a case for using the same price relationship now in view of the great changes which have taken place, both in agriculture and industry since the 1909–1914 period." The congressman believed it entirely possible that a better formula could be devised, but

37. Schapsmeier and Schapsmeier, "Farm Policy," 364; Anderson to Dan Burross, November 19, 1945, Alphabetical Correspondence file, Clinton P. Anderson Papers, Harry S. Truman Library (hereafter cited as Anderson Papers).

38. Hope to Esther E. Voohies, May 22, 1945; to J. Frank Grimes, May 16, 1945; to Margaret Justin, May 25, 1945; for comments on OPA, to C. E. Hadley, May 19, 1945, FF, Hope Papers.

he was troubled by the government "control and regimentation" that seemed inevitable if farmers were guaranteed a "desirable price level." "I am satisfied that farmers don't want this," he continued,

> but more than that, I grow more fearful every day of the future of our country if we continue along the line of our present trend toward fixing prices and monopolistic practices in every field. . . . I feel that the final solution of the farm problem does not lie in that direction. Rather, it lies in the restoration of free enterprise in industry and labor.
> . . . It may be that farmers will have to accept regimentation and price-fixing and limitation of competition as their lot but if they do it will be to their detriment, I am sure.
> There isn't any question but what we can through governmental action maintain any price level we want to on agricultural products but, of course, along with it there will have to be controls over production and marketing which will be more rigorous and intensive as the sought-after price level advances. This may be the answer to the farm problem but at this time it is not to me a satisfactory answer.[39]

The Truman administration, almost from day one, also was obliged to give some thought to postwar agricultural policy. On April 16, four days after FDR's death, Albert S. Goss, president of the National Grange, wrote Truman requesting a meeting for the purpose of discussing "four chief distinct approaches to the farm problem and how they would affect the place of agriculture in our postwar economy."[40] Not to be outdone, Farm Bureau president Edward A. O'Neal provided the chief executive with a formal statement and related materials outlining his position on the "many difficult problems of reconversion and readjustment" facing American agriculture. "We must not repeat the mistakes following World War I when the bottom dropped out of farm prices and farm income and hundreds of thousands of farm families lost their farms." O'Neal, an Alabama cotton planter, was of the opinion that Congress had acted wisely in recent years; and, although "some adjustments and improvements" might

39. Hope to John J. Dillon, June 2, 1945, FF, Hope Papers.
40. A. S. Goss to Truman, April 16, 1945, Official file, Harry S. Truman Papers, Harry S. Truman Library (hereafter cited as OF, Truman Papers).

be needed, he advised the president that the AFBF would "strongly oppose any attempts to destroy and emasculate any of these basic laws"—laws that, it should be added, reflected considerable bureau influence.[41]

Despite this early interest and anxiety, Congress and the administration had some time before they had to give the issue serious attention. President Truman did not declare an official end to the hostilities until December 31, 1946. Thus, thanks to Steagall, the government was pledged to high price supports for both basic and nonbasic commodities until the end of 1948.

In light of the revolutionary change in the productive capacity of American agriculture, this could have created a disastrous surplus problem. Fortunately, abnormally high demand, partially the result of wartime devastation in Europe, relieved the country of the burden of high support payments and provided farmers with a favorable economic climate. With the commencement of the two-year transition period, however, increased concern was expressed that the government for political and economic reasons could not indefinitely continue to support farm prices at wartime levels. A new, more permanent program reflecting modern conditions was called for, and soon, it seemed, Congress would be forced to act.[42]

41. "Statement of Edward A. O'Neal...to President Harry S. Truman, at the White House, August 20, 1945," OF, Truman Papers. During his first months in office, the president also had several meetings with James G. Patton, president of the National Farmers Union (President's Personal file, Truman Papers [hereafter cited as PPF, Truman Papers]). For a biographical sketch of O'Neal (1875–1958), who took over the leadership of the AFBF in 1931 and who had been intimately involved in the development of New Deal agricultural policy, see *Current Biography*, 1946, 51.

42. Rasmussen, "Impact of Technological Change," 578; Schultz, *Agriculture in an Unstable Economy*, 81; Matusow, *Farm Policies and Politics*, 110; Donald R. McCoy, *The Presidency of Harry S. Truman*, 109; Benedict, *Farm Policies of the United States*, 472.

2

THE SEARCH BEGINS

Spearheading administration efforts to influence farm legislation in 1947 was Clinton P. Anderson, secretary of agriculture. His role and the role of his successor in 1948, Charles F. Brannan, are particularly important because the president took only marginal interest in the formulation of policy in this field. Historian Allen J. Matusow seemed somewhat surprised that "the first president since Ulysses S. Grant to work part of his adult life as a dirt farmer" abdicated his executive authority in this area and let his subordinates do the real job of policy making. Finding that Truman also yielded his authority in other policy areas during the troubled days of his first administration, Matusow critically observed: "Even in farm matters where he might have legitimately claimed special interest or knowledge, Truman was a minor figure who intruded only infrequently into the realm of policy."[1] Truman biographer Alonzo L. Hamby agreed with Matusow's assessment. He found that the president "apparently had little interest in or time for agricultural problems" and, as a result, delegated considerable responsibility to his cabinet secretary. Hamby, however, appeared less surprised by these developments than did Matusow. He attributed Truman's attitude to the idea that the farm was a "symbol of failure" for the Truman family.[2]

1. Matusow, *Farm Policies and Polititcs,* 1; McCoy, *Presidency of Harry S. Truman,* 109; Alonzo L. Hamby, *Beyond the New Deal: Harry S. Truman and American Liberalism,* 75; Hamby, *Man of the People: A Life of Harry S. Truman,* 25–42, 92–93.
2. Hamby, *Beyond the New Deal,* 75. Richard S. Kirkendall, who convincingly argues that the farm was actually a positive and successful experience for

Whether we ascribe Truman's peripheral role in agriculture policy formulation to Hamby's quasi-psychological explanation or Matusow's "abdication of executive authority" criticism, the fact remains that Truman talked in general terms about the need to treat farmers fairly and left the detailed work to the Department of Agriculture. Truman, a practitioner of cabinet government, was not impressed with the administrative methods of Franklin Roosevelt. Rather than depend on "powerful White House operatives" as did his predecessor, Harry Truman encouraged his cabinet secretaries to formulate their own policies and expected them "to shoulder their own burdens."[3]

To his credit, the president lent his support to two very capable secretaries of agriculture. Faced with numerous problems related to postwar reconversion at home and a vastly expanded role for the country internationally, Truman realized that the nature of the modern presidency made administration by delegation a necessity. The president's decision to remain on the periphery can be interpreted as a realistic grasp of new trends in organization. But he no doubt also realized that time constraints prohibited his becoming intimately familiar with all the complexities of the many issues involved in farm policy formulation in the midst of the ongoing structural transformation taking place in the agricultural economy.

Typical of Truman's vague but frequent exhortations for improvements in agricultural legislation was his 1947 State of the Union address. In a brief statement devoted to agriculture, the president called for swift movement toward the passage of permanent legislation to provide stability in farm prices. "The farmer," Truman insisted, "is entitled to a fair income." Efforts must be made to utilize his new productive capacities and "to expand his markets at home and abroad."[4] It was Clinton Anderson who was to turn these broad executive goals into workable policy.

Truman, undermines the legitimacy of this interpretation (Kirkendall, "Harry S Truman: A Missouri Farmer," 467). See also David McCullough, *Truman*, 101; Robert H. Ferrell, *Harry S. Truman: A Life.*

3. Patrick Anderson, *The President's Men: White House Assistants of Franklin D. Roosevelt, Harry S. Truman, Dwight D. Eisenhower, John F. Kennedy, and Lyndon B. Johnson*, 92.

4. Truman, *Public Papers of the President, 1947*, 8.

Anderson, who enjoyed the complete confidence and consistent support of the president, was appointed secretary of agriculture in May 1945, within weeks of Truman's ascension to the presidency. Convinced that it was wise for him to compose his own cabinet, the new president quickly began shaping a Truman administration.[5] One of his first opportunities came when Claude Wickard, secretary of agriculture under FDR during World War II, was appointed to a less demanding post as the head of the REA. Anderson, explained Truman a decade later, "was on the special committee of the House of Representatives to investigate food shortages and had been instrumental in the passage of a great deal of legislation in the House. I invited him to breakfast at the White House one morning and asked him if he would consider being Secretary of Agriculture, and he accepted."[6]

Always conscious of the political climate and implications of his decisions, Truman had not failed to notice that Anderson was emerging as the administration's chief critic with regard to food policy and had received a great deal of favorable press for his committee's efforts. What better way to deal with this particular situation than to make his chief critic his chief administrator? As Anderson himself explained, "On May 23, the day after my special committee released a report critical of the Administration's handling of the sugar shortage, President Truman summoned me to the White House.... I wondered how badly I was going to be burned for the report." Instead, Anderson was surprised to find that the president wanted to offer him a job. "The President liked the way I handled the food investigation and, when he asked me to join him, I could not refuse."[7]

5. "Appointment Sheet," May 19, 1945, in Robert H. Ferrell, ed., *Off the Record: The Private Papers of Harry S. Truman,* 30.

6. Truman, *Memoirs by Harry S. Truman: Year of Decision,* vol. 1, 326; Ferrell, ed., *Off the Record,* 30. On Wickard, see Walter W. Wilcox, *Farmer in the Second World War;* Dean Albertson, *Roosevelt's Farmer: Claude R. Wickard in the New Deal;* Virgil W. Dean, "Claude R. Wickard, U.S. Secretary of Agriculture, 1940–1945," in John A. Garraty and Mark C. Carnes, eds., *American National Biography,* 23:329–30; Milton S. Eisenhower, *The President Is Calling,* 88, 90. Eisenhower, the youngest brother of the general and future president, who served three presidents and four secretaries while working at USDA, called the January 20, 1941, appointment of the "inept" Wickard "a ghastly mistake" (90, 88).

7. Clinton P. Anderson, *Outsider in the Senate: Senator Clinton Anderson's Memoirs,* 56; Matusow, *Farm Policies and Politics,* 8.

There were other factors that, in Truman's estimation, qualified the forty-nine-year-old, two-term congressman from New Mexico for this new assignment. Although by his own admission not an expert in agriculture, Anderson was a loyal Democrat who had helped secure the vice-presidential nomination for Truman in 1944, and he was considered a man of significant administrative ability. Born in South Dakota, the son of an immigrant Swedish farmer, Anderson was a strong willed individual who had overcome a life-threatening struggle with tuberculosis to become a successful businessman, politician, and public servant in his adopted home state of New Mexico.

After entering the House of Representatives in 1941, he forged a friendship with Senator Harry Truman—according to Anderson, this friendship developed partly because they held two interests in common: Masonic Lodge membership and poker. The latter kept the two in close contact during the three months of Truman's vice presidency and helped draw Anderson into the inner circle of close Truman advisers after he joined the cabinet. Anderson and Truman pitched horseshoes together behind the White House, and the secretary of agriculture became a regular at the president's celebrated poker games. Anderson also became part of the group that met with the president for lunch on Tuesdays and that had considerable influence on administration policy. In addition to Anderson, the coterie included Secretary of State James Byrnes, Secretary of the Treasury Fred Vinson, Secretary of the Navy (later Secretary of Defense) James Forrestal, Postmaster General R. E. Hannegan, and Attorney General Tom Clark. "Jocularly," Anderson said, "we referred to ourselves as the 'intellectuals,' chiefly because we were not."[8]

Anderson, who impressed Milton Eisenhower, then president of the Kansas State Argicultural College and a veteran of many years in the USDA, as "a man of probity, charming personality, and disarming forthrightness," faced many crises as he settled into his new administrative position. The immediate problems caused by food shortages at home were compounded for the new secretary by the sudden

8. Anderson, *Outsider in the Senate,* 77. For an in-depth look at Anderson's background and relationship with Truman, see Matusow, *Farm Policies and Politics,* 9; James L. Forsythe, "Clinton P. Anderson: Politician and Businessman as Truman's Secretary of Agriculture."

surrender of Japan on August 14, 1945. Reconversion policy for peacetime agricultural production and a serious world food crisis made Anderson's tenure as secretary of agriculture difficult and often controversial.[9]

Initially, however, the secretary received high marks, even from future critics such as Farmers Union President James G. Patton, for his leadership role in departmental reorganization.[10] Appalled by the sprawling bureaucracy that was the USDA over which he had to preside, Anderson the successful businessman wanted to streamline the department by centralizing authority and by eliminating many of the agencies with overlapping responsibilities. To help with this job, Secretary Anderson drew on the talents and experience of Milton Eisenhower, who was appointed chairman of an advisory committee. In addition to working out a plan for the reunification of the War Food Administration and the Department of Agriculture, the committee proposed the creation of a new agency, the Production and Marketing Administration (PMA), which replaced the New Deal's Agricultural Adjustment Administration. The reorganization acquired its own critics, but Anderson was pleased with the "fine job" Eisenhower accomplished for him during the late summer of 1945. During the first eighteen months of Anderson's tenure, the USDA was completely reconstituted.[11]

Although many agreed that reorganization was long overdue, the character of the restructured department soon joined the list of factious issues, and Anderson lost favor with some of his early supporters. In addition, Secretary Anderson's opposition to the Pace bill for

9. Eisenhower, *The President Is Calling,* 172; Robert J. Donovan, *Conflict and Crisis: The Presidency of Harry S. Truman, 1945–1949,* 110–11; Matusow, *Farm Policies and Politics,* 68; Hamby, *Beyond the New Deal,* 75–76; James Ashe to Anderson, October 20, 1945, and Anderson to Ashe, November 19, 1945, Alphabetical Correspondence file, Anderson Papers.

10. Patton to Truman, August 8, 1945, PPF, Truman Papers. For more on Jim Patton, whose organization continued to identify itself with the interests of the family type farm as opposed to the larger commercial farm represented by the AFBF, see *Current Biography,* 1945, 450, and *Current Biography,* 1966, 308; Flamm, "National Farmers Union and the Evolution of Agrarian Liberalism," 54.

11. Forsythe, "Clinton P. Anderson," 466, 503; Eisenhower, *The President Is Calling,* 172–74; Matusow, *Farm Policies and Politics,* 72–73; Wayne D. Rasmussen and Gladys L. Baker, *The Department of Agriculture,* 57.

modernization of the parity formula and his close ties with the conservative Farm Bureau, political activities, and running battle with Chester Bowles of the OPA made him a controversial member of the administration and brought harsh criticism from many quarters. By the fall of 1945, Anderson was under attack, and some of his detractors, most notably state and national Farm Union officials, were demanding his immediate resignation.[12]

Nevertheless, Truman's support for his agricultural secretary was unwavering. On May 4, 1946, in response to a letter from Jim Patton containing a forceful call for Anderson's resignation, Truman expressed his "regret" that Patton was "at odds with my able Secretary of Agriculture." He reminded the president of the Farmers Union that decisions concerning cabinet posts belonged to the president of the United States and continued: "I think you are entirely misinformed on his attitude. I think he is as able a Secretary of Agriculture as the Country has ever had and I intend to keep him." Later that same year, in response to persistent rumors of Anderson's pending resignation (something that was almost constant throughout his three years in office), Truman wrote Edward O'Neal: "He is one of the ablest of my Cabinet members and I am sure he will stay with me."[13]

In spite of what were actually the more pressing problems of his office, Anderson did give at least some attention to "long-time" administration policy for agriculture for the period to follow the expiration of the Steagall amendment. As early as October 1945, Anderson was receiving recommendations for such a policy from his department's Bureau of Agricultural Economics (BAE), which insisted on an over-

12. Anderson to Dan Burross, November 19, 1945 (attached to James Ashe letter), Alphabetical Correspondence file, Anderson Papers; Waldo R. McNutt to Truman, November 21, 1945, OF, Truman Papers; Darrell Cady, "The Truman Administration's Reconversion Policies, 1945–1947," 149–58. In November, Bowles urged Truman to cut rations of meat, fats, and oils by 10 percent so that more could be sent to Europe to combat a severe food shortage. The decision was left up to Anderson, however, and "with the interests of American farmers and consumers in mind and still hopeful about supplies, Anderson not only rejected Bowles' suggestion but brought about the end of rationing of meat, fats, and oil" (Donovan, *Conflict and Crisis,* 124–25).

13. Truman to O'Neal, November 9, 1946, President's Secretary's file, Truman Papers (hereafter cited as PSF, Truman Papers); James Patton to Truman, May 2, 1946, and Truman to Patton, May 4, 1946, National Farmers Union file, Anderson Papers.

hauled parity system.[14] In addition, by December he had written an article for the *Saturday Evening Post* that spelled out his ideas for a prosperous peacetime agriculture program.

The opportunity to write the *Post* article had first arisen in July when Ben Hibbs, the magazine's editor, contacted the secretary. The journalist explained that he thought it would be a good time for the new secretary of agriculture to express his views on the food situation, and he mentioned that former Secretary Wickard had established the precedent by writing several articles for the periodical during his tenure at USDA. Anderson, who had been an aspiring young journalist in the late 1910s and early 1920s, responded with interest and mentioned that he had long wanted to publish in the *Post;* indeed, he had rejection slips dating back to 1918. His article, which was not to appear in print until December, was completed in early October. On October 10, Hibbs wrote to Anderson expressing his approval of the finished work. Hibbs took exception only with the title, "Farmers Plan for Plenty." In light of all the gloomy speculation about agriculture, the editor explained, would a title such as "I Don't Expect a Farm Depression" be acceptable? Anderson responded two days later with his own substitution, "What's in Store for Agriculture?"[15] When the article appeared on December 22, 1945, it carried the title "Is the Farmer Heading for Trouble Again?" How this relatively minor difference of opinion was resolved is unclear, but it does show a concern with appearance that reflects a belief that attitudes, as well as economic realities, were an important aspect of economic development in agriculture during the troubled postwar period.

Of greater import is the content of Anderson's article. The secretary described his emerging policy of abundance in regard to American agriculture. This policy, echoed by the president at every opportunity thereafter, stressed the need for abundant farm production, as opposed to the planned scarcity of the early New Deal, and optimistically predicted that with proper national emphasis on such factors as

14. Raymond Smith to Anderson, "Report on Post-War Programs," October 2, 1945, and report by USDA Inter-bureau Committee on Post-war Programs, September 5, 1945, Official Correspondence file, Anderson Papers.

15. Ben Hibbs to Anderson, July 9, 1945; Anderson to Hibbs, July 19, 1945; Hibbs to Anderson, October 10, 1945; Anderson to Hibbs, October 12, 1945, Alphabetical Correspondence file, Anderson Papers.

On June 4, 1946, administration and congressional farm-state leaders looked on as President Truman signed the National School Lunch Act, which made the program a permanent part of the USDA's activities. Pictured here, from left to right, are Representative Clarence A. Cannon; Secretary Clinton P. Anderson; Representative Malcolm C. Tarver; Senator Richard B. Russell Jr.; Senator Allen J. Ellender; Representative Clifford R. Hope; Senator George D. Aiken; Representative John W. Flannagan Jr.; Under Secretary of Agriculture Nathan Koenig; Director of Food Distribution Paul C. Stark; Under Secretary of Agriculture N. E. Dodd; and PMA administrator, Robert A. Shields. USDA photograph, courtesy of the Kansas State Historical Society.

full employment and nutritionally sound diets, Americans could consume the country's farm produce. Effective marketing and government efforts to make America's low-income population a greater part of the consuming public would remain important factors in administration policy toward postwar agriculture. Anderson admitted that technological developments would continue to reduce the total number of farmers needed, and that the government would have to encourage "large shifts in kinds of crops" produced to avoid surplus problems in some areas. He insisted, however, that programs such as health and food education and an expanded school lunch program, along with full employment, would make the farmer's future bright.[16]

Greatly underestimating the world demand that was soon to take the form of a food crisis, Anderson insisted that American farmers should produce primarily for the home market. While stressing the philosophy of abundance, Anderson revealed his concern with over-production. He insisted America should not get into the practice of "exploiting land" to meet foreign demand that in the long run would be modest at best. This point led to an additional emphasis on soil conservation programs, a policy that allowed the government to take land out of production (theoretically reducing total output) while still encouraging full production. On an optimistic note, Anderson concluded: "It is clear that plenty of food for all can come only from a fully productive industry and a fully productive agriculture. These are part and counterpart of a prosperous, well-fed United States. I believe we are going to attain them, just as we did our war goals."[17]

The secretary's optimism, at least for the short run, was unwarranted; and, if anything, 1946 was a more trouble packed year than was 1945. Nevertheless, Secretary Anderson survived and came out the winner in several intra-administration power struggles. For example, Director Harold Smith of the Bureau of the Budget (BOB) became increasingly critical of administration policy in general, and of Anderson in particular, during the first half of this election year. Smith pointed out that the administration had been talking about a food surplus problem just weeks before it was forced to change its tune and express concern about a food shortage. He insisted, according to Truman biographer Cabell Phillips, that "these administrative deficiencies were primarily the fault of Secretary Anderson who was determined to protect the interests of the American farmers first and did not give sufficient consideration to the needs of consumers at home and abroad." Like many of the experts, Anderson misjudged the nature of the postwar reconversion, and he assumed a serious recession would follow and feared deflation rather than inflation. He

16. Clinton P. Anderson, "Is the Farmer Heading for Trouble Again?" 95. See also "School Lunch Programs," OF, Truman Papers. A bipartisan legislative effort, the school lunch program (H.R. 3370, which became PL 396), was approved June 4, 1946.
17. Anderson, "Is the Farmer Heading for Trouble Again?" 96.

failed to foresee the extent of the damage inflicted on world agricultural production and to recognize for a critical period (until early
1946) that there was no world surplus.[18] Anderson stayed on the job,
however, while Smith lost influence with the president and finally
resigned in July.

On another front, the internecine wrangle between Director Bowles
of the OPA and Secretary Anderson intensified during the spring of
1946 as the nation neared the June 30 expiration of all price controls.
This was an extraordinarily contentious matter, especially with the
approach of the fall congressional elections, and everyone had an
opinion. According to Clifford Hope, his mail indicated that many
people were "irked with OPA restrictions" and seemed "to be willing to take a chance on inflation in order to get rid of it." He was personally against keeping the agency "indefinitely" and believed "we
ought to get rid of it as soon as plentiful supplies make it unnecessary. I feel, however, it would be disastrous to stop it on June 30th."[19]
Ultimately, Congress passed an amended OPA extension bill that seriously crippled the agency; Truman vetoed the measure despite the
contrary advice of congressional leaders and the majority of his cabinet officers; Director Bowles resigned; inflation swept the country
during the summer of 1946; and a new anti-inflation bill, little better
than the first, was passed and became law without the president's
signature.[20]

Anderson survived this and other crises. Inflation and shortages,
however, undoubtedly contributed to Democratic setbacks in the 1946
congressional elections that gave Republicans control of the Eightieth
Congress, and calls for Anderson's resignation continued. Regardless,
the secretary retained the support of his boss, and when asked to
appear before the House Committee on Agriculture in April of 1947,

18. Cabell Phillips, *The Truman Presidency: The History of a Triumphant
Succession,* 295; Harold F. Gosnell, *Truman's Crises: A Political Biography of
Harry S. Truman,* 276–77.

19. Hope to V. E. Keller, April 2, 1946, and to Elmer Case, April 4, 1946,
FF, Hope Papers. See also Patton to Truman, May 2, 1946, National Farmers
Union file, Anderson Papers; Hamby, *Beyond the New Deal,* 75–76, 90–91;
Phillips, *Truman Presidency,* 105–8.

20. Phillips, *Truman Presidency,* 109; Barton J. Bernstein, "Clash of Interests:
Postwar Battle between the Office of Price Administration and the Department of
Agriculture," 45; Bernstein, "The Postwar Famine and Price Control, 1946," 235.

he was ready to present at least the general outline of an administration plan for a long-range farm policy. Anderson had weathered the storms of his first two years in office and had solved, at least for the time being, the shortage problem while pursuing a policy that served the interests of American agriculture.[21] Now, with the emergence of an unprecedented show of unity among agricultural interest groups, it appeared he might be able to add a comprehensive farm policy to his list of accomplishments.

Following Truman's call for "permanent legislation to provide stability of farm prices and general farm welfare and guarantee adequate markets at home and abroad," Anderson prepared to deliver his department's ideas that had been some time in the making. Although he had initiated a long-range planning study early in 1946, it was not until December 30, 1946, when Assistant Secretary of Agriculture Charles F. Brannan was made chairman of a departmental program and policy committee, that work in this area began in earnest. "The main task of the new committee," according to Matusow, "was to take the vision of abundance so well enunciated by BAE and accommodate it to reality."[22]

Writing to the president a month before his committee appearance, Anderson confirmed the importance of the Brannan committee's work. It had been "developing the Department's conception of a proper pattern for agriculture," the secretary explained. "Time is running against us in the present program of agriculture support prices. It is urgent that we develop an adjusted pattern of peacetime agriculture with the greatest speed."[23] The policy committee's efforts were critical to the successful attainment of this objective. The process revealed some divergent opinions within the department—in particular, a split between advocates of income parity (involving the use of direct payments) and the traditional price parity—but Anderson was generally favorable toward the committee report.[24]

---

21. Matusow, *Farm Policies and Politics,* 34–36; Forsythe, "Clinton P. Anderson," 252, 361.

22. Matusow, *Farm Policies and Politics,* 133; *Congressional Digest* 26 (January 1947): 166.

23. Anderson to Truman, March 11, 1947, OF, Truman Papers.

24. According to Brannan, his committee's report was accepted in toto by Anderson and presented at the congressional hearing, with the exception of

Anderson's congressional testimony reflected his and the nation's increasing concern that the government could not continue indefinitely under a policy of rigid 90 percent parity support for agriculture. The popular press had become critical of New Deal remedies for dealing with the farm situation, and in January 1947 *U.S. News* labeled commodity loans at 90 percent parity a " 'heads I win, tails you lose' proposition" for farmers. The magazine approvingly indicated, however, that Secretary Anderson was beginning to worry about the cost of supports, which USDA estimates placed at $500 million to $1 billion for 1947.[25]

The most important cause of this general anxiety regarding the exorbitant cost of the farm program resulted from the government's effort to support the price of potatoes as required under the Steagall amendment. While almost all the other Steagall commodities remained above parity, and thus required no price supports during the immediate postwar period, domestic demand for potatoes decreased and production continued to increase. No satisfactory method was found to ship this perishable product to the literally starving European market. Consequently, prices fell, and the government had no alternative; Uncle Sam, in the form of the Commodity Credit Corporation, became the potato producer's primary market. In 1946 potato growers marketed 484 million bushels; the CCC, which lost $91 million as it sought to dispose of the surplus outside regular commercial channels, purchased 108 million of these bushels.[26]

The potato situation is a classic example of the dilemma that faced agriculturalists during the second agricultural revolution and of the problem of inelastic demand, which had plagued many farm commodities since World War I. While the corporation fought farm surpluses, the USDA's various research bureaus were helping producers

---

Brannan's recommendations on price supports. Anderson substituted his own more conservative proposals here (Charles F. Brannan, interview with author, August 9, 1985, Denver, CO).

25. "New Aid Ahead for Farmers," 44. In the same issue, the magazine called Truman's December 31 proclamation terminating hostilities "unexpected" and claimed it "was prompted in part by the administration's alarm over threatened costs of the farm program" (45). Others have suggested that the timing was political; by forcing the newly elected Republican Congress to enter the farm policy quagmire, Truman was virtually ensured a winning issue for the 1948 campaign.

26. Matusow, *Farm Policies and Politics,* 125–28.

increase their yields. "For their part," explained Matusow, consumers "had slowly been turning away from the potato to fruits and other vegetables. In 1910 the average American ate 190 pounds of potatoes a year;... in 1946, only 128. Meanwhile the inflexible provisions of the Steagall amendment greatly overpriced potatoes and assured continued overproduction for at least two more years."[27]

This disastrous state of affairs led Secretary Anderson to seek a new potato program from the Republican Eightieth Congress in 1947. As Congressman Hope indicated, however, the secretary's request for controls on Steagall commodities "puts a Republican Congress in a rather tough spot, because many Republicans have been urging the removal of all controls, and have gone on record as being opposed to imposing regimentation generally as far as agricultural producers were concerned." Nevertheless, Hope recognized the seriousness of the situation and indicated that without controls "the Treasury will be faced with the possibility of paying out vast sums of money in the way of supports."[28]

In a February 17 "Report on Legislative Developments Relating to Agriculture," Anderson informed the president of his appearances on January 22 and 23 before the House and Senate agricultural committees. With the potato situation, which had generated such unfavorable publicity, uppermost on his mind, the secretary had discussed "problems regarding price supports" and had "recommended that the Congress enact legislation clarifying the authority of the Secretary of Agriculture under the so-called Steagall Amendment, with particular reference to authority to impose adjustment production requirements as a condition of eligibility for price support." Anderson also had "recommended that Congress give consideration to the question of what the long range program of the Government should be with respect to price support and also to a revision of the parity formula."[29]

27. Ibid., 127–28.

28. Hope to Congressman Francis Case (R-SD), January 23, 1947, and to George VerSteeg, January 29, 1947, FF, Hope Papers.

29. Report from Anderson on agriculture developments, February 17, 1947, OF, Truman Papers. See also Anderson to Arthur Capper, February 26, 1948, Agricultural Correspondence, Arthur Capper Papers, collection 12, Manuscripts Department, Kansas State Historical Society (hereafter cited as Capper Papers).

Although Congress was not forthcoming on Anderson's request with regard to the potato program, his early efforts to influence congressional action on general policy were received favorably. Fundamental differences as to approach remained and would become manifest in the months ahead, but on April 21, 1947, when Anderson appeared before the House Committee on Agriculture, the atmosphere appeared conducive to constructive change in farm policy; nearly everyone was demanding some modification in the old support system.

Indeed, when the committee convened and the hearings commenced, they did so, according to Chairman Hope, "On the theory that the best time to fix the roof is while the sun is shining." This was to be a nonpartisan affair, for the sole "purpose of discussing and considering our postwar agricultural policy." As long as the prosperity held, there was some chance for agreement on the nature of postwar farm legislation. There was no sense of immediate urgency, and the new chairman of the House agricultural committee sought to continue his long commitment to bipartisanship in the search for effective farm legislation.[30]

Clifford Hope was chairman by virtue of GOP gains in the election of 1946; after many long years in the minority, Republicans were eager to have an impact on national policy. The desire for bipartisanship in farm policy formulation, though, was genuine on both sides of the aisle. In the wake of his party's defeat, Congressman Pace of Georgia wrote to Hope: "I am sure you know that I take no special delight in the defeat of the Democrats, but I want you to know that it does give me a great deal of satisfaction to know that in the change we have you as Chairman of the House Committee on Agriculture." In reply, Congressman Hope assured his Democratic colleague that he had never known the committee to be partisan, "and I certainly don't want it to be in the next two years. I don't know of a single member on your side of the committee that I can't work with wholeheartedly, and that is what I want to do."[31] Early in the new year,

30. House Committee on Agriculture, *Long-Range Agricultural Policy,* 80th Cong., 1st sess., 1947, 1; James L. Forsythe, "Clifford Hope of Kansas: Practical Congressman and Agrarian Idealist," 406.

31. Pace to Hope, November 19, 1946, and Hope to Pace, November 25, 1946, General Correspondence, Committee on Agriculture, Hope Papers.

Hope reaffirmed his commitment to bipartisanship in another letter to the Georgia lawmaker by expressing his pleasure with their past work together and his anticipation of "an equally pleasant association during the coming two years. As a matter of fact," Hope wrote, "I am counting very heavily upon your cooperation and support in the efforts which we must make to work out a postwar agricultural program."[32]

This program would have to address many different issues, such as crop insurance, marketing (both foreign and domestic), and soil conservation. But the issue that consistently attracted the most attention was the level and methods to be used in supporting commodity prices. As it began to contemplate its policy choices, Congress faced a difficult task, explained Chairman Hope, "because while many plans are being offered to us, and most of them look fine on paper, further study always seems to disclose some defects and difficulties which were not apparent at a first glance." Every method had its potential pitfalls and trade-offs, and, ultimately, farmers would have to decide which was best for them. "That is one reason I want to have rather extensive hearings, so that we can give publicity to all the plans which are proposed, and give farmers an opportunity to express themselves as to the merits or demerits of these various programs."[33]

Despite years of intensive study and labor in this area, Congressman Hope remained in something of a quandary with regard to the farm problem. A fairly typical western or plains state Republican, Hope was relatively conservative on most issues but had long espoused the philosophy of agrarianism, which occasioned his support for the principles of New Deal farm legislation. He was a conscientious, hardworking farm legislator who sought what was best for his constituents. Although philosophically opposed to government interference in the marketplace, he came to accept the necessity of government price supports for agricultural commodities. In this respect, Hope reflected a general GOP dilemma. His was a pragmatic position dictated by the realization that farmers had been unable to solve the farm problem on their own, through such preferred methods as cooperation,

32. Hope to Pace, January 4, 1947, General Correspondence, Committee on Agriculture, Hope Papers.
33. Hope to Sam Spahr, February 4, 1947; to to W. L. Gooding, January 25, 1947; to Charles R. Robertson, February 25, 1947; and to John L. Dean, March 1, 1947, General Correspondence, Committee on Agriculture, Hope Papers.

for example. Some type of federal support system seemed the only way to compensate for agriculture's inherently unequal competitive position in relationship to the nonfarm sector of the economy.[34]

On January 25, 1947, Hope commented on two specific and frequently suggested price supporting methods: fixing prices at the marketplace through government purchases or loans and direct payments to the farmer from the federal treasury. In the process, he expressed some commonly held fears with regard to farm policy that would have significance for several years to come. Hope believed that farmers "generally" preferred the former method.

> The difficulty of course with a program of that kind is that if the support price is as high as a good many people want it—say, 90% of parity (and some want it higher)—it must usually be accompanied by rigid controls. That is because in most cases, when we get away from war prices, 90% of parity will probably be an incentive to production. This means that such a program must be accompanied by rigid controls and regimentation. It also has the effect of freezing production in the pattern of some former period.... The other plan of making direct payments to the farmer of differences between the going market price and the rate at which it is desired to stabilize the price has the advantage of permitting us to use the existing marketing system. It would also not interfere with the export market. However, most farmers seem to object to such a plan, for the reason that they regard the government payment as a dole. Frankly, I cannot see any difference between the two plans from that standpoint.... Certainly, one of the chief benefits to be derived from the plan of direct payments is that it would require nothing like as much regimentation and control as the other plan.[35]

In writing favorably about direct payments early in 1947, Hope was expressing a view that enjoyed wide currency among the nation's agricultural economists. At this time, though, it was generally assumed that a compensatory payments scheme would support farm income considerably below high wartime levels. "Rather," explained Willard

34. For additional information on Hope's views and his relationship to the New Deal, see Forsythe, "Clifford Hope of Kansas," 407; Clifford R. Hope Jr. to Virgil Dean, February 5, 1990.
35. Hope to Frank Blecha, January 25, 1947, FF, Hope Papers.

W. Cochrane, then with the Bureau of Agricultural Economics, this preferred approach could be tailored "to effect adjustment in the agricultural plant. *The objectives of such an income payments program would be to assist producers to shift (1) into commodity lines for which they are more efficient relative to equilibrium prices or (2) into nonagricultural pursuits.*"[36]

In the spring of 1947 there was still time for study as Congress did not have to make an immediate policy choice. It had made a "solemn promise" to America's farmers in the form of the "Steagall guarantee" that applied through the 1948 crop year. A decade had passed since the Committee on Agriculture had conducted general hearings on farm policy, during which time many fundamental changes had taken place in the industry. Chairman Hope and others believed it was "necessary for this Congress to resurvey the entire farm program" before devising "a permanent postwar agricultural policy."[37]

In early April when he announced the opening of the committee investigation, Chairman Hope informed the press that the "hearings will be the most comprehensive to be held on the agricultural program for many years." The committee did not intend to introduce legislation during this session but to thoroughly study the new problems facing American agriculture. It would determine the appropriate policy course, and, most likely, new legislation would follow during the second session of the Eightieth Congress.[38]

The atmosphere for such deliberations was favorable that spring; there seemed to be plenty of time for a thoughtful and thorough investigation, and an unprecedented unanimity appeared to exist among

36. Willard W. Cochrane, "Income Payments as a Substitute for Support Prices," 1029 (emphasis his); Schultz, *Agriculture in an Unstable Economy;* American Farm Economic Association, "Toward a Better Parity," 42; Geoffrey S. Shepherd, *Agricultural Price Policy.* For further discussion of the views of agricultural economists such as Cochrane, Schultz, Howard Tolley, and especially Shepherd during this era, see Lauren Soth, "Agricultural Economists and Public Policy," in Richard H. Day, ed., *Economic Analysis and Agricultural Policy,* 46–56.

37. Hope to Dale Stucky, January 24, 1947, and to A. V. Zink, January 6, 1947, FF, Hope Papers.

38. Quote from House Committee on Agriculture Press Release, April 3, 1947, Speech file, Hope Papers; House Committee, *Long-Range Agricultural Policy,* 1; House Committee on Agriculture, News Release, January 17, 1947, and News Release, April 16, 1947, Legislative Correspondence, Hope Papers.

agricultural interest groups. Ironically, in light of subsequent developments, Hope's brief opening statement to the Committee on Agriculture included the following:

> ... these hearings have been called when agriculture is prosperous and while current programs have some time yet to run. We *will not be working under pressure* as has been the case in the formulation of most agricultural programs in the past. In conducting these hearings we want to learn of the changes which have taken place in agriculture since general legislation was last considered in 1938. We want to study the progress of mechanization. We want to consider the effect of improved techniques and new methods of production which have come into effect in recent years. We want to study the question of if and how agriculture can continue its present expanded production.
>
> We will want to check up on existing legislation and see whether it fits present-day conditions. Our objectives will be constructive. We want to retain the good and discard that which is outmoded and ineffective. ... We want the best ideas and suggestions we can get.[39]

With these rather perceptive remarks, which posed the right questions and revealed considerable understanding of the revolutionary changes taking place in American agriculture, the committee was ready to hear the testimony of its first witness—Secretary of Agriculture Anderson.

Before getting into the heart of his proposals, Anderson commended the congressmen for their wisdom in initiating "this comprehensive search for the right long-range agricultural policy" and stressed the importance of their task. He also said that his purpose was to present "one practical policy for American agriculture" that reflected an approach of "organized, sustained, and realistic, abundance." The secretary emphasized the need to tap the potential market of the nation's poor, the wisdom of highlighting livestock production, and the importance of soil conservation. He then outlined the "broad requirements" that the USDA believed were essential to any "forward-looking" policy.[40]

Anderson's suggestions included the need for full employment

39. House Committee, *Long-Range Agricultural Policy,* 1 (emphasis added).
40. Ibid., 2–8.

and government programs to promote better medical and educational facilities in rural America, but most significant was his call for a flexible price support approach to replace the "rigid system" that threatened to price "our commodities out of the markets." He insisted, "Prices are and should be an effective means of encouraging changes in production as the conditions of production and demand change. To this end, the parity formula should be modernized." An astute political practitioner who understood the politics of agricultural policy formulation, Anderson told the committee that he preferred to allow farm organizations and Congress to work out the exact details on this last point. But when he was pressed during questioning toward the end of the day's hearings, Anderson tentatively replied that he was "inclined to feel . . . that something of a moving average needs to be added to the ordinary fixed base, in order to make it more flexible, more useful."[41]

The secretary did not provide "the program requirements for the proposed policy," partly because "the Policy and Program Committee of the Department" was still working out the details. But his appeal for congressional adoption of the "goal of organized, sustained, and realistic abundance as our national agricultural policy," with an emphasis on livestock production, "which is an aid to soil conservation and future productivity," struck a responsive cord with most committee members. Representative August Andresen (R-MN) expressed his delight "that the Department is going all out for an abundant production program rather than the philosophy of scarcity." Congressman Reid F. Murray (R-WI) also was interested, especially in the secretary's "approach to a future program" that recognized "the importance of the livestock industry in connection with soil conservation, and . . . as one of our principal agricultural activities."[42]

Chairman Hope had been singing the praises of abundance for some time. In early January 1947, while discussing the Research and Marketing Act of 1946, he made mention of the fact that government

41. Ibid., 27. For an excellent discussion of various approaches to price supports, including flexible supports, see Willard W. Cochrane, *Farm Prices: Myth and Reality,* 138.
42. House Committee, *Long-Range Agricultural Policy,* 5, 8, 12, (Andresen) 16, and (Murray) 19. Andresen's remark about scarcity was, by implication, a not so subtle criticism of New Deal farm policy.

research in the area of production was nothing new. Indeed, it had been quite successful. Marketing and distribution had become agriculture's real problems. Scientific research should now focus, he explained, "on the problem of distributing and using the food and other farm products which we now know how to produce in ample quantity."[43] Anticipating the administration's position as expressed by Secretary Anderson on April 21, Hope insisted that with proper research and education and with adequate incomes the overproduction enigma could be solved; "the expansion of consumption, rather than the limitation of production, is the basic answer to our problems."[44]

Anderson's philosophy of abundance and a relatively prosperous state of affairs in agriculture (a sharp contrast with the farm crisis that came on the heels of World War I) contributed to the surprising harmony that existed in 1947 among farm groups and the government. A healthy farm industry, largely sustained by the government's willingness to make foreign loans for the purchase of farm products after 1945, coupled with increasing public antagonism toward expensive and wasteful farm programs, made farm leaders more inclined to tinker with the old support system.

As a result, reaction to Secretary Anderson's relatively vague statement of policy objectives was generally favorable, and the major farm interest groups found common ground with the administration. During the ensuing three weeks, as the hearings continued, a procession of witnesses came before the committee to express a variety of ideas and concerns. Anderson's testimony was immediately followed by that of the national leaders of the four major farm interest groups: Edward A. O'Neal, president of the American Farm Bureau Federation; John H. Davis, executive secretary of the National Council of Farmer Cooperatives; Albert S. Goss, master of the National Grange; and James G. Patton, president of the Farmers Educational and Cooperative Union of America.[45] Although each of these leaders presented

43. Speech to the National Council of Farmer Cooperatives, Chicago, January 8, 1947, Speech file, Hope Papers.

44. Quoted in House Committee on Agriculture Press Release, April 3, 1947, Speech file, Hope Papers.

45. House Committee, *Long-Range Agricultural Policy,* 29–154: O'Neal, April 22, 1947, 29–50; Davis, April 23, 1947, 69–90; Goss, April 25, 1947, 91–130; Patton, April 29, 1947, 131–54.

his organization's plan for a sound agricultural program, there was considerable agreement on basic principles.

One area of consonance was reflected in the May 1 statement of H. K. Thatcher, executive secretary of the National Association of Commissioners, Secretaries, and Directors of Agriculture. All agreed with Thatcher who said that parity was basic to any agricultural policy. "True parity price" and how to achieve it was a "debatable question," but the concept itself was "fundamental to agriculture and to the Nation as well.... Any long-range agricultural program that is not based upon the premise that agricultural production be paid its equitable price will be of little value to the Nation."[46] Agricultural interest groups and their representatives might disagree on how best to achieve parity and on the appropriate levels of support, but virtually no one, whether liberal or conservative, questioned the viability of the concept or the responsibility of the federal government to maintain an active role in the farm economy.[47]

The NFU, which had been feuding with the administration over various issues for two years, even found reason for optimism. After Anderson's address to the Committee on Agriculture, Jim Patton uncharacteristically rallied to the support of the administration's latest proposals. On April 23, 1947, Patton wrote President Truman to applaud Anderson's "brilliant statement." Patton assured the president that he fully supported the principles outlined in the secretary's statement and intended to give them his strongest endorsement when he appeared before the committee. Truman, undoubtedly with great pleasure, replied the same day that he was "certainly happy" that Patton had changed his mind about Anderson. The president continued, "I told you ... that he was a good Secretary of Agriculture and knew what he was doing and that I was certain the farmers would eventually find it out."[48] Patton was mainly in accord with the administration

46. Ibid., Thatcher, May 1, 1947, 181.
47. The viability and efficacy of a national farm policy built on commodity price supports certainly has been questioned and debated ever since. In addition to public misconceptions about agriculture and agricultural policy, cost/benefit analyses have been the focus of much work and debate in the ongoing dialogue among agricultural economists since the late 1940s and 1950s. Some of this work and the issues raised will be discussed in subsequent chapters.
48. Patton to Truman, and Truman to Patton, April 23, 1947, OF, Truman Papers.

policy of abundance, a philosophical underpinning of the NFU backed full-employment bill of 1945–1946; but he was true to his word and strongly endorsed "the principles enunciated by Secretary Anderson" in his (Patton's) testimony of April 29. To be sure, in concrete policy terms basic disagreements still existed, but this was as close to concordance as Patton and Anderson ever came.[49]

The Farmers Union, which drew most of its support from plains state farmers, was in accord with Secretary Anderson's position at least partly because it was sensitive to urban concerns and criticism of the farm program. Patton realized that urban goodwill toward the farmer was crucial to the success of any farm program and that a hostile reaction could lead to the destruction of all price supporting techniques. Flexible supports, as proposed by Anderson and later incorporated in Senator George Aiken's 1948 bill, were a "means of deemphasizing price supports" and a step in the direction of the real NFU position—direct or income subsidies for farmers.[50] In addition, Patton had long held out hopes for the building of a farmer-worker coalition. It would appear that the NFU's position in 1947 and early 1948 was a transition stance for the organization between its former commitment to high fixed supports and its late 1948 and 1949 commitment to production payments, such as those proposed by Secretary Brannan.

Interestingly, the nation's largest farm organization, the American Farm Bureau Federation, was more tentative in its initial reaction to the Anderson program. Although President O'Neal recognized the need for new farm legislation, he was not convinced the old support system should be abandoned. During much of 1947, Anderson found himself in an unlikely position; the NFU supported the key provisions

49. House Committee, *Long-Range Agricultural Policy,* 131; Angus McDonald, "Anderson's Program," 30. Patton was a key player in the development of the original full-employment bill, which embodied the liberal consensus' rationale for government intervention in the postwar economy. When finally passed, however, the Employment Act of 1946 was a grave disappointment; Patton believed the administration had compromised away any real commitment to full employment (Flamm, "National Farmers Union and the Evolution of Agrarian Liberalism," 55, 78–79; Clinton P. Anderson, "'Work Conquers All Things': Full Employment First Requisite for Farm Prosperity," 661; Hamby, *Man of the People,* 366–67).

50. Hall, "Aiken Bill," 22; Hamby, *Beyond the New Deal,* 223–24.

of the administration's proposal, while the AFBF was, at best, skeptical about the plan.[51]

On June 19, 1947, during a break following the opening round
of committee hearings, Congressman Hope managed to escape the
nation's capital long enough to deliver a speech in Syracuse, New
York. Addressing the annual meeting of the Dairymen's League, Hope
had an opportunity to assess his committee's progress. Although there
was much to be done, Hope assured his audience that

> the hearings have brought out some very fine and constructive
> ideas and suggestions and, in many ways, a surprising unanimity
> of opinion. Perhaps the greatest unanimity existed on the sub-
> jects of soil conservation and research. Everyone who appeared
> put these problems high on the list for solution. Nearly everyone
> thought there must be a revision of parity. . . .
>
> Most of the witnesses suggested the need of price or income
> supports, although there were wide differences of opinion as to
> levels of support and the methods to be used.
>
> Cooperative marketing and financing were discussed and rec-
> ommended by many witnesses. Many recommended a program
> of abundant production, although not many explained what they
> meant by the term.[52]

There was also agreement on the need to seek out new markets and
general endorsement of the school lunch program.

Two days after Chairman Hope's Syracuse analysis, the *Saturday
Evening Post* reflected on the committee's efforts and discussed the
general farm problem for its readership. Although prices were high,
according to the popular weekly magazine, Congress had renewed

51. In his April 22, 1947, testimony, Edward O'Neal claimed a membership
of 1,128,000 for the AFBF (House Committee, *Long-Range Agricultural Policy,*
29). According to Robert L. Tontz, the AFBF had nearly 1.5 million family mem-
berships in 1950 (710,416 of these in the Midwest and 477,290 in the South);
the National Grange had 442,728 (more than half of them coming from the
northeast); and the NFU (1953 figures) could claim 216,406 (more than half
from the plains states) ("Membership of General Farmers' Organizations, United
States, 1874–1960," 143). See also William R. Johnson, "National Farm Organizations and Reshaping Agricultural Policy in 1932," 35; Morton Rothstein,
"Farmers Movements and Organizations: Numbers, Gains, Losses," 161.

52. "A Long Time Program For American Agriculture," June 19, 1947, Speech
file, Hope Papers.

the "twenty-five-year quest for an effective farm program." Experts
worried about agriculture's future without the unusually high demand
levels of the past few years. A new program was needed to replace
the second AAA, which had proven inadequate even before the
beginning of World War II. Most agreed this was made imperative
by the productive forces unleashed during the war that promised
ever-increasing supplies. In light of these and other developments,
particularly the estimated $80 million spent on the 1946 potato pro-
gram, the *Post* predicted that if price supports were retained they
would likely be placed "on a sliding scale to act as a brake on overproduction." The national interest would be served by a good agricultural program, the article concluded, that provided for farm stability and the security of the U.S. food supply, promoted a better
national diet, and implemented a national land program emphasizing
soil conservation.[53]

In a somewhat more critical tone, Angus McDonald told *New Republic* readers that Hope's effort to "mend the roof while the sun
was shining" was a bit optimistic in light of the fact that under the current program some farmers benefited more than others. "The trouble
with price support is that it doesn't give aid in proportion to the
need," McDonald insisted. "In certain instances it can even be com-
pared with some of the Republican help-the-rich schemes."[54] Since
the top 10 percent of the producers sold 50 percent of the farm commodities, they obviously stood to get the most support.

McDonald favored the more radical approach, partially reflected
in the testimony of Jim Patton, in which the parity formula would be
revised but the government would guarantee farmers a minimum
income. There also was to be an emphasis on increasing the number of
family-size farms through an active program of government purchase
and resale. "As large farms came on the market," McDonald explained, "they were to be bought up by the government and resold to
farmers." In addition, "Small farms were to be enlarged and mecha-
nized so they could produce efficiently." Although "Patton's plan"
undoubtedly had "some flaws and inconsistencies in it," McDonald

53. "New Farm Program is in 'Blueprint Stage,'" 160.
54. Angus McDonald, "Toward a New Plan," 31.

was enthusiastic about its possibilities and insisted that "it is a thoroughgoing effort to show how the American family-size farm may be preserved."[55]

While the USDA worked out the details of Anderson's proposal, the House Committee on Agriculture was preparing to take its show on the road "to give farmers themselves in every part of the country an opportunity to present to the Committee their ideas on a long-range program for American agriculture."[56] After hearing the specific proposals presented by the department and other groups in Washington, the committee traveled across the country, holding meetings in twelve cities from Durham, New Hampshire, to Fresno, California, and visiting farms to observe agricultural methods and to get "grass roots" opinion. A subcommittee of the Senate Committee on Agriculture and Forestry, chaired by George Aiken, followed a similar course of action, hearing from farm organizations, USDA officials, and more than three hundred actual farmers before submitting a report on its findings that was to serve as the basis for the Senate long-range farm policy bill.[57]

In a letter to Charles M. Hardin, professor of political science at the University of Chicago, Hope, who had just reviewed a "rough draft chapter" from Hardin's "book covering the field hearings," commented on the "difficulties inherent in holding hearings of this kind." In general, Hope thought they had been as successful as possible under the circumstances. More time would have been propitious, and he was disappointed that more committee members had not participated, but those who did attend got a more accurate picture of real grassroots opinion "than could be secured from cold print." "With respect to the general value of the hearings," Hope believed "that at least half of the value came from the contacts obtained with farmers outside of the formal hearings. . . . One of the advantages of traveling in a bus, as we did for a good part of this trip, was the opportunity

55. Ibid., 31, 32. For Patton's proposal, see House Committee, *Long-Range Agricultural Policy,* 132, 138.

56. Press Release, July 28, 1947, Agricultural Legislation; Hope to Lee Hannify, radio farm editor, United Press, August 15, 1947, Speech file, Hope Papers.

57. Aiken, *Congressional Record* (hereafter cited as *CR*), 80th Cong., 2nd sess., Senate, June 15, 1948, 94, pt. 7: 8301–02.

afforded to stop at wayside farms or in Court House squares and talk individually with farmers or small town people. This balanced up in many ways the witnesses that appeared at the formal hearings."[58]

In October 1947, the administration's plan was fleshed out and presented to the Congress. "Anderson's program" was well received in most quarters and, according to Angus McDonald, brought together many ideas endorsed by the major farm groups. Although it reflected considerable agreement with the AFBF, the program also contained some concepts supported by the NFU: a revision of parity, a food-allotment plan, and the election of county agricultural committees. It neglected the family-size farm, but the Anderson proposal contained many good features, McDonald admitted, and "nearly everybody has endorsed most of the program."[59]

"Everybody," as McDonald correctly pointed out, included the AFBF. The bureau's accord with the administration's approach to farm policy, which allowed for this brief brush with virtual unanimity, occurred as a result of a change in the AFBF's national leadership. After an internal power struggle between the southern and midwestern wings of the organization, the AFBF came under the leadership of a conservative Iowan, Allan B. Kline, one of the country's most vocal critics of an inflexible parity price policy. Reflecting the southern position, the outgoing president, Edward O'Neal, had openly attacked the policy of abundance; he considered the USDA program impracticable and advocated high, fixed parity support levels. O'Neal had led the AFBF since 1931 and helped craft New Deal policies that were especially generous to cotton and tobacco growers. In contrast, Kline, the former president of the Iowa Farm Bureau, advocated a policy of abundance, much like what the Brannan committee had recommended.

58. Hope to Hardin, January 27, 1949, FF, Hope Papers. The book about which Hardin and Hope corresponded appears to have been Hardin's *The Politics of Agriculture: Soil Conservation and the Struggle for Power in Rural America,* 198. Hardin was generally complimentary of the effort to reach out for farm opinion but critical of the procedure that he said really allowed the committees to hear only from farm leaders (Hardin, "Politics of Agriculture in the United States," 571–583).

59. McDonald, "Anderson's Program," 31. McDonald, who can be considered an unofficial spokesman for the NFU, was convinced that despite its support the program would not become law. "There is no more chance of Congress passing the food-allotment program than there is of Taft turning Communist."

He also opposed crop controls, called for full production and a thriving foreign trade, and favored some subsidized consumption, but he believed in relatively low levels of parity support.[60]

The change in leadership marked a shift in national Farm Bureau policy from high to flexible supports and amounted to an endorsement of the Anderson approach. The split between O'Neal and Kline (or the southern and midwestern wings of the AFBF) also reflected the differences that existed among commodity interests. The change in the AFBF's policy position did not mean that southern congressmen would abandon their own long-held beliefs. Many continued to support the 90 percent of parity principle, despite the national position of the South's dominant farm organization. By doing so, they helped make the House of Representatives, where they had their most power, a formidable obstacle to significant farm policy change in 1948.[61]

During a period of relative prosperity, many grain farmers in the Midwest were willing to risk a freer market to avoid more government control. More dependent on a single crop, however, southern cotton producers were willing to accept controls if they guaranteed high market prices for their vital commodity. With the election of Kline at its annual federation meeting, the AFBF convention endorsed flexible price supports, and, like the USDA, the bureau began to turn "its back on the farm program of the New Deal."[62] While the NFU was endorsing flexibility as a transition to production payments and an ever-increasing government role in agriculture, the AFBF saw its similar position as part of a move in the opposite direction: to the complete elimination of government support for agriculture and a return to the free market.[63]

---

60. Matusow, *Farm Policies and Politics,* 137; *Current Biography,* 1948, 24.

61. Theodore Saloutos, "Agricultural Organizations and Farm Policy in the South after World War II," 388–89.

62. Matusow, *Farm Policies and Politics,* 136, 138.

63. Kline's election, wrote Samuel Berger, marked the ascendancy of "the Farm Bureau's generation of agri-business executive leaders." Their concern was primarily with the nation's commercial producers, not with subsistence farmers (a group that had been receiving increasing attention from reform-minded members of the USDA). The "turning point in Farm Bureau history" came at its 1948 convention when a "clean break" was made with the government farm program. This move split the AFBF off from other farm groups and started the bureau down the road of trying to "purge the federal government from agriculture"

Despite some fundamental philosophical differences, in 1947 Patton, Kline, and most of the other farm leaders could support the administration's policy of abundance and flexibility. By the end of that year, there seemed to be an emerging consensus with regard to certain aspects of the farm program. Flexible supports, linked to a modernization of parity, appeared to many to be the best solution to the troubled price support system. Their commitment to this plan hinged on the prosperity of the moment, though, and would not continue in the face of price declines. Congress failed to take advantage of this rare display of harmony, and the passage of a new farm bill was delayed until 1948. By that time a downturn in crop prices, the fear of imminent depression, and political posturing were destroying the basis for agreement.

Although farm organizations, the administration, and much of the Congress had been in agreement on the principle of flexibility, the underpinning for this fleeting period of accord was the idea of abundance. This economic philosophy was not unique to agriculture, but, by the beginning of 1945, it had become a panacea adopted and espoused by farm leaders throughout the country. The theory, which was at the heart of Theodore Schultz's influential plan for agriculture, maintained that with full employment and enough money the American consumer could and would, in the words of Allen Matusow, "eat most of the so-called surpluses. . . . The word *abundance* came to summarize a hopeful view of the farm problem, a view holding that not crop controls but full industrial employment in the coming peace was the best farm program. By rejecting restrictionist economics, the advocates of abundance broke sharply with the New Deal and created in effect a new liberalism."[64] This is a simplification of Schultz's analysis of the problem and its solution, but Matusow's observations are enlightening. As he explained, the adherents to this "new liberalism" seriously underestimated the "dimension of the technological change" that had already transformed agriculture in the United States. They did not understand that the increases in pro-

and "return the farm economy to the 'free market'" (Berger, *Dollar Harvest: The Story of the Farm Bureau,* 107–8; John Mark Hansen, *Gaining Access: Congress and the Farm Lobby, 1919–1981* , 112–47).

64. Matusow, *Farm Policies and Politics,* 115–16; Schultz, *Agriculture in an Unstable Economy.*

duction, which came in 1946 and 1947, were only the beginning of what was to come.

The new liberals saw the philosophy of abundance and full employment as the solution. With proper government programs, any surplus that did occur could be used to feed the poor. They held to the position that expanding consumption could solve the farm problem and foresaw an end to the old parity formula, because they believed full employment would keep farm incomes at these levels without it. They were convinced, explained Matusow, that "the peculiar marriage of parity and price supports stood as the foremost obstacle in bringing production into line with the desires of the consuming public. . . . By abandoning price supports and parity, the Government would restore sanity to farm prices and keep American agriculture competitive in international trade."[65] The new liberals were different, however, from traditional advocates of free enterprise, for they saw the need for a significant government role in the transition and expected it to act as a protector in times of economic downturn. They had no plans for the government to abandon the farmer but simply did not want that support tied to the old parity formula. Instead, the new liberals saw direct payments, or what Schultz called "compensatory payments," based on a "predepression price," rather than price supports determined by an "historical parity formula," as the best approach.[66]

Despite some agreement on the basic precepts, Congress reached no legislative consensus in 1947; indeed, it had no intention of acting decisively until the next session, which was to convene in January 1948. Secretary Anderson could be faulted for not pushing harder for legislation during the first session of the Eightieth Congress, but he was a political realist and may have been right to encourage Congress

65. Matusow, *Farm Policies and Politics,* 117–18.
66. Schultz, *Agriculture in an Unstable Economy,* 228. In his contribution to Day's volume, a collection of essays dedicated to Geoffrey S. Shepherd, Lauren Soth wrote that at this time many economists "explored proposals for compensatory payments to farmers in lieu of price supports. The economists were attracted to a plan for stabilizing farmers' incomes without interfering with commodity markets and thus avoiding unmanageable surpluses." They also "attributed the farm problem first to loss of foreign markets, then to slack domestic demand. They were slow to appreciate the consequences of the technological revolution in farming" (Soth, "Agricultural Economists and Public Policy," in Day, ed., *Economic Analysis and Agricultural Policy,* 50).

and the farm organizations to take the initial lead in working out specific policy to go with his general principles. As a political realist, Anderson should have known that the partisan climate of a presidential election year would not prove conducive to constructive legislative action. Compounding this problem was the fact that the apparent farm prosperity of 1947 and early 1948, which made some farm groups uncharacteristically willing to tinker with the old parity system, began to give way to price declines and fears of imminent depression.[67] When a new farm policy, the Hope-Aiken Act, finally did emerge from Congress, it reflected the diversity of opinion that was more characteristic of the American farm community.

67. Throughout 1947 food shortages were the major concern, not surpluses. In September, the president received advice from his cabinet committee on a world food program, and he appointed a Citizens Food Committee to advise on ways to conserve food at home and supported international efforts to this effect undertaken by the FAO. The administration also called on U.S. consumers to observe meatless days and took steps to allocate grain for the manufacture of alcoholic beverages (see, for example, Goss to Truman, September 25, 1947, and Truman to Goss, September 27, 1947, OF, Truman Papers; Anderson speech to "American Life Convention," October 9, 1947, Official Correspondence file, Anderson Papers; Citizens Food Committee Program, Anderson Speech, October 5, 1947, and Executive Order, December 30, 1947, OF, Truman Papers; "Report [from Secretary Anderson] on Consumer Program Conference," February 5, 1948, PSF, Truman Papers).

3

THE EIGHTIETH CONGRESS
TRIES TO "FIX THE ROOF"

The politically explosive year of 1948 opened with farm legislation promising to be a central issue of the legislative session and, possibly, of the campaign. In his message to the special session of Congress called in late 1947, Truman did not address the issue of long-range farm policy but instead focused on the crucial issues of foreign aid and inflation.[1] The president expanded his usual remarks on agriculture, however, in his "Annual Message to Congress on the State of the Union," delivered on January 7, 1948, and called for legislation patterned after USDA recommendations. Implementing a well-conceived political strategy in this policy area, the president challenged the Republican Congress to make good on its promises to the American farmer.[2] Everyone knew the time for action was at hand.

The president laid out an aggressive domestic program, including a call for a new farm program, but assured the nation that farmers were better off than ever before. Nevertheless, farm families still had a long way to go to "catch up with the standards of living enjoyed in the cities." High wages and full employment, along with "adequate diets for every American family," would help to achieve this goal. "[O]ur farm program," Truman insisted, "should enable the farmer to market his varied crops at fair price levels and to improve his standard of living." The administration's comprehensive program for

1. Truman, *Public Papers of the Presidents, 1947,* 498; Phillips, *Truman Presidency,* 326.
2. Truman, *Public Papers of the Presidents, 1948,* 1–10.

agriculture included the continuation of "price supports for major farm commodities on a basis which will afford reasonable protection against fluctuations in the levels of production and demand." To this end, Truman insisted, "The present price support program must be reexamined and modernized." The proposal also provided for improvements in federal crop insurance, better marketing techniques, support for cooperatives, expansion of the school lunch program, continued emphasis on rural electrification, and aid and encouragement for greater soil conservation efforts. "All these are practical measures," Truman asserted, "upon which we should act immediately to enable agriculture to make its full contribution to our prosperity."[3]

Many Republicans expressed concern about the potential cost of Truman's overall program, but few farm leaders objected to the basic elements of his farm proposal. In his January 14 economic report to Congress, the president elaborated on each of these points, placing a great deal of emphasis on abundant production. With respect to the controversial issue of commodity price supports, Truman insisted that they were "desirable as assurances against special dislocations which might arise in case of recession" but emphasized "the need for keeping support levels flexible."[4]

Secretary Anderson also began to apply considerable pressure during the early months of the 1948 session. In a letter to Senator Arthur Capper, chairman of the Committee on Agriculture and Forestry, Anderson wrote: "Once again I find it necessary to call to the attention of Congress certain basic problems involved in the mandatory price support provisions for farm commodities, and the administration of programs to carry out these legislative provisions. Potatoes are the crop of most immediate concern, but the basic principles apply to the other commodities which are covered by the Steagall Amendment and related legislation." Anderson reminded Capper that he had been calling for "prompt and thorough consideration" of the "whole question of price support policy" since November 1946, but,

3. Ibid., 5–6. For an interesting discussion of this phase of the search for agricultural policy, see Clarence Poe, "The Next Great Fight For Equality for Agriculture," *Progressive Farmer* (December 1947) in Thomas G. Abernethy (D-MS), Extension of Remarks, *CR,* 80th Cong., 2nd sess., House, January 26, 1948, 94, pt. 9, *Appendix:* A413.

4. Truman, *Public Papers of the Presidents, 1948,* 93.

"unfortunately, no legislative action has yet been taken. We are still operating under the same inflexible provisions which held eighteen months ago." Anderson insisted that he was not suggesting the revocation of postwar guarantees. "Farmers deserved this protection, and it would have been unthinkable to go back on the promise. At the same time, our farmers do not want production to continue under a frozen pattern which results in waste of production effort, money, and soil." What the secretary wanted was "action to achieve those adjustments in price support provisions which would be generally beneficial, while staying within the spirit of the price support commitments." Congress, Anderson averred, had to decide as soon as possible what was to happen after December 31, 1948, so that farmers would know how to plan their production. Action of this type was "important for all crops which are under price support; it is urgent for potatoes. The need for greater flexibility of methods and price levels should be considered."[5]

Congressional efforts to address the major farm issues discussed by Anderson and outlined by the president were already under way. Farm congressmen might have relished even more time for study, but they realized the clock was ticking. Both houses had thoroughly studied the issues in 1947, and their respective agricultural committees had renewed their efforts early in the second session. Unfortunately, as the debate progressed, it became apparent that the previous agreement on the principle of flexibility was breaking down, and the road ahead promised to be a rocky one.

On March 15, 1948, Senator George Aiken (R-VT), an old Truman friend, introduced a long-range program in the upper chamber.[6] The president and the senator, who was considered something of a "G.O.P. Rebel" during the first session of the Eightieth Congress, had developed a mutual respect and friendship during their service together on Capitol Hill.[7] This relationship continued after Truman's ascension to the White House. Aiken's farm bill embodied most of the

5. Anderson to Capper, February 26, 1948, Agricultural Correspondence, Capper Papers.
6. *CR,* 80th Cong., 2nd sess., Senate, March 15, 1948, 94, pt. 2: 2800.
7. "G.O.P. Rebels' Key Position: Four Who Could Prevent Overriding of Vetoes on Labor and Taxes," 20; Donovan, *Conflict and Crisis,* 15; Ken Hechler, *Working with Truman: A Personal Memoir of the White House Years,* 25.

administration's recommended farm program and thus had the support of the president and the secretary of agriculture. Clinton Anderson registered his support, if not complete endorsement, in an April 26 letter to Senator Capper. The secretary complimented the committee, which had "made a splendid start in attempting to accomplish a difficult task."[8]

The Aiken bill (S. 2318) made provision for a flexible support system and the modernization of the parity formula. Price supports were to be based on an adjustable scale from 60 to 90 percent of parity depending on the levels of production. Historians generally agree that the Aiken bill was a bipartisan measure. It also enjoyed significant support in all the agricultural regions of the country, with the exception of the cotton South, and had the distinction of gaining the endorsement of all the major farm organizations, including the NFU and the AFBF, shortly after its introduction.[9]

Unfortunately for the proponents of flexible supports and Aiken's sliding scale, as Allen Matusow explained, "the real strength of the farm bloc lay in the House of Representatives," and one could find precious little support for the plan there.[10] Consequently, on April 14, Congressmen Clifford Hope introduced a bill that revealed the farm bloc's continued attachment to high-level price supports. Reflecting the strength of southern interests in the House, the Hope bill (H.R. 6248) provided for 90 percent parity on basic commodities and flexible supports on certain other farm products at not less than 60 percent of parity. There appeared to be no grounds for compromise and the battle, which was to be waged into the summer and the closing days of the session, commenced.[11]

To the chagrin of the high support camp, advocates of flexibility

8. Anderson to Capper, April 26, 1948, Legislation 1, General Correspondence, 1948, Office of the Secretary of Agriculture, Record Group 16, National Archives and Records Administration, Washington, DC (hereafter cited as Office of the Secretary of Agriculture, RG 16, NA).

9. Agricultural Act of 1948, Correspondence, George D. Aiken Papers, Special Collections, Bailey/Howe Library, University of Vermont (hereafter cited as Aiken Papers); Hall, "Aiken Bill," 15–16, 21.

10. Matusow, *Farm Policies and Politics,* 141.

11. *CR,* 80th Cong., 2nd sess., House, April 14, 1948, 94, pt. 4: 4474; Benedict, *Farm Policies of the United States,* 473, 475.

had captured the political high ground. With the high cost of living on the national mind in 1948, the blame for inflated food prices was frequently, if unfairly, laid at the farmer's doorstep. A sensitivity to this urban criticism, according to historian Tom Hall, and the awareness that they were in the minority, helped make plains state farmers and senators unusually receptive to the Aiken bill's flexible support philosophy. Jim Patton, "chief spokesman for Plains farmers," realized that urban goodwill toward agriculture was crucial to the success of any farm program and that a hostile reaction, or urban revolt, could lead to the destruction of all price support programs. At a time when another agricultural depression seemed very possible, the Aiken plan, which at least offered relief in case of an emergency, was much better than no plan at all.[12]

Many blamed the antifarm bias of the eastern press for the misconceptions city people harbored about the high cost of groceries. High support advocates sought to counter these charges, insisting that consumers had reaped the benefits of the postwar farm program in the form of increased production. According to Harvard University's John D. Black, one of the country's leading agricultural economists, the charge that farm prices were causing high inflation was totally erroneous. Supply and demand, plus commodity speculation, had been holding some wholesale prices up, Black explained, but virtually all prices were well above parity and would stay so even if the support system were abolished. "Domestic demand," Black reasoned, was "almost solely responsible" for the high retail prices consumers were having to pay.[13] But the 90 percenters, such as Black, who supported the continuation of the existing program during this uncertain period of transition, had a difficult time convincing the general public that there was a large gap between farm prices and consumer prices that was responsible for high grocery bills.[14]

12. Hall, "Aiken Bill," 21–22.

13. J. D. Black, "Why Farm Prices Have Been High," *Christian Science Monitor,* entered by Representative Hope in *CR,* 80th Cong., 2nd sess., House, March 31, 1948, 94, pt. 10, *Appendix:* A2039–40. See also Black to Aiken, March 3, 1948, Agricultural Act of 1948, Correspondence, Aiken Papers.

14. See, among others, Arthur Lewis (R-NE), "The High Cost of Living," in *CR,* 80th Cong., 2nd sess., House, April 21, 1948, 94, pt. 4: 4622.

Despite the apparent growing dissatisfaction with the price support program, as the time of decision approached many farm leaders and legislators began to express an interest in the idea that the complete overhaul of the farm program should be further delayed. Some of the more vocal proponents of flexible supports were leaning toward a temporary extension of the transitionary program. In testimony before the Senate agricultural committee in late January, Allan Kline said the Farm Bureau now believed that revision of the existing farm program "should be deferred for the present in order that postwar conditions in which the legislation will have to operate will be more clearly appraised, and additional consideration can be given to needed changes." Previously, Albert Goss had stated a similar position for the National Grange before the House Committee on Agriculture, and Senator Capper echoed this sentiment: "The common point at which we seem to have arrived," he told a Kansas radio audience, "is that world conditions, . . . especially when our American Agriculture has been geared to enormous production for export, . . . still are so unsettled, that it probably will be necessary to pass over to a new Congress the job of revising the long range farm program."[15]

Thus, during the late winter and early spring of 1948, while the major farm groups remained in basic agreement with the principles enunciated in the Aiken bill, few seemed disturbed by the prospect of extending the Steagall guarantees if a satisfactory long-range policy could not be achieved during the current session. As for the many other facets of a truly comprehensive agricultural program, it appeared that these too would be delayed until the next session.

While the two houses of Congress sought in vain to hammer out a reasonable compromise on farm policy during the late spring, a changing of the guard was taking place at the Department of Agriculture. Undoubtedly weary after a difficult, but reasonably successful, three years as secretary of agriculture, Clinton Anderson decided to leave the cabinet and run for the Democratic senatorial nomination in his home state of New Mexico. Whether Anderson decided to leave his post in early 1948 to escape the apparently sinking Truman ship or, as Anderson himself insisted, because he believed he had "fulfilled

15. Quoted in Arthur Capper's WIBW Radio Speech, February 1 and March 28, 1948, Speeches, Capper Papers.

the mission" the president had given him, Truman was sorry to lose his friend and trusted lieutenant.[16]

The rumors of Anderson's imminent departure had begun anew in early March of 1948. When the president was asked about the reported resignation at his March 11 news conference, two days before the secretary told him of his decision to run for the Senate, the president said he had not seen Anderson and would thus not comment. When asked if he would be agreeable to this resignation, Truman responded abruptly: "I would not. I hope Secretary Anderson stays in the Cabinet. He is a good Secretary of Agriculture, and has done an excellent job."[17] There is no reason to question Truman's sincerity about this issue. He agreed to Anderson's initial suggestion that he stay at his job until the end of the session so he could "press for the adoption of a program of permanent farm legislation."[18]

Nevertheless, as word of Anderson's pending resignation spread, the president was deluged with letters and telegrams recommending a number of different men as replacements. But Truman was in no hurry to make a new appointment, and in late March he seemed to display an uncharacteristic pessimism about the prospects for a second Truman administration. On March 25, 1948, he informed Senator Harley M. Kilgore of West Virginia that Anderson had agreed to stay at his post until Congress adjourned. As a result, Truman explained, he might not need a new secretary.[19]

Circumstances changed, however, when Anderson found that he would have to wage a primary campaign. Consequently, the effective date of his departure was moved up, and Truman formally accepted Anderson's resignation on May 10. The secretary admitted that his

16. Anderson, *Outsider in the Senate,* 84–90. In 1985, former Secretary of Agriculture Brannan was emphatic in his conviction that Anderson left the administration because of the political outlook. He resigned and ran for the Senate because he did not think Truman had "a snowball's chance of being elected" (Brannan, interview). Senator Robert Taft also interpreted Anderson's resignation as an indication that Democrats recognized coming defeat (AP, "Flat Dixie No to Truman's Renomination," *Topeka Daily Capital,* March 14, 1948).

17. Truman, *Public Papers of the Presidents, 1948,* 179.

18. Anderson to Truman, March 13, 1948, PSF, Truman Papers; AP, "Flat Dixie No to Truman's Renomination," *Topeka Daily Capital,* March 14, 1948. The Anderson announcement was presented with reports of an intensification of the southern Democratic revolt as bad news for Truman's reelection campaign.

19. Truman to Kilgore, March 27, 1948, OF, Truman Papers.

three years had been "tough ones" for the department, but he wrote, "It has been a great pleasure to serve in your Cabinet." Anderson's "decision to leave" was especially difficult because Truman had "always given earnest attention to the interests of farmers." The New Mexican predicted that "when the farmers of this country reflect on how they have progressed during the Roosevelt and Truman administrations . . . they will quickly see how much they have gained by your friendly consideration of their problems, and by your steady personal interest in the long range welfare of agriculture. You deserve well at their hands."[20]

Although quite controversial at times, Anderson left the administration in rather good shape with respect to agriculture. After a rocky start, administration efforts to confront the European famine and other reconversion crises were relatively effective. Secretary Anderson had laid the groundwork for a successful campaign to win farm support in 1948, and when judged in the context of the time, according to James Forsythe, he "emerges as a strong Secretary." Anderson "brought a businessman's ideas of efficiency and coordination into the chief governmental agency which needed these reforms."[21]

Columnist Drew Pearson, a frequent critic of the administration, complimented the outgoing secretary. He credited Anderson with almost single-handedly saving Italy from communism with his postwar farm policy decisions and for increasing grain supplies in time to feed much of the remainder of Europe. "Clint Anderson has been one of the most refreshing and variegated personalities in the turbulent Truman Administration," wrote Pearson. "Though Anderson says he was a better congressman than cabinet member, actually he did an outstanding job as secretary of agriculture. . . . Most people think that running the Department of Agriculture is a matter of putting out booklets on soil conservation, boll weevil and how to preserve vegetables. But it isn't. And in these days where crop shortages can cause Communism, the U.S.A. has been lucky to have as secretary of agriculture a farsighted statesman."[22] With this and several other equally

20. Anderson to Truman, May 7, 1948, OF, Truman Papers.
21. Forsythe, "Clinton P. Anderson," 9–10.
22. "Drew Pearson on the Washington Merry-Go-Round," *Washington Post,* May 13, 1948, clipping in Alphabetical Correspondence file, Anderson Papers.

flattering send-offs, Anderson left the USDA in the hands of his trusted lieutenant, Charles F. Brannan, and went home to New Mexico.[23]

Meanwhile, on Capitol Hill, work continued on a farm policy package. Price supports were the most controversial feature, but fundamental differences existed on certain other basic issues. Soil conservation, everyone agreed, had to be a part of any complete farm program. But below this surface level of accord, differences—rooted in history, tradition, and ideology—ran deep. On one side were the proponents of the Aiken bill. As introduced, Titles I and II of this proposed legislation "would have decentralized administration" of government conservation efforts, explained Charles Hardin, "in a manner highly satisfactory to the colleges of agriculture," the extension service, and the Farm Bureau.[24] The other camp included the major farm organizations that did not enjoy the bureau's close ties with the county agents. Ably led by Congressman Hope who introduced a separate bill (H.R. 6054), this latter coalition "expected to make every effort to substitute" the provisions of Hope's bill "for the soil conservation features of the Aiken bill."[25]

Hope insisted that H.R. 6054 reflected the thinking of many experts and farmers throughout the country, and he maintained that it did not "give the Soil Conservation Service [SCS] or the Secretary of Agriculture one bit of power which they do not have at the present time." Nevertheless, the bill elicited the "bitter opposition" of the AFBF, which, according to Hope, wanted the Extension Service to "take over

23. Anderson went on to wage successful primary and general election campaigns, returning to the nation's capital in January 1949 as the junior senator from New Mexico. Senator Anderson wasted little time in getting back in the battle for permanent agricultural legislation and fought, during the first session of the Eighty-first Congress, for a bill in many ways similar to the program he championed while serving in the cabinet. But by this time the Truman-Brannan administration had departed from the course charted by Truman and Anderson. To his consternation, the former secretary found himself opposing a new administration farm plan embraced by his old boss and championed by his former assistant.

24. Hardin, *Politics of Agriculture,* 26, 104–42, for an excellent discussion of the relationships among the various organizations, agencies, and interest groups involved in the formulation and administration of farm policy.

25. Hope to Jack E. Reynolds et al. (Grant County Supervisors), May 24, 1948, and to Blackwell, May 22, 1948, FF, Hope Papers.

the soil conservation service." He argued that "the present successful cooperation" between these two agencies was critical, with the Extension Service responsible for the educational work and the SCS for the action programs. Hope believed the country could not have an effective soil conservation policy if it were broken "up into 48 state programs or 3,000 county programs. Erosion problems don't stop at state and county lines." Notwithstanding the apparent logic of Hope's argument, the opposition remained adamant. As for the Kansas congressman, he was unwilling to make "substantial compromises" and thus believed no such legislation would pass during the current session.[26]

In general, Hope agreed with those who questioned the advisability of moving too fast toward a final farm program. "I am not satisfied with the Aiken bill which is now pending in the Senate," he wrote on May 28.

> In fact, I am not sure this is the time to write a long range program. My present thinking is that it might be better to extend the present program for another year and then write a long range program in the next Congress.
> ... In the main, farmers seem to be pretty well satisfied with the way things are going now and apparently they aren't urging any action on the part of Members of Congress. In the preparation of any bill there have to be a good many compromises and changes, and as long as there isn't much interest it's hard to get Members to agree to the compromises which must be made. Furthermore, I think there is just as much justification for continuing the present plan, on the theory that under the Marshall Plan agriculture is still pretty much on a war basis in this country.
> The present Steagall program was written to take care of the war period and, in view of the current situation, it may be just as well to operate under it for another year.[27]

26. Hope to Representative Charles A. Halleck, May 25, 1948; to Harry F. Stitt, June 3, 1948, and to James Murphy, May 24, 1948, FF, Hope Papers. The proposed "National Land Policy Act," officially "A Bill to establish conservation and orderly development of the Nation's agricultural land and water resources as a basic policy of the United States," was not introduced by Hope until July 1948. The Eightieth Congress delayed action on a new soil conservation program and simply extended the Soil Conservation and Domestic Allotment Act during the closing hours of its second session (See copy of H.R. 6054, Legislative Correspondence, Hope Papers).
27. Hope to Vandie Richie, May 28, 1948, FF, Hope Papers.

Other congressmen expressed similar sentiments, especially those from the South and the West. Representative Ezekiel Gathings of Arkansas, a Democratic member of the House Committee on Agriculture, defended the committee's decision to extend the postwar support program for another year. He too was convinced "that these unsettled times" were "not the proper time to draw up a long-range program which would commit the farmer for years to come, regardless of the world situation."[28]

Nevertheless, with only weeks left before the expected June 19 adjournment, Republican leaders in the Senate and the House faced increasing pressure for action. On June 1, Congressman Stephen Pace expressed his desire to cooperate with the GOP majority and insisted that he did not want to promote partisanship. He forcefully reminded his colleagues, however, that the Eightieth Congress had to act on at least three vital aspects of the farm program that were scheduled to expire at the end of the year: (1) the 90 percent support program, (2) the Commodity Credit Corporation charter, and (3) the Soil Conservation and Domestic Allotment Act. With Republicans such as H. Carl Andersen of Minnesota echoing agreement, Pace asserted that "the support program is the heart of the farm program" and that Congress must, at the very least, extend the three programs he listed.[29]

Members of both parties in the Senate were also expressing analogous concerns. On June 2, Senator Aiken, who was ready to stay all summer if necessary, insisted that it was "absolutely unthinkable that the Congress would adjourn and go home without enacting" proposed long-range farm legislation. Senator Scott Lucas, an Illinois Democrat, agreed that action of this type was crucial. "I certainly hope," he told members of the upper chamber, "that the Republican policy committee will include in their 'must' program the long-range farm and agriculture program bill."[30]

While some continued to hold out hope for a genuine long-range bill, it soon became clear that differences ran too deep for a satisfactory compromise at this late date. Clifford Hope believed that "price

28. *CR,* 80th Cong., 2nd sess., House, April 30, 1948, 94, pt. 4: 5116–17.
29. *CR,* 80th Cong., 2nd sess., House, June 1, 1948, 94, pt. 5: 6839.
30. *CR,* 80th Cong., 2nd sess., Senate, June 2, 1948, 94, pt. 5: 6921.

supports should be on a flexible basis" when the long-range program was finally enacted, but he insisted that this could not, and should not, be attempted during the current session. He also argued that, despite the fears expressed by some consumers, "extending support prices on agricultural commodities at 90% of parity" would not cause any further rise in the cost of living. This was true because "practically every agricultural commodity is now considerably above 90% of parity. . . . In other words," he wrote on June 7, "if the price of all agricultural commodities were to come down to 90% of parity and be supported at that price, it would mean a considerable drop in the cost of food."[31]

Hope's assurances notwithstanding, the cost-of-living issue surfaced frequently in the halls of Congress. On June 11, during debate on House Resolution 638, which provided for consideration of H.R. 6248, opponents often appeared driven by the belief that high price supports were contributing to high consumer prices, while supporters insisted that they held prices down by ensuring abundant production.[32] Congressman Ross Rizley (R-OK) applauded farmers for their vital role in helping to win the war and secure the peace and praised the existing price support programs. He insisted that they had "been conducted without cost to the tax-payer" and had "aided materially in checking the inflationary spiral by assuring at all times an adequate food supply." He also believed that the committee had acted wisely in extending the program because "the domestic and foreign demand for most agricultural commodities has been so great that producers have not had the 2-year period to readjust production to peacetime conditions as was contemplated in the original law establishing price support."[33]

After reminding the House that the bill to be considered had been unanimously reported by the Committee on Agriculture, Rizley closed

31. Hope to W. F. Levy, June 7, 1948, FF, Hope Papers.
32. *CR*, 80th Cong., 2nd sess., House, June 11, 1948, 94, pt. 6: 7891. The arguments directed against Republicans during this debate focused on the fact that they were advocating a support program that was not really needed in light of the high cost of living and rising farm incomes. During the election campaign that followed, the GOP was attacked in general for attempting to scuttle the support system altogether.
33. *CR*, 80th Cong., 2nd sess., House, June 11, 1948, 94, pt. 6: 7891.

with an appeal to agrarian fundamentalism and the memory of a departed colleague:

> Mr. Speaker, no one who has made any study of the past period of our history in respect to its economic stability can successfully dispute the fact that when we have a healthy agriculture in this country, when agriculture is prosperous, we have a healthy and prosperous business. This bill is absolutely as necessary now as it was in the days when the late lamented Congressman Steagall, whom we all knew and loved, fostered this idea. He was the daddy of it. These conditions with which we are confronted today I think demand that this bill have our full support.[34]

Reflecting the concerns of many of the bill's opponents, especially those representing predominantly urban districts, George G. Sadowski, a Democrat from Detroit, Michigan, asked, "in view of the high prices that the consumers in the cities must pay for food today, is not this bill just a guaranty for a continuation of the high cost of living to the consumers in the cities?" Despite Rizley's assurances to the contrary, Representative Chester E. (Chet) Holifield, a Los Angeles, California Democrat, came back with a comment that aptly expressed the political concerns of many urbanites. "I am in somewhat of a quandary," he admitted, "about supporting this program in view of the fact I have no farms in my district and the people in my district are paying 97 cents a pound for ordinary beef."[35]

Before the formal introduction of H.R. 6248, the debate turned a bit more partisan. Democrats Adolph J. Sabath of Illinois and Helen Gahagan Douglas of California, both of whom said they would vote for the bill mainly because it was an extension of a New Deal program, criticized their Republican colleagues for being insensitive to the high cost-of-living problem. Congressman Sabath accused the GOP of championing the interests of big business while being unable to find the time "to help the needy and deserving people who should have their support." In fact, Sabath continued, "the remedy suggested by one of the Republican candidates for the Presidency [Senator Robert Taft] to combat the high cost of living was for the people to eat less. . . . Today the Republican candidates, instead of being interested

---

34. *CR,* 80th Cong., 2nd sess., House, June 11, 1948, 94, pt. 6: 7892.
35. *CR,* 80th Cong., 2nd sess., House, June 11, 1948, 94, pt. 6: 7892.

in feeding the people with food, are feeding them with the fear of communism and more communism." He also blasted Republicans for emasculating the price control system and called on the "gentlemen whose constituents will be the beneficiaries under this legislation" to "show some reciprocity" by supporting such things as increased wages for urban workers.[36]

Subsequently, Chairman Hope introduced H.R. 6248, a bill for the purpose of stabilizing prices of agricultural commodities, and proceeded to explain its basic provisions. As the congressman indicated, his bill mainly sought "to taper off wartime price support and build a bridge to a comprehensive long-range program." The Hope bill was an extension of the existing program and was to be in effect from January 1, 1949, to June 30, 1950. It provided for price supports of 90 percent parity on basic commodities (wheat, corn, tobacco, rice, cotton, and peanuts) and at least 60 percent parity support for the so-called Steagall commodities, down from the 90 percent minimum of the existing law. An exception with regard to the latter group of commodities was made for milk and its products, which were to be supported at 90 percent of parity. As directed by the Committee on Agriculture, Hope also offered a committee amendment that stipulated that hogs, chickens, eggs, and potatoes (harvested before January 1, 1949) be added to the list of "commodities to be supported at not less than 90 percent of parity." An additional provision of some significance, not contained in the existing law, gave the secretary of agriculture the "authority to require compliance with production goals and marketing regulations as a condition to eligibility of producers for price support." This provision, Hope expounded, made it possible for the secretary to deal with commodities that were "in overproduction or threatened overproduction; in other words, it will give him some authority to deal with a situation like the potato situation with which we have been confronted for the past 3 years."[37]

36. *CR,* 80th Cong., 2nd sess., House, June 11, 1948, 94, pt. 6: 7893–95, 7899–7900. Senator Taft's remark, referred to by Congressman Sabath, had been made in September 1947. Not surprisingly, since "Mr. Republican" was a leading contender for the GOP presidential nomination, it had been distorted by the press and repeated frequently for partisan purposes throughout 1948 (see Richard Norton Smith, *Thomas E. Dewey and His Times,* 478–79).
37. *CR,* 80th Cong., 2nd sess., House, June 11, 1948, 94, pt. 6: 7900, 7901.

Hope realized that the provision in the new bill for potatoes produced in 1948, regardless of when they were marketed, was especially controversial. He insisted, however, that it was necessary because the Steagall 90 percent guarantee expired on December 31. Without the proposed change, there almost certainly would be a glut of potatoes sold before the deadline.[38] Despite the apparent logic behind this new provision, the debate that followed focused primarily on the potato program and its cost to the taxpayer.

In addition to the concern expressed with regard to the dogged potato issue, opposition of a more general nature was voiced by a quartet of conservative Republicans. Leading the assault on the Hope amendment was Chester Gross of Pennsylvania. "I am sorry," he began, "that I should have to rise in opposition to a committee amendment. I am also sorry that the Committee on Agriculture has become the tool and spokesman and the mouthpiece of a gang of 'do-gooders' and New Dealers down in the Department of Agriculture, who lay awake at night trying to find ways of doing things to help the people of this country." The congressman insisted that "this whole parity program is wrong": first, the program was too costly; second, parity was intended to protect against major losses, not to guarantee profits or encourage production; and third, farmers did not even want the program.

Representatives Fred Busbey of Illinois, Ellsworth Buck of New York, and Leon Gavin of Pennsylvania echoed Congressman Gross's position. Busbey insisted that the GOP was not staying true to its commitments to economy when it supported these subsidy programs. Buck was somewhat more imaginative in his attack on a bill that he insisted "ought to be [entitled], 'A bill to guarantee that the high cost of living will not go down for 2 years, and for no other purpose.'" Gavin, who reminded the House that America was built on free enterprise, was surprised that the Republicans were "now picking up where the New Deal left off." In principle, he insisted, his party opposed subsidies but continued them just the same.[39]

38. *CR,* 80th Cong., 2nd sess., House, June 12, 1948, 94, pt. 6: 7983.
39. *CR,* 80th Cong., 2nd sess., House, June 12, 1948, 94, pt. 6: 7985, 7986, 7989. Only one of the four Republicans mentioned here returned to Washington as a member of the Eighty-first Congress. Gross and Busbey were unsuccessful candidates for reelection in November 1948, and Buck was not a candidate

The remarks of these four maverick Republicans might be considered insignificant. But it is interesting to note that they opened the door for an opportunistic Democratic attack on the apparent inconsistencies in the GOP position on farm issues. Following a comment by Iowa congressman Charles B. Hoeven, who insisted that this was not a "party matter" and that members of his party should remember that "the backbone of the Republican Party is in the agricultural States of the Midwest," former Majority Leader John W. McCormack (D-MA) expressed his hope that "the backbone of the Republican Party, the farmers," would remember who gave them farm legislation. Calling up the specter of Hooverism, the Massachusetts Democrat recalled how Republicans had allowed farmers to be "prostrated" during the early depression years. "It was only after we Democrats came in under the leadership of the immortal Franklin D. Roosevelt that a real farm program was put into operation. It is most pleasing to know that the Republican Party has finally been converted." McCormack emphasized the benefits derived by farmers from this New Deal legislation and continued by driving home his main point: "despite all of the characterizations of past years the great majority of the Republican Members of Congress are now coming in falling over one another to try and show their farmer constituents that they favor this legislation which is strictly New Deal legislation proposed by Franklin D. Roosevelt and put on the statute books by a Democratic-controlled Congress against the severe opposition of the Republican Party in Congresses of the past."[40]

When Clarence J. Brown (R-OH) reminded the former majority leader that some Republicans had helped pass farm legislation after the first AAA was invalidated, McCormack retorted: "The gentleman is trying to hang his hat on the gentleman from Kansas [Mr. Hope], who is one of the real outstanding Members of Congress and who as a Republican was constantly repudiated by his own party in bygone years when he was trying to cooperate with the Democratic majority in getting through a real, sound, stable agricultural program.

for renomination. Only Gavin successfully defended his congressional seat (see *Biographical Directory of the American Congress, 1774–1961,* online at http://bioguide.congress.gov/biosearch/biosearch.asp).

40. *CR,* 80th Cong., 2nd sess., House, June 12, 1948, 94, pt. 6: 7990.

It is very pleasing now to note our Republican friends are converted to good Democratic policies."[41] There can be little doubt that these remarks, coming as they did on the eve of the 1948 election campaign, had definite political overtones; indeed, this interlude of partisan rankling was a harbinger for the acrimonious presidential contest to follow later that year.

In the House, cooler heads prevailed, at least to some extent, and debate on H.R. 6248 was subsequently limited to thirty minutes; the bill then passed with bipartisan support.[42] Even so, Congressman Hope recognized the concerns of those who articulated the pervasive inflationary argument. Making specific reference to the recent fall in the price of wheat, Hope told a constituent that "the public generally seemed to rejoice," believing as they did that "it might reduce living costs somewhat" and decrease the burden on the federal treasury. But it simply did not work that way where wheat was concerned. "Of course, the situation varies with different commodities," Hope admitted, "and in the case of some of them the farm price exerts a great deal more influence on the price the consumer pays than on others." "The fact is," he continued,

> we are going to have a very difficult time in keeping government price supports on agricultural commodities. If there is any one subject in the world that people are stirred up about now, it is the high cost of living. People have a lot of erroneous ideas on that, but that doesn't make any difference. . . .
>
> The farm population of this country is now only 19% of our total population and is going down all the time. We can't have a farm program in this country unless we can convince the rest of the people that it is for their benefit also. Here in the East and, in fact, in the cities everywhere, East or West, everybody is jumping on the farmers because of the high cost of living.

Unfortunately, when it came to this sensitive pocketbook issue, "most people are not inclined to listen to reason or logic on the matter."[43]

The congressman went on to register his trepidation regarding the Senate's long-range agricultural program that had recently been

41. *CR,* 80th Cong., 2nd sess., House, June 12, 1948, 94, pt. 6: 7990.
42. *CR,* 80th Cong., 2nd sess., House, June 12, 1948, 94, pt. 6: 8014.
43. Hope to L. M. Baer, June 15, 1948, FF, Hope Papers.

reported with the unanimous support of its agricultural committee. In particular, he was troubled by the provision that pegged "price supports at from 60% to 90% of parity." Not only would the regular support level be 75 percent rather than 90 percent of parity, "the Senate bill also revises parity in such a way," Hope explained, "that instead of wheat parity being $2.20 a bushel as it is under the present formula, it would be $1.79 a bushel; so that the support price would not be 75% of $2.20, but 75% of $1.79." Hope did not think the Aiken bill would pass, but he recognized that the Senate held the political advantage with regard to national attitudes and that trouble lay ahead for farm producers. "No one knows how long the taxpayers of this country are going to be willing to put up money to ship food stuffs overseas," and the hard reality was this: "We cannot keep up our present volume of wheat production without exporting three hundred to five hundred million bushels as we have been doing. So the time is coming when the wheat producers of this country will be confronted with the proposition of having overproduction or going through a drastic reduction of acreage. We simply can't continue producing over a billion bushels a year, as we have been doing lately, and expect to sell it at anything like the prices we have been getting."[44]

Hope's consternation regarding the Aiken bill (S. 2318) was warranted. On the evening of June 15, the same day Hope penned his concerns, the Senate resumed consideration of its long-range farm bill with Senator Aiken delivering the committee's preliminary statement. He assured his Senate colleagues that the committee had worked long and hard on this program and that it had "acted as a unit." Partisanship, he insisted, had not entered into the deliberations, and S. 2318 was being "reported out of the committee unanimously." In fact, "we have acted unanimously all the way through, from the very beginning, almost 9 months ago."[45]

As explained by Senator Aiken, Titles I and II of the proposed bill dealt with "reorganization and reassignment of functions performed by the United States Department of Agriculture," specifically pertaining to soil conservation. This was an especially controversial aspect of

44. Ibid.
45. *CR,* 80th Cong., 2nd sess., Senate, June 15, 1948, 94, pt. 7: 8301.

the new bill and a point of considerable contention between the two houses. Under the Senate provisions, soil conservation programs were to be "decentralized so as to bring their exercise closer to farmers, provide for greater farmer participation, and to coordinate services at the local level." A new agency, the Bureau of Agricultural Conservation and Improvement, was to be created to take over many of the functions carried out by the Soil Conservation Service, which essentially was abolished. The bill also provided for an expanded role for the extension service and experiment stations, with an emphasis on state and local control, especially as it related to educational, informational, and research activities. Programs were to be administered through a new group of community, county, and state committees.

Title III of the Aiken bill amended the price support provisions of the Agricultural Adjustment Act of 1938; the new plan, as the senator demonstrated, "base[d] price supports on the supply as well as upon market prices, thus giving flexible price supports." The method of computing parity was to be "changed to the extent necessary to give appropriate recognition to changes in relationships between the agricultural commodities themselves occurring since the base period from 1910 to 1914, such as those resulting from the discovery of new uses or new methods of production."

In an attempt to further untangle the parity enigma, Senator Aiken elaborated:

> S. 2318 would provide a formula which, while preserving the 1910–14 relationship between farm and nonfarm prices, will reflect the developments of recent years. Thus, while parity prices on the average would be based on the differences between the 1910–14 and the present prices of things that farmers buy, the new parity price formula in S. 2318 accepts the prices of individual farm commodities for the 10 immediately preceding years as reflecting the current relative supply of and demand for different farm products better than the price relationships between different farm commodities in 1910–14. However, the period 1910–14 is retained as the base period in showing the over-all relationship between the prices of things farmers buy and the prices of farm products.[46]

46. *CR*, 80th Cong., 2nd sess., Senate, June 15, 1948, 94, pt. 7: 8303.

After listing many of the newly calculated parity prices, Aiken continued, using corn as an example: "The 10-year average price of corn—1938–47—was $0.953. Average prices of all farm products during the last 10 years is 168 percent of the average prices of all farm products during the 1910–14 base period. Thus, $0.953 is divided by 1.68 to show the parity price of corn in 1910–14, which would amount to $0.567. Since the prices of things farmers buy are now 250 percent, or 2.50 times as high as in 1910–14, the current parity price of corn would be 2.50 times $0.567, or $1.42."[47] Although some parity prices would be higher and others lower under the new formula, Aiken indicated that the average for all commodities would be "the same under the old and new formulas."

The Aiken bill sought to ensure that price supports would reflect changes in market price and supply. It also would limit mandatory supports to storable commodities; seek to "encourage producers to shift part of their productive resources to those products in short supply or greatest demand"; and provide adequate discretionary power so that adjustments could be made "to meet changing or unforeseen conditions." Specifically, S. 2318 gave the secretary of agriculture considerable "flexibility in the choice of methods to be used in supporting prices," authorizing him to support "any agricultural commodity through loans, purchases, [direct] payments, or other operations." In addition, explained Aiken, "Compliance with acreage allotments, production goals, and marketing practices may be required as a condition of price support on either basic or nonbasic commodities." To avoid increasing demands on the federal treasury and to encourage farmers to consider market conditions in making their production decisions, the bill established a "flexible price support schedule" that varied "inversely to supply" to "encourage farmers to adjust production to demand." Basic commodities were to be supported between

---

47. *CR,* 80th Cong., 2nd sess., Senate, June 15, 1948, 94, pt. 7: 8304. If anything, the new parity formula was more complicated than the old. Some congressmen were willing to admit that they really did not understand it. "When I first came to the House in 1939," Representative William J. Miller (R-CT) confessed, "some of my friends from the agricultural districts attempted to explain the so-called parity formula to me. I do not expect to live long enough to understand all of the detals [*sic*] of the parity formula" (*CR* [House], June 12, 1948, 94, pt. 6: 7991).

60 and 90 percent of parity for cooperating farmers, with a minimum support level of 50 percent in cases where marketing quotas had been disapproved. Price supports on nonbasic commodities were left to the discretion of the secretary of agriculture but were not to exceed 90 percent of parity. If the "national interest" required, however, "price-support operations at levels in excess of 90 percent of parity" were "permitted with respect to either basic or nonbasic commodities."[48]

Debate on the Aiken bill commenced the following day, June 16, 1948. Although the program enjoyed considerable support, numerous efforts were made to alter specific provisions. Senator Allen J. Ellender (D-LA) voiced his basic agreement with the bill, which "streamlines and continues what we are now doing," but pointed out that "it is not in itself a complete farm program." He mentioned for example the need for action on the Commodity Credit Corporation charter bill. Ellender also indicated his intention to support an amendment that would add a provision allowing farmers to chose between the old and new parity formulas.[49]

The most significant opposition came from a small group of senators from the cotton and tobacco South. On June 17, Kentucky senators John Sherman Cooper and Alben Barkley, who was destined to become Truman's vice presidential running mate in less than a month, successfully offered an amendment to the bill providing for the continuation of 90 percent support on tobacco. Interestingly, after the close 41 to 40 favorable vote on the amendment, Republican senator Aiken attacked his Democratic colleagues for their failure to support the president on this issue. "I realize," lamented the usually calm and genial New Englander, "that this vote, giving special privilege to a single agricultural commodity, and possibly to be followed by votes which will give special privilege to other commodities, may be the start of the break-down of this bill." He also understood that many members were opposed to the enactment of a long-range program and preferred "the stopgap bill of the House of Representatives." Regardless, it was, Aiken believed, "a most ridiculous spectacle for the President of the United States to be traveling thousands of miles around the country advocating the enactment of this bill, as he did

48. *CR*, 80th Cong., 2nd sess., Senate, June 15, 1948, 94, pt. 7: 8306.
49. *CR*, 80th Cong., 2nd sess., Senate, June 16, 1948, 94, pt. 7: 8438.

by name in Los Angeles only the other evening, and then have only three or four members of his own party support him in the Senate. I think it is a sorry spectacle to see a great party disintegrate to that extent, to see how little regard they have for the opinions of their leader."[50]

Despite this Republican appeal for Democratic party loyalty, it was becoming clear to many during the closing days of the session that a long-range bill, which would take immediate effect, was not in the cards for this Congress. Senator Aiken's uncharacteristic reaction to this round of opposition obviously reflected his frustration and was an attempt to rescue a lost cause. If anything, his tactics had the opposite effect, and the rancorous debate continued. The Vermont Republican did receive some Democratic support, most notably from Senators Ellender, Elmer Thomas of Oklahoma, and Scott Lucas of Illinois, all members of Aiken's subcommittee. Lucas emphasized the painstaking efforts made by the committee and the fact that members had succeeded in keeping the issue nonpartisan, until now. He also echoed Aiken's fear: "once we permit one commodity to have preferential treatment under the bill, as has been done in the case of tobacco, then there is no reason why I should not offer an amendment to give the corn producers of my State the same kind of treatment. There is no reason why the Senator from North Dakota [Mr. Young] should not offer an amendment to do the same for the wheat producers of his State. So we shall go down the line of basic and nonbasic commodities, and give them all preferential treatment."[51]

These appeals for deference to the committee report notwithstanding, Senator Richard B. Russell of Georgia offered an amendment that substituted the House bill extending the Steagall amendment until June 30, 1950, for the Senate's long-range bill. Justifying his action, Senator Russell explained:

> The question before the Senate at this time is [not] between the Aiken bill and the House bill. As I view the situation, the ques-

50. *CR,* 80th Cong., 2nd sess., Senate, June 16, 1948, 94, pt. 7: 8557, (comments of Senators Barkley and Claude Pepper) 8558–59. The presidential speech referred to by Aiken was delivered on June 14 (Truman, *Public Papers of the Presidents, 1948,* 352).

51. *CR,* 80th Cong., 2nd sess., Senate, June 17, 1948, 94, pt. 7: 8563.

tion is between the House bill and nothing; because if we do not pass the House bill, but, instead, pass the Aiken bill and send it to conference, knowing that the House committee has held long and extended hearings on this entire question, and that the House has decided that due to the unnatural conditions which obtain in the American economy we should carry on with the wartime legislation for the time being, it is obvious that the House will not readily yield to our position.

Russell reminded the chamber that adjournment was only three days away and explained his concern by posing a question: "Is it wise to gamble with a matter which is important not only to the farmer but to the Nation and to the world, to gamble with a new and revolutionary bill of this kind? I submit, with all respect that the bill is far too complicated and too far reaching to be considered under conditions existing in the Senate today."[52]

A year and a half after the beginning of the postwar transition period and after months of effort on the part of both agricultural committees, many believed there was not enough time to work out the details of a compromise measure that could muster needed support. Congressman Hope had come to accept this reality several weeks before; Senator Aiken fought the battle to the end. Having misjudged the mood of the Senate, the latter continued his fight by appealing in vain for his colleagues to exhibit confidence enough in their committee to accept its recommendations.

Ultimately, the Russell substitute was defeated by a vote of 27 to 55, H.R. 6248 was passed 79 to 3 after substituting the language of S. 2318 as amended, and a conference committee was constituted. The following day, Friday, June 18, the House rejected the Senate action but agreed to a conference. In the waning hours of the session the joint committee hammered out a peculiar compromise measure that became the Agricultural Act of 1948, more commonly known as the Hope-Aiken Act. Explaining the conference report on H.R. 6248 to the lower house, Hope pointed out that Title I extended the present program through 1949 and included "substantially all of the provisions

52. *CR,* 80th Cong., 2nd sess., Senate, June 17, 1948, 94, pt. 7: 8570. See also Ben F. Jensen (R-IA), "Long-Range Bill for Agriculture," Extension of Remarks, *CR* (House), June 19, 1948, 94, pt. 12: A4271–72.

The Republican Eightieth Congress struggled to find a solution to the post-war farm problem, but the best it could do was the Agricultural Act of 1948, a compromise measure that pleased very few. Senator George D. Aiken (above left) and Representative Clifford R. Hope (above right) are pictured here in Albany, New York, on September 18, 1948, with their party's 1948 presidential candidate, Governor Thomas E. Dewey. Some were predicting that "President" Dewey would name Hope the next secretary of agriculture. Courtesy of the Kansas State Historical Society.

of the House bill." The remaining titles, II and III, which President Truman described as the portion that approached long-range planning, were the Senate's share of the compromise package. Of the original four titles that made up the Aiken bill, two were out. This version, Hope explained, contained "substantially all of titles 3 and 4 of the Senate long range bill, which provisions deal with a long range price support program." The two eliminated titles had dealt with the reorganization of the USDA, "which in effect would have eliminated the Soil Conservation Service and turned its functions over to the Extension Service, the land grant colleges, and the Production and Marketing Administration, under a new name, however."[53] The most

53. *CR,* 80th Cong., 2nd sess., House, June 19, 1948, 94, pt. 7: 9344.

significant features of the two remaining titles were a new formula for computing parity and a plan for a flexible support system on a sliding scale that, in practice, would range from 72 to 90 percent of parity for most major crops. The secretary of agriculture also was given authority to impose production controls and to support other crops at his discretion.[54]

Few members of the Eightieth Congress were happy with the final package, but at least they had a farm bill. Republicans could take solace in the belief that, after their anticipated victory in November, they would have two more years to work out the bugs (or at least until January 1, 1950, when the provisions of the Aiken bill took effect). Some members, especially those from the South who feared Aiken's flexible supports, raised some strenuous objections before the final vote was cast. Congressman John W. Flannagan, an eighteen-year veteran of the House and former chairman of the agricultural committee, had "gone through" his "strangest and most unusual experience since yesterday [June 18] at 2 o'clock." The Democrats on the conference committee had "stood pat," he asserted, "but the Republican members went over to the Aiken bill." The House conferees accepted the Senate portion of the bill about which they actually knew very little. "Now," Flannagan asked, "why did these things happen? I do not want to inject politics into this discussion, but evidently the Philadelphia Republican Convention had to have a farm program, and in order to give that convention a farm bill, they had to rape the conferees in order to give the convention a program."[55]

Harold D. Cooley (D-NC) agreed: "For long hours the conferees labored and they brought forth a monstrosity. It is neither bird nor beast nor fish nor fowl. It has the head of an elephant, but the heart of the Republican long-range farm program has been torn from the monster's body." Congressman Cooley lamented the fact that House members were so eager to vote they would not listen to the explanation given by "the great and noble chairman of my great committee, the very able and alert and distinguished gentleman from Kansas." The Democratic Congresses of the New Deal years had been "called rubber stamps," Cooley said, but "this is a super duper case of rubber

54. *CR*, 80th Cong., 2nd sess., Senate, June 15, 1948, 94, pt. 7: 8305.
55. *CR*, 80th Cong., 2nd sess., House, June 19, 1948, 94, pt. 7: 9345.

stamp. Take it for TAFT so that he can talk about it. Do it for Dewey so that he can dangle it before the people. Write it into law for Warren, and mark it for MARTIN. Stay here late for Stassen, and win a victory for VANDENBERG. Whoop it up for the Old Guard, so that you may have a hot time in the old town on Tuesday."[56]

Despite these remonstrances, a vote was taken, and the conference report was agreed to by a vote of 147 to 70.[57] House Democrats had registered observations and objections that undeniably contained some validity, but there was also no doubt that the Senate bill had bipartisan support. It had its faults, but it was hardly the "monstrosity" the Flannagans and Cooleys made it out to be. The Aiken bill embodied much of the administration's recommended program for agriculture and was endorsed by all four major farm organizations. "There is greater unanimity on the part of the farm organizations of this country on this bill," Congressman Hope told the House during the final debate, "than on any important agricultural bill with which I have been familiar."[58]

Walter W. Wilcox, professor of agricultural economics at the University of Wisconsin, judged the 1948 act "an improvement," albeit a small one, "over the 1938 AAA Act." Speaking before the annual meeting of the American Farm Economic Association on September 15, 1948, Wilcox said: "It seems to me that this legislation compares

56. *CR,* 80th Cong., 2nd sess., House, June 19, 1948, 94, pt. 7: 9346. In addition to the obvious front-runners, Cooley alluded to four additional contenders for the Republican presidential nomination: governors Earl Warren (CA) and Harold Stassen (MN), Speaker of the House Joe Martin (MA), and the president pro tempore of the Senate, Arthur Vandenberg (MI). James L. Forsythe substantiates the Flannagan-Cooley contention that a decree from GOP leaders in Philadelphia was the impetus for the Hope-Aiken compromise (Forsythe, "Postmortem on the Election of 1948: An Evaluation of Cong. Clifford R. Hope's Views," 341). See also AP, "Farm Plank of Interest," *Evening Kansan-Republican* (Newton, KS), June 21, 1948.

57. *CR,* 80th Cong., 2nd sess., House, June 19, 1948, 94, pt. 7: 9347. There was no roll call vote on the conference report but, according to Hope, virtually all the Republicans voted for it. All but four Democrats followed the "lead of Messrs. Flannagan, Cooley and [Stephen] Pace, voting against it" (Hope to Gene Worrell, July 2, 1948, FF, Hope Papers).

58. *CR,* 80th Cong., 2nd sess., House, June 19, 1948, 94, pt. 7: 9344. See also Senator Aiken's "Farm Bill Correspondence, 1948," and clipping from the *Farmers Union Herald* (St. Paul, MN), July 16, 1948, Agricultural Act of 1948, Correspondence, Aiken Papers.

with our pre-war legislative model about like the post-war automobile models compare with the pre-war models. To say that the similarity is easily recognized is conscious understatement." Nevertheless, Wilcox found merit in the Aiken bill's "formulas for determining loan levels" and in its new modernized parity formula—"an outstanding improvement." Although he was generally unimpressed with the new farm law and believed his views reflected those of most agricultural economists, Wilcox acknowledged the fact that "the four farm organizations—the Farm Bureau, the Grange, the Farmers Union, and the Cooperative Council—supported the 1948 legislation with considerable enthusiasm."[59]

Like many of his House colleagues, Congressman Hope was disturbed by the fact that the "normal process for the consideration of the Senate bill" had been bypassed and that, as a result, "not two per cent of the Membership of the House knew what the Senate bill contained at the time the conference report was adopted." As he wrote Allan Kline on June 29, his objection to the final package was based more on the procedure than on the "merits or demerits of the legislation."

> It may be true, as contended by you and by Senator Aiken, that it will be more difficult to pass long range legislation in the next Congress than in this one; and if that is true, then by accepting the revision of parity and price support provisions contained in the Aiken bill, we have gained a great deal of ground. I have not felt that way about it, but I could easily be mistaken.
>
> I am expecting that Governor Dewey will be elected President and I believe that, with a Republican House and Senate, and a President who is as familiar with and sympathetic to the agricultural problems of the country as Governor Dewey, we could work out a good bill. Of course, we can still make any necessary changes and have the Aiken bill to tie to as an anchor. I would not be surprised if further study of the Aiken bill doesn't disclose the need for some revision and I know our Committee will want to go over it very carefully in the next Congress.[60]

59. Unpublished paper, "Additional Legislation Needed," sent to Hope, September 18, 1948, General Correspondence, Hope Papers.

60. Hope to Kline, June 29, 1948, General Correspondence, Hope Papers. See also Kline to Aiken, telegram, June 18, 1948, Agricultural Act of 1948, Correspondence, Aiken Papers.

Had Congressman Hope's election analysis proven correct, it is quite possible that the Hope-Aiken Act would have enjoyed a happier life. The Democratic Eighty-first Congress, however, felt no obligation to provide the corrective surgery that members of both parties thought the act would need from the moment of its birth. In theory, one can make a case for both portions: the House's desire to further extend wartime supports during a continuing extraordinary postwar period of high demand; and the Senate's eagerness to get on with a new plan that promised to guard against a potential drain on the treasury, to assuage consumer concerns about the high cost of living, and to encourage farm production adjustments reflective of peacetime demand. Republicans found that they could not have it both ways. To be sure, this was not a simple Republican versus Democrat contest, but the election campaign that followed made it appear that way. At best, the Hope-Aiken Act emerged from the campaign as a symbol of Republican incompetence and, at worst, a subtle GOP assault on the foundation of the farm price support program.

As Lauren Soth, an editorial writer for the *Des Moines Register* and the *Des Moines Tribune* explained: "The 1948 farm-price Act was one of those last minute compromises between bitter opponents that is inherently unstable."[61] Supporters of the compromise, such as Clifford Hope, found that promises for an opportunity to change the law during the next session, made even before its passage, only contributed to that instability. It can be argued that the Hope-Aiken bill was not a compromise at all; if Congress had reached some middle ground for agreement, then the word *compromise* could be used to describe the bill. As Congressman Pace pointed out, in this instance "the House passed a bill, the Senate passed a bill, and the compromise is to enact both of them." Despite his continued respect for Congressman Hope, the Georgia lawmaker, who had been so eager for nonpartisanship during the hearings, could not support a confer-

61. Lauren Soth, "Conflicts in Farm-Price Policy," 60; see also H. C. M. Case, "The Agricultural Act of 1948," 227. Case, a University of Illinois agricultural economist, worked as adviser with the Senate agricultural committee during the spring of 1948 (Aiken to Dean Rusk, University of Illinois, Department of Agriculture, June 21, 1948, and to "Doc" Case, July 26, 1948, Agricultural Act of 1948, Correspondence, Aiken Papers).

ence report, with its admittedly "serious mistakes," just because "the Republican leadership says it must pass now."[62]

The much-maligned Hope-Aiken Act, then, reflected the deep policy differences that persisted throughout the agricultural community during the postwar era, making rational policy formulation extremely difficult. Everyone had come to accept the principle of farm-price protection in some form, but preferred methods of support for agriculture were nearly as divergent as the farm industry itself.[63] Under the best of circumstances, which seemed to exist during 1947 and early 1948, Congress had been unable to make satisfactory repairs in the nation's basic farm program; at best, the roof had only been patched, despite a workmanlike effort.

It is unfortunate that legislation was not passed during this early period of harmony, but it is hard to fault thoughtful deliberation. There was no necessity for rushing toward final action in 1947. By the time Congress got around to passing the badly needed legislation in the summer of the following year, however, time had run out, and the favorable climate had turned stormy. It is not surprising that the Truman administration found the atmosphere in 1949, even with its own party in control of Congress, no more conducive to building a consensus. In 1948, though, it was the Republican Eightieth Congress that mishandled the farm policy ball and fumbled away a golden opportunity to write permanent agricultural legislation. By the time the Eighty-first Congress convened, the nature of the traditionally nonpartisan farm policy debate had changed, with agriculture destined to be a political football during much of Harry Truman's second term of office.

---

62. *CR,* 80th Cong., 2nd sess., House, June 19, 1948, 94, pt. 7: 9346, 9347.
63. For a good, concise analysis of the political groupings on farm policy issues, see Spencer Rich, *U.S. Agricultural Policy in the Postwar Years, 1945–1963: The Development of U.S. Farm Problems; an Eighteen-Year Legislative Review* and Hansen, *Gaining Access,* 79–97.

4

Farm Policy and
the Election of 1948

The Republican Eightieth Congress closed out its second regular session on June 19, 1948, two days before the opening of the party's national nominating convention in Philadelphia. Political maneuvering and campaigning had been under way for some time, but now all attention could be focused on the national conventions and the selection of presidential and vice-presidential candidates. When this work was finished, and the politically inspired special session of the Eightieth Congress had come to a merciful end, the fall campaign took center stage. No one, besides the president himself, attracted more attention or received more deserved credit for the Truman victory than did the president's new secretary of agriculture.[1] Charles Brannan, who had quietly settled into his new job during the closing weeks of the regular session, shattered the preconceived notions about his nonpolitical nature and became a real force in the campaign. He contributed substantially to the Truman victory and, with the president's support and assistance, plunged the traditionally nonpartisan farm policy debate into the political arena with a vengeance.

The events of the spring of 1948 proved to be good luck for the political future of the Truman administration. In mid-March Secretary Anderson, who had been tabbed by some as a likely vice-presidential (if not presidential) nominee, informed Truman of his decision to

1. Gosnell, *Truman's Crises,* 292, concluded that Brannan, Maurice J. Tobin, who was appointed secretary of labor after the June 10, 1948, death of L. B. Schwellenbach, and Attorney General Tom Clark were the only cabinet members that helped Truman during the campaign.

leave the cabinet.[2] Word of his impending resignation spread quickly, and interest in a replacement for the outgoing secretary intensified during the month of April. This interest is somewhat surprising because many considered the new secretary, whoever he might be, a mere interim appointment. Truman, however, did not suffer from a lack of candidates or unsolicited advice.

Virginia Congressman John W. Flannagan, the former chairman of the House Committee on Agriculture, and Under Secretary of Agriculture Norris E. Dodd both garnered considerable support.[3] Although Flannagan was anathema to many liberals, Dodd's support was widespread and nonpartisan. J. Howard McGrath, chairman of the Democratic National Committee, informed the White House that he had "received innumerable endorsements for Mr. N. E. Dodd to succeed Clint Anderson" from "large farm organizations" and many senators.[4] In responding to a letter from the president of the Kansas Farmers Union endorsing Charles Brannan, Arthur Capper, chairman of the Senate Committee on Agriculture and Forestry, wrote that he considered "Mr. Charles Brannan a very fine man." But, the elderly senator continued, Under Secretary Dodd was a "dirt farmer" with many years of experience in the USDA, and Capper had already expressed his support for him.[5]

Despite Dodd's credentials and impressive list of backers, the man who garnered the widest support—in addition to the endorsement of his boss, the outgoing secretary of agriculture—was Assistant Secretary of Agriculture Charles F. Brannan. Brannan emerged as the

2. Forsythe, "Clinton P. Anderson, 578; Ayers's entry for November 22, 1947, in Robert H. Ferrell, ed., *Truman in the White House: The Diary of Eben A. Ayers,* 211. When asked if he thought Anderson would have stayed on as secretary of agriculture had he believed Truman would be reelected, Brannan was emphatic: "Oh I know he would have! I actually think that Anderson could have been Mr. Truman's selection for vice-president. . . . As far as I could tell [Truman] thought quite well of Anderson, and Anderson was an attractive person" (Brannan, interview).

3. See, for example, A. S. Goss to Truman, telegram, April 27, 1948; Sam Rayburn (and twenty-nine other members of the House) to Truman, April 22, 1948; Senator H. R. O'Conor to Truman, March 25, 1948; Congressman John H. Kerr to Truman, April 5, 1948, OF, Truman Papers.

4. McGrath to Donald S. Dawson, April 1, 1948, OF, Truman Papers.

5. Capper to E. T. Fortune, March 29, 1948, Agricultural Correspondence, Capper Papers.

odds on favorite toward the end of April.[6] Although President Truman remained noncommittal for some weeks and delayed the Brannan appointment for another two weeks after formally accepting Anderson's resignation on May 10, the assistant secretary had a great deal going for him. Brannan had paid his dues and was highly qualified. But even more important during this election year, the liberal westerner had the wholehearted support of the National Farmers Union and fitted perfectly into the campaign strategy that had guided the administration's conduct since late 1947.[7]

Although there was significant opposition to Brannan's appointment, one would have been hard pressed to make a credible case against his qualifications for the office. Described by *Time* magazine as a "balding, bespectacled man" who looked "like a banker" and was "politically left of center," Brannan was only forty-four years old but had already had a rich and varied career in government service.[8] A native of Denver, Charles Brannan received a law degree from the University of Colorado in 1929. He established a private practice specializing in irrigation and mining law before joining the Department of Agriculture in 1935 as an attorney for the Resettlement Administration. An ardent New Dealer, Brannan's initial work with the USDA was to make arrangements for the purchase of drought-stricken land in the mountain states and to provide for the relocation of destitute dust bowl farmers. In 1937, Brannan was promoted to regional attorney in the office of the solicitor and, in this capacity, assisted in a number of cooperative efforts undertaken with farmers striving to solve their land and water problems, including the formation of irrigation districts.[9]

During most of World War II, Brannan served the needs of indigent families as regional director of the Farm Security Administration. Then, after nearly a decade with the department, he accepted an ap-

6. Truman, *Public Papers of the Presidents, 1948,* 228. See also *Washington Post* news clipping, May 26, 1948, Anderson—Office folder, Anderson Papers.

7. Allen Yarnell, *Democrats and Progressives: The 1948 Presidential Election as a Test of Postwar Liberalism,* 29.

8. *Time* 51 (May 31, 1948): 17.

9. Unattributed two-page biographical sketch, filed "by Mr. Dawson," June 2, 1948, OF, Truman Papers; Eleanora W. Schoenebaum, ed., *Political Profiles: The Truman Years* 51; *Current Biography,* 1948, 57.

pointment as assistant secretary of agriculture under Claude Wickard. Brannan carried out numerous specialized assignments in the following four years, including vice chairman of the Commodity Credit Corporation's board of directors and chairman of the department's program and policy committee. In addition, Brannan had some international experience as agricultural adviser to the U.S. delegation to the United Nations conference in San Francisco in 1945. In March 1948, he also was selected by Secretary of State George Marshall to serve on the U.S. delegation to the Ninth International Conference of American States.[10]

Although he had never held elective office and was not well known by the general public, Brannan was widely respected on Capitol Hill, and his value to the Department of Agriculture had not escaped Anderson's notice. Assistant Secretary Brannan was made chairman of the Program and Policy Committee in late 1946, at least partly because Anderson did not want to lose him. In early 1947 when President Truman nominated Brannan for one of three positions on the recently created Indian Claims Commission, Anderson persuaded his assistant to stay at his post in agriculture. Anderson wrote the president urging him to "reconsider and withdraw" Brannan's nomination in light of his vital role at USDA. The problems of agriculture at home and abroad "are such that I simply cannot spare Mr. Brannan," Anderson explained. The secretary stressed the importance of Brannan's work as "chairman of a policy committee which is developing the Department's conception of a proper pattern for agriculture." A change at that point would have adversely affected the work of the department, and thus, Anderson wrote, "I have urged Assistant Secretary Brannan to request the withdrawal of his name and he has generously agreed to do so. I recognize the industry, integrity, and sound thinking in his work here commend him to you for the post to which you have nominated him. While I appreciate his right to advancement, I am faced by so many problems at home and abroad that I cannot let him go. If it will not embarrass you or inconvenience you too greatly, I ask that you withdraw his nomination."[11]

10. *Current Biography,* 1948, 57; Marshall to Truman, March 25, 1948, OF, Truman Papers.
11. Anderson to Truman, and Brannan to Truman, March 11, 1947, Indian Claims Commission, OF, Truman Papers.

Truman complied with the request, and Brannan continued his work on long-range programs. The programs that he helped develop became the basis for the administration's recommendations to the Eightieth Congress.

Brannan was a loyal supporter of department policy while serving in a subordinate role, but he was by no means an Anderson clone. A New Deal liberal, Brannan came to his new post with the strong endorsement of several key liberal constituencies. In addition to support from conservative Colorado senator Edwin C. Johnson, Brannan received hearty recommendations from several prominent congressional liberals like Wright Patman of Texas.[12] In light of the 1948 campaign strategy that targeted labor, farmers, and blacks as key to Truman's success, it is also important to note the endorsements received by the president on May 11 from Dr. F. D. Patterson, president of the Tuskegee Institute, and Claude A. Barnett, founder of the Associated Negro Press in Chicago. Both men were prominent African Americans who had served the administration as special assistants to the secretary of agriculture on the problems facing black farmers and supported Brannan because of his commitment to small farmers. In his endorsement, Barnett informed the White House that "the President should know I feel that Mr. Brannan's selection would find great favor among colored farmers and colored people generally, his outstanding ability and sincere interest in the problems of small farmers have helped farm programs reach down in greater degree to all farmers especially in the South."[13]

Of all his friends and admirers, however, Brannan's greatest champion was undoubtedly fellow Coloradoan James Patton, president of the liberal National Farmers Union. On March 17, Patton began by

12. Johnson to Truman, March 16, 1948, and Patman to Truman, April 23, 1948, OF, Truman Papers; Brannan to Eugene H. Mast, April 22, 1948, James G. Patton folders, Subject file, 1938–1988, Charles F. Brannan Papers, Harry S. Truman Library (hereafter cited as Brannan Papers).

13. Patterson to Truman, and Barnett to Truman, May 11, 1948, OF, Truman Papers. Patterson also had been a member of Truman's Commission on Higher Education, which had completed its work and issued a report in December 1947 (*Current Biography,* 1947, 495; W. Augustus Low and Virgil A. Clift, eds., *Encyclopedia of Black America,* 167). In mid-April 1948, according to Herbert S. Parmet, Truman received word that black voters were moving toward the Wallace camp (*The Democrats: The Years after FDR,* 78).

lobbying Brannan's boss, Clinton Anderson. After wishing the secretary well in his upcoming senatorial campaign and complimenting him on his "sustained work in support of the long-range program for agriculture," Patton expressed his hope that Anderson would sponsor Brannan's appointment. "Charles is a Western man," Patton emphasized. "He would be able to continue the understanding of Western agriculture, and of reclamation and conservation interests, which have been excellent features of your administration." Patton felt "very deeply about this matter" and thought there were "very few people who are both professionally and politically qualified to give progressive leadership in the Department. Charles is the outstanding one."[14]

In short, when Brannan took over the helm of the mammoth USDA on June 2, 1948, he enjoyed a wide base of support.[15] He was enthusiastically liked and endorsed by a variety of labor, consumer, minority, and liberal farm organizations and accepted by most people interested in agriculture. The National Grange, which had not supported the Brannan appointment, had "found him very cooperative" and expected that same cooperative relationship to continue once the Senate approved his appointment. The National Council of Farmer Cooperatives, which claimed to have been neutral during the selection process, had experienced "very satisfactory" relations with Assistant Secretary Brannan. The American Farm Bureau Federation, also claiming neutrality regarding the nomination, "expected to cooperate as fully as possible with whoever is secretary of agriculture."[16] The honeymoon was short lived, however, and before the end of the fall campaign, many were taking a closer look at their new secretary of agriculture.

Although the direction in which the Brannan administration would attempt to steer agricultural policy remained unclear for some time,

14. Patton to Anderson, March 17, 1948, Alphabetical Correspondence file, Anderson Papers. Much evidence of Jim Patton's efforts on behalf of Brannan's nomination, including copies of numerous letter and telegrams sent in March 1948 by Patton to senators, representatives, farm leaders, etc., are in James G. Patton folders, Brannan Papers.

15. Brannan's appointment was confirmed by the U.S. Senate on May 28, 1948 (*Current Biography,* 1948, 58).

16. J. T. Sanders, legislative counsel, National Grange, to Capper; John H. Davis, executive secretary, National Council of Farmer Cooperatives, to Capper; Roger Fleming, director, Washington office, AFBF, to Capper, all dated May 26, 1948, Agricultural Correspondence, Capper Papers.

Brannan soon revealed a political combativeness that might well have worried some of his supporters. Those who knew him were probably not surprised and were already aware that the new secretary, unlike his predecessor, was a thoroughgoing liberal.

Brannan had close ties with Jim Patton and his Farmers Union, far and away the most liberal of the major farm organizations. Organized during the first decade of the twentieth century, the union was in the tradition of agrarian radicalism that characterized the Farmers Alliance of the nineteenth century. Its style, according to John A. Crampton, "has long been marked by belligerence and by optimism. The Union's casual rhetoric bristles with the language of struggle."[17] The Farmers Union considered itself the effective voice of the old agrarianism and, although its membership was primarily middle class, its ideology appealed to the poorer farmer. "Drawing its membership mainly from the mountain and plains states," explained Alonzo L. Hamby, "the NFU saw itself as a representative of the small farmer and drew upon a neopopulist ideology which celebrated the virtues of agrarian life and the fundamental social importance of the small landholder."[18]

The union had been a militant supporter of the embattled Farm Security Administration (Brannan's former agency) and also concerned itself with issues affecting the urban disadvantaged. As a result, Patton had supported many New Deal and Fair Deal programs and was a leader in the fight for full-employment legislation. His organization worked diligently with labor and other liberal groups for the creation of a farm-labor party. Although some state unions were supporting Henry Wallace's third party bid in 1948, Patton opposed the third party movement. He remained loyal to Truman and retained considerable influence with the administration.

In addition to this liberal relationship, which led to his acceptance of a position as general counsel for the NFU after he left the USDA in 1953, Brannan developed close ties with other progressives in the administration. As early as January 1947, Brannan began meeting regularly with officials who shared similar beliefs and were concerned with what appeared to be a conservative drift in administration policy. The coterie, which included Special Counsel Clark Clifford, Assistant

17. Crampton, *National Farmers Union,* 4.
18. Hamby, *Beyond the New Deal,* 33.

Secretary of Labor David A. Morse, and Administrative Assistant Charles S. Murphy, was devastated by the Democratic defeat of 1946 and believed that if Truman was to win in 1948 he had to support a liberal program.[19] The key men in this group, which Hamby called the Fair Deal's "liberal caucus," were Brannan, Oscar Ewing, a Democratic party leader, and Leon Keyserling of the President's Council of Economic Advisers. Although it is probably true that Truman did not need a committee to tell him the right liberal choices to make, it is difficult to assess the group's influence, and "a number of actions [the president] was to take did correspond with positions recommended by the liberal group."[20] According to Clifford, who acted as the coterie's liaison with the president, "the group was very valuable to me. I was dealing with problems on behalf of the President, week in and week out, and to have a group with whom I could discuss these problems in complete confidentiality, and in the knowledge that they were working toward the same goal that I was, made it very valuable."[21]

Despite the liberal background and connections of its new cabinet secretary, in the immediate aftermath of Anderson's resignation the administration was not prepared to alter its course on long-range policy, and Truman continued to press Congress for passage of a new legislative program along the lines established by the outgoing secretary. On May 14, 1948, four days after Anderson left office, President Truman sent a special message on agriculture to the Congress. The message, according to Anderson, was "designed as a campaign document for the months ahead. We knew that the Republican Eightieth Congress would not enact its recommendations. But we saw it as the recitation of a record and the extension of a promise."[22]

19. For discussions of this liberal clique, or "Monday-Night Group" as Clifford called it, see Clifford, *Counsel to the President: A Memoir*, 84; Hamby, *Man of the People*, 430–31; Phillips, *Truman Presidency*, 162; Donovan, *Conflict and Crisis*, 271; Hechler, *Working with Truman*, 60; Keyserling, "Harry S. Truman: The Man and the President," in William F. Levantrosser, ed., *Harry S. Truman: The Man from Independence*, 238; Irwin Ross, *The Loneliest Campaign: The Truman Victory of 1948*, 163.

20. Donovan, *Conflict and Crisis*, 272; Hamby, *Beyond the New Deal*, 295.

21. Quoted in Hechler, *Working with Truman*, 60–61; Clifford, *Counsel to the President*, 84–85.

22. Anderson, *Outsider in the Senate*, 90; Truman, *Public Papers of the Presidents, 1948*, 256.

Indeed, the message was in perfect step with an overall campaign strategy that had been implemented in several other policy areas. Inspired by James H. Rowe, an advisor to Bureau of the Budget director James E. Webb, and revised and directed by Clark Clifford, the course was charted in a November 19, 1947 memorandum that Clifford prepared for the president. This blueprint for Truman's comeback victory reflected the concerns of Clifford's "liberal caucus" as well as a no-holds-barred attitude toward politics; victory was the driving force. The so-called Clifford memorandum included a no compromise approach toward Congress on key domestic issues. "The Administration," read the document, "should select the issues upon which there will be conflict with the majority in Congress. It can assume it will get no major part of its own program approved. Its tactics must, therefore, be entirely different than if there were any real point to bargaining and compromise. Its recommendations—in the State of the Union Message and elsewhere—must be tailored for the voter, not the Congressman; they must display a label which reads 'no compromises.'"[23] The Clifford memo "shaped a strategy in which rhetoric was going to play the key role," explained Allan Yarnell. "The art of politics was practiced not to achieve compromise, but to achieve victory."[24]

Regarding the State of the Union message specifically, the memorandum read: "There is little possibility that he will get much cooperation from the Congress but we want the President to be in a position to receive the credit for whatever they do accomplish while also being

23. Quoted in Clifford, *Counsel to the President,* 193; Dean, "Farm Policy and Truman's 1948 Campaign," 505. Gary A. Donaldson, "Who Wrote the Clifford Memo? The Origins of Campaign Strategy in the Truman Administration," convincingly demonstrated that Rowe authored the Clifford memorandum. "Clifford did make some additions" and alterations, but it was Rowe's "brilliant grand strategy, along with a number of prophetic predictions and the important advice furnished to the president that made the memo the important historical document it has become" (751). See also McCullough, *Truman,* 589–93; Ferrell, *Harry S. Truman: A Life,* 275.

24. Yarnell, *Democrats and Progressives,* 38. Many authors discuss the importance of Clifford (and his forty-three page confidential memorandum) to the 1948 campaign. See, for example, Anderson, *President's Men,* 119; Harvard Sitkoff, "Years of the Locust, Interpretations of the Truman Presidency since 1965," 91. Rowe's involvement was ignored until the publication of Clifford's memoir in 1991 (Clifford, *Counsel to the President,* 189–91).

in position to criticize the Congress for being obstructionist in failing to comply with other recommendations. This will be a fertile field for the development of campaign issues."[25] Truman enthusiastically embraced this strategy, and in many areas it proved to be a self-fulfilling prophecy.

In his State of the Union address, Truman called for the enactment of his "10-point anti-inflation program" and action on a wide array of domestic initiatives, including the long-range farm bill. The total package, Republicans believed, would be a budget buster, but the president did not stop there. He also proposed a "cost of living tax credit of $40 for each individual taxpayer and an additional credit of $40 for each dependent," with the loss in government revenue to be made up by a corporate tax increase.[26] For Republicans, as well as some Democrats, of the Eightieth Congress, many of whom were already committed to support an expensive foreign policy program, this was simply too much. In a radio address broadcast in Kansas on January 11, Senator Capper alleged, "If Congress should enact legislation putting his social—I might say state socialistic—program into effect, there would be no tax reduction for many years to come—if ever." Thanks to Senator Vandenburg, Capper continued, legislation supporting the Marshall Plan would probably pass in February, but the "Eightieth Congress is becoming increasingly 'dollar conscious.'"[27]

The political implications of the president's address were not lost on observers inside or outside the government. Republicans generally dismissed the message as purely political, as did many newspapers. The *Washington Post* described it as "unmitigatingly demagogic" and a "transparently political move." Harold Ickes, secretary of interior from 1933 to 1946, wrote that to call this "political harangue a State-of-the-Union Message is akin to slander.... The words purported to be that of the Roosevelt New Deal, but the voice was the voice of Esau."[28] More than a year later, Congressman Clifford Hope explained the

25. Quoted in Yarnell, *Democrats and Progressives,* 42. See also Robert Underhill, *The Truman Persuasions,* 236.

26. Truman, *Public Papers of the Presidents, 1948,* 9.

27. WIBW speech, January 11, 1948, Speeches, Capper Papers.

28. Quoted in Jules Abels, *Out of the Jaws of Victory,* 4–5.

administration's ongoing strategy to a constituent: "The President's policy is that of sending bills up which he knows Congress won't pass, in order that he can still use them in the next campaign."[29]

Although Truman continued to advocate a farm program similar to that which had won the endorsement of all major farm organizations late in 1947, his program was thrust into partisan politics when he implied that it might require additional revenue. To counter this undesirable trend back to politics as usual, Republican congressman Reid Murray quickly introduced a bill designed to extend the current support program and the charter of the Commodity Credit Corporation (CCC) to the end of 1950. The advantage, Murray admitted, was that his bill would "take the question of a support program out of partisan politics" so that "neither party will be called upon to place the support program in their platforms."[30] A few weeks later, however, in an early attempt to define the political issues for the 1948 campaign, Democrat George Grant of Alabama did not shy away from the politicization of farm policy. Congressman Grant claimed that Republicans were already attacking the farm program. As evidence he cited a recent Omaha, Nebraska, speech delivered by an unnamed Republican congressional leader who reportedly said that if there was to be a price support program it would have to be less than 90 percent parity. "Is this an advance notice to the farmers of the country as to what will happen if a Republican administration is elected next fall?" If the U.S. had a GOP president and Congress, Grant averred, "Our great farm program" would be destroyed.[31]

As for the president, he followed his 1948 State of the Union address with a series of special messages to Congress designed to keep the administration program in the press. According to Irwin Ross, "Truman was thereby exploiting one of the major prerogatives of Presidential office which no congressional rebuff could deny him: the power to generate publicity, for any utterance of a President is news."[32] Messages on a wide range of issues were sent to Congress almost weekly during January and February and continued intermittently through May. In the case of agriculture, the president's May 14

29. Hope to Perkins, July 16, 1949, FF, Hope Papers.
30. *CR,* 80th Cong., 2nd sess., House, January 27, 1948, 94, pt. 1: 587.
31. *CR,* 80th Cong., 2nd sess., House, February 19, 1948, 94, pt. 1: 1422.
32. Ross, *The Loneliest Campaign,* 60.

communiqué does indeed appear to be the opening blow in his 1948 campaign against the Republican Congress, as well as the beginning of a major effort to capture farm support. Truman credited Democratic agricultural legislation of the prewar era with the farm prosperity that followed World War II. This was in sharp contrast, he reminded Congress, to the farm depression that came in the wake of the first war. Truman saw no need to drastically change or "overturn this sound legislative base," but he believed that it was imperative that Congress move ahead with necessary "extensions and improvements in the program we already have."[33]

Truman reiterated the administration's call for a policy of "organized, sustained, realistic abundance" and proceeded to outline a five-point program. The president insisted that "Congress should [first] enact legislation providing on a permanent basis for a system of flexible price supports for agricultural commodities." This was of prime importance because the supports then in existence were designed to expand production during the war. These had been remarkably successful. In peacetime, however, the farm economy could be improved only with orderly shifts in production that could best be accomplished with flexible price supports. The president's other points stressed the need for the expansion of soil conservation and consumption and the distribution of programs. He also emphasized the importance of supporting and protecting cooperatives and improvements in rural living standards. Truman closed with a call for the prompt enactment of all these measures.[34]

In essence, the president continued to advocate the program embodied in the Aiken bill, which had been introduced in the Senate on March 15. Truman's message did not attract a great deal of national attention, and the *Commonweal* characterized it as rather undramatic. According to the periodical, it was delivered "with a marvelous lack of emphasis" and apparently designed more to annotate a record than to urge a program.[35] Nevertheless, the Democratic administration had begun to plot its political strategy, and in the area of agriculture it "bore the imprint of [Secretary] Anderson." The emphasis was on

33. Truman, *Public Papers of the Presidents, 1948,* 256.
34. Ibid., 258.
35. "Also the Farm Problem," *Commonweal* 48 (May 28, 1948): 152.

the farm prosperity that had existed under two Democratic administrations and the possibility that a Republican president would block
pending legislation if not passed before the election. These Democratic moves and the president's insistence on immediate action
"placed the [farm] program into the arena of partisan politics."[36]

As Truman expected, Congress did not act promptly. At first there
seemed to be no real need. Many believed it would be better to pass
a simple extension, and Congressman Hope, for one, was "convinced
that we do not have the time to work out the right kind of a program."[37] On June 3, however, Truman embarked upon a "nonpolitical" tour with stops in fourteen middle West and western states, and
these opening rounds of his famous 1948 bout with the Republican
Eightieth Congress began to change the political climate.[38]

Although the administration was in basic agreement with the Republican Senate's agricultural bill (the Aiken bill) and House opposition was made possible with considerable Democratic support, Truman had little trouble placing the entire blame for congressional
procrastination on the Republican Party. On June 5, in a major farm
policy speech delivered in Omaha, Nebraska, and carried on a nation-
wide radio broadcast, the president reminisced about the tragic circumstances that faced America's rural population after World War I.
Reiterating the points made in his special message to Congress, Truman reminded his listeners "that prosperity can be lost if we fail to
safeguard it." He closed by placing the burden for positive and crucial action on a balky Congress.[39]

Leaving Nebraska the next day, the president's train rolled through
the Rocky Mountains to the Pacific Northwest, then south to California, where Truman delivered the commencement address at the Uni-

36. Forsythe, "Clinton P. Anderson," 542, 544.
37. Hope to Tom Leadley, editor, *Nebraska Farmer,* June 2, 1948, FF, Hope
Papers.
38. Truman decided he had to take his program directly to the people,
explained Hechler. "He considered this a shakedown cruise to prepare for the
1948 campaign. . . . To preserve the fiction that the trip was nonpolitical, officials
from the Democratic National Committee and other political leaders were
scrupulously excluded" from the traveling party aboard the president's railroad
car, the *Ferdinand Magellan* (Hechler, *Working with Truman,* 69–70; Truman,
Public Papers of the Presidents, 1948, 284–379).
39. Truman, *Public Papers of the Presidents, 1948,* 292.

Administration insiders considered President Truman's spring 1948 western tour a "shake down" for the fall campaign. As he prepared to embark on that critical trip, the president was photographed with several men who would play key roles in the upcoming campaign (left to right): Tom C. Clark, attorney general; Charles F. Brannan, secretary of agriculture; Senator Scott W. Lucas; Senator J. Howard McGrath, chairman of the Democratic National Committee; George C. Marshall, secretary of state; James V. Forrestal, secretary of defense. Abbie Rowe, National Park Service, courtesy of the Harry S. Truman Library.

versity of California at Berkeley on June 12. Three days later, Truman was in New Mexico praising former Secretary Anderson and endorsing his senatorial candidacy; and in Newton, Kansas, on the sixteenth, a "smiling, jovial" president paid tribute to the state's farmers and, before an estimated crowd of two thousand, repeated his call for adequate farm legislation from this session of Congress.[40]

40. Ibid., 336, 356, 361; *Evening Kansan-Republican* (Newton, KS), June 16, 1948.

Returning to Washington via Missouri and the Ohio Valley, the president's party arrived back on June 18, the day before Congress passed the Agricultural Act of 1948 (the Hope-Aiken Act) and adjourned its regular session. As he expected and probably wanted, considering the fact that the administration made little effort to influence the legislative outcome during the final critical weeks, the bill Truman received fell far short of his recommendations. The administration's influence was recognizable in the Senate's part of the compromise, but Truman was not pleased with the package. In the statement issued upon signing the bill, July 3, 1948, the president scolded Congress for acting on "only one" of his "major recommendations" and for not implementing an effective long-range policy.[41]

To raise issues that he expected to play an important part in the upcoming campaign, Truman emphasized the many things the Eightieth Congress had not done for American agriculture. "In signing H.R. 6248," the president explained,

> I wish to make it plain once again that legislation for price supports is only part of the action this Congress should have taken to meet the problems of American agriculture.
>
> The 80th Congress did not enact legislation nor provide adequate funds for strengthening the soil conservation program.
>
> The 80th Congress did not grant adequate funds for marketing research; it did not enact a standby program for improving the diets of low-income families.
>
> The 80th Congress did not act on the International Wheat Agreement, negotiated after years of effort to assure United States wheat producers of export outlets. . . .
>
> The 80th Congress did nothing to meet the serious problems of rural housing, health, and education.

Truman closed with a severe indictment that would be hammered home throughout the campaign. "In the field of agriculture, as in so many others, most of the business of the 80th Congress was left unfinished."[42]

41. Truman, *Public Papers of the Presidents, 1948,* 399.
42. Ibid., 400.

As Truman prepared this early assault on the "Do-Nothing" Republican Congress, the GOP was in Philadelphia busily going about the business of nominating the next president of the United States. New York governor Thomas E. Dewey captured the Republican Party nomination on June 24, after holding off strong challenges by Harold E. Stassen, former governor of Minnesota, and Ohio senator Robert A. Taft. For the second spot on this seemingly unbeatable ticket, the convention chose Governor Earl Warren of California. Dewey's acceptance speech "was short—less than fifteen minutes—and dignified," wrote his biographer Richard Norton Smith, "a return to the high road abandoned in 1944, the speech of a man already elected. When it was over, the hall responded warmly if without passion. It was a sobering speech, in a bleak time, suggestive of the campaign to follow."[43]

The contrast came during the week of July 12, also in Philadelphia. After holding off a dump Truman movement and enduring a sectional platform fight over civil rights that led to the creation of the State's Rights Party, the president accepted the Democratic nomination. At 2 a.m. on July 15, Truman tried to rally the weary delegates, most of whom were already resigned to their seemingly inevitable fate: their first presidential defeat in twenty years.[44] The president began by thanking the convention for its "unanimous nomination of my good friend and colleague, Senator [Alben] Barkley of Kentucky" for vice president. "Senator Barkley and I will win this election and make these Republicans like it—don't you forget that!" He then proceeded to deliver a bombastic assault on the GOP and the Eightieth Congress that was nonpartisan only in its selfish insistence that "partisanship should stop at the water's edge." Before closing, the president announced that he was calling Congress back into session on July 26—"Turnip Day."[45] With this, and a few parting shots, Truman left little doubt as to the tone of his campaign.

43. Smith, *Thomas E. Dewey and His Times,* 500.
44. For a more detailed discussion of the Democratic Convention and platform fight, see McCoy, *Presidency of Harry S. Truman,* 156; Abels, *Out of the Jaws of Victory,* 91; McCoy and Richard T. Ruetten, *Quest and Response: Minority Rights and the Truman Administration,* 124.
45. Truman, *Public Papers of the Presidents, 1948,* 406–10.

Many members of his own party opposed the calling of a special session, but Truman played a hunch, and the result was a "brilliant political coup."[46] The press judged the twelve day session that opened on Turnip Day a standoff, but the president, who knew he had placed the Republicans in a no-win situation, used it to his advantage. On July 27 Truman addressed the session, focusing primarily on the need for positive action to curb inflation and the passage of a comprehensive bill "to help in meeting the acute housing shortage"; but he also recommended federal aid to education and the enactment of civil rights legislation and an array of other items. The president's comments on agriculture were limited to a call for the ratification of the International Wheat Agreement, which promised to "guarantee American farmers an export market of 185 million bushels of wheat at a fair price during each of the next 5 years."[47] As expected, the Turnip session accomplished little, and the president had even more ammunition to fire at the Republican Party and its Do-Nothing Congress.

Although Truman barely raised the farm problem in his address, the price support system, which many urban congressmen saw as a major factor in the high cost of living, inevitably came up in floor debate. Congressman Murray broached the issue on opening day by accusing the administration of playing politics with the consumer and the farmer. On August 5, responding to another Republican attack on the USDA's handling of the controversial potato program, Senator Scott Lucas blamed the majority party that had delayed the enactment of a flexible support system. The remarks pertaining to agriculture during the special session consisted of Democratic assaults on and Republican defense of the farm record of the past Congress.[48]

As the president indicated in his July 3 message, price supports

46. Abels, *Out of the Jaws of Victory,* 122; R. Alton Lee, "The Turnip Session of the Do-Nothing Congress: Presidential Campaign Strategy," 256; Phillips, *Truman Presidency,* 226; Underhill, *The Truman Persuasions,* 270.

47. Truman, *Public Papers of the Presidents, 1948,* 420; Underhill, *The Truman Persuasions,* 271–72.

48. *CR,* 80th Cong., Special sess., House, July 26, 1948, 94, pt. 8: 9353; *CR,* 80th Cong., Special sess., Senate, August 5, 1948, 94, pt. 8: 9802–3, 9851–54; Senate (August 6, 1948) 9956, 9959, 10102, 10137; Christian A. Herter, Extension of Remarks, *CR,* 80th Cong. 2nd sess., House, July 27, 1948, 94, pt. 12, *Appendix:* A4650; Helen Gahagan Douglas, Extension of Remarks, *CR,* 80th Cong., 2nd sess., House, August 7, 1948, 94, pt. 12: A5288.

were only one aspect of a good long-range farm policy, but they proved to be the most potent issue in the debate that followed. The depth of the disagreement on this old bugaboo was quite clear, and the prospects for a renewed search for farm policy loomed large for the next Congress.[49] The campaign and election of 1948, as it turned out, removed any doubt. Differences on this issue, however, were not as clearly partisan as Truman tried to portray during the campaign. As the political rhetoric intensified and talk of inflationary pressures dominated the economic news, farm legislators from both parties tried to calm the fears of farmers who were afraid that the whole support system was in jeopardy. While Republicans attacked Democrats and Democrats attacked Republicans on the campaign trail, congressmen on both sides of the aisle found themselves defending the basic principles of the farm program against an increasingly hostile onslaught by the "metropolitan press."[50]

In a statement released on August 27, Congressman Stephen Pace of Georgia protested:

> During the last few days the newspapers have published reports out of Washington to the general effect that efforts may be made to reduce the ninety per cent of parity support program for farm commodities for next year, inasmuch as the farmers have produced so abundantly this year.
>
> Of all the absurd, unsound and unreasonable suggestions I believe that this one tops the list. This assurance of support and protection which the Congress has given the farmers of the nation should not and must not be reduced or modified. . . .
>
> Parity is a fair price for farm commodities. The farmer is entitled to full or 100 per cent parity. The support price is only ninety per cent of parity. . . .
>
> Those who would reduce or destroy the present support price program have given little thought to what such action would bring about. There could be no more certain or quicker way to throw the economy of this nation into a tailspin than to break down farm commodity prices and the farmers' purchasing power.

49. Saloutos, "Agricultural Organizations and Farm Policy," 390; McCoy, *Presidency of Harry S. Truman,* 112; Matusow, *Farm Policies and Politics,* 143.

50. Hope to Pace, September 1, 1948, Legislative Correspondence, Hope Papers.

Pace airmailed a copy of this release to his colleague, Congressman Hope, along with a request that he too "speak out on this subject."[51]

Hope, whose mail also reflected a growing anxiety about 1949 support levels, needed no encouragement. In a statement released to the press on August 29, the man many believed would be the next secretary of agriculture insisted that city people would have to bring down the prices of things farmers buy before they could expect a decline in agricultural prices. He told reporters there was no reason for government to consider cutting supports and that city people should learn how the farm program operates. "There is a lot of hysteria, not justified by fact, blaming the farm-price support program for high food prices. The fact is," Hope insisted, "the support guarantees have served to encourage larger farm production that has stopped food prices from going much higher... There is nothing in the picture now to make us have any concern about price supports." In a letter dated August 31, Hope's Democratic colleague from Georgia expressed his approval: "Naturally it pleases me that we are in agreement on the fundamentals and I want you to know that I am ready to work with you in trying to protect the farmers of the nation and the general economy."[52]

A few days later Hope reiterated his earlier position when he wrote a constituent that the potato situation had given "a black eye to all price supports." This was caused primarily by poor administration, and Congress had taken steps in the new law to correct the problem in 1949. He concluded by saying that "this agitation about food prices" was already "being overdone" and predicted that "with thousands of candidates talking about it... every day between now and election, we probably haven't seen anything yet!"[53]

Congressman Hope was correct, of course, and as he and others defended the farm record of the Eightieth Congress, Democrats raised

51. Pace to Hope, August 27, 1948, and copy of "Statement by Stephen Pace, M.C.," Legislative Correspondence, Hope Papers.

52. Pace to Hope, August 31, 1948, and Hope statement quoted in the *Telegraph* (Macon, GA) clipping with Pace's letter, Legislative Correspondence, Hope Papers.

53. Hope to Richard W. Robbins, September 2, 1948, Legislative Correspondence, Hope Papers.

many questions that challenged the viability of the new farm law. Among the critics on the campaign trail, the administration's new secretary of agriculture was possibly the most effective. This came as a surprise to many because Charles Brannan, widely respected as a diligent public servant, revealed an unfamiliar political side to his personality.

This facet of Brannan's temperament was not evident while the secretary settled into his new job. At the end of the regular session, Republican senator Aiken expressed his appreciation and thanks for the department's cooperation and assistance during the recent work on the long-range farm bill. On July 6 Brannan responded in kind: "The pleasant and cooperative working relations between the Department and the Congress on this farm legislation has been of much pleasure to me."[54] The department was, in fact, genuinely cooperative and even supportive during the last weeks of June. In attempting to quiet the fears of a Kansas wheat farmer who believed the Aiken bill would mean disaster for his area of the state, an assistant to the secretary explained the new legislation and assured his correspondent that Congress had made a real effort with hearings to reflect popular attitudes.[55] The USDA made little effort to influence the final outcome of the legislation and, although he expressed some objections, Secretary Brannan was not particularly troubled by the new law. As he told Budget Director Webb, "It should be pointed out that this schedule [sliding scale] of price supports is a minimum level, and that the Secretary has authority to support prices of these commodities up to 90 percent of parity."[56]

In a matter of weeks, the situation had changed dramatically. Brannan began to attract attention as an effective political voice for

54. Brannan to Aiken, July 6, 1948, Public Relations 2, General Correspondence, 1948, Office of the Secretary of Agriculture, RG 16, NA; Aiken to Brannan, June 21, 1948, and to R. S. Gilfillan, July 26, 1948, "Agricultural Act of 1948, Correspondence," Aiken Papers.

55. W. A. Minor to H. F. Sutton, June 22, 1948, Legislation 1, Office of the Secretary of Agriculture, RG 16, NA.

56. Brannan to Webb, June 25, 1948, and Brannan to Hope, June 18, 1948, Legislation 1, Office of the Secretary of Agriculture, RG 16, NA. See also Reid F. Murray, Extension of Remarks, *CR,* 80th Cong., 2nd sess., House, June 19, 1948, 94, pt. 12, *Appendix:* A4377.

the administration at a time when few were left (other than the president himself) to fill that role.[57] In addition to delivering numerous sharp attacks on the Eightieth Congress himself, Brannan and his subordinates supplied the president with some effective ammunition. The secretary's most cogent efforts in this regard came early in September. Despite the pleadings of several GOP farm leaders, the Dewey campaign had moved slowly to solidify its natural base of support in the farm regions. Then, on September 2, after a meeting with the candidate, Harold Stassen criticized the administration for intentionally keeping consumer prices high. "At a time of housewives' revolts over the cost of sirloin and pork chops," wrote Richard Smith, "this seemed like smart politics." But to the politically astute secretary of agriculture, it looked like political dynamite. Within a few hours, Secretary Brannan issued his own statement in which he called Stassen's remarks "typically deceptive" and "inaccurate." "This is in essence an attack on the price-support system," Brannan charged.[58]

The following day, the secretary was even more direct. "Mr. Dewey and the Republican leadership have now openly launched a very sinister attack on the price support phases of farm programs." Brannan accused the Eightieth Congress of conducting a two-year assault on a variety of farm programs and, as Alonzo Hamby explained, quickly claimed that Stassen "had been detailed the job of sending up a trial balloon against price supports."[59] The Republican leadership, Brannan insisted, "intends to destroy the farmers' price supports by falsely attributing to that legislation the exorbitantly high prices of certain foods."[60] Brannan had taken off the gloves, ignored the well-known

57. L. W. Barringer to Truman, July 22, 1948, OF, Truman Papers.

58. Smith, *Thomas E. Dewey and His Times,* 511. For Brannan's statements of September 2 and 3, see Joseph O. Parker to Hope, September 3, 1948, Legislative Correspondence, Hope Papers. Parker, an aide to Congressman Hope, forwarded these materials to Hope's home in Garden City, along with a cover letter reacting to some of the specifics of this "very partisan approach."

59. Hamby, *Beyond the New Deal,* 249.

60. Brannan's press release, September 3, 1948, Legislative Correspondence, Hope Papers. When interviewed in 1992, the eighty-five-year-old Stassen had no recollection of the furious exchange sparked by his September 2 remarks other than to say that often what one said was subject to misinterpretation; he did, however, repeatedly emphasize that his record on agricultural policy was clear and consistent. Stassen favored parity price supports up to a certain level of production because he believed farm policy should be oriented toward the

positions of Republican leaders such as Aiken and Hope, and falsely accused the Eightieth Congress of trying to destroy the farm program.

The secretary also had skillfully crafted another issue raised only vaguely in the president's bill signing address of July 3. It pertained to a provision in the bill that renewed the Commodity Credit Corporation's charter and, according to Truman, restricted the CCC in its efforts to provide, at reasonable cost, adequate storage facilities for farm commodities.[61] Since the full implications of this provision were not clear at the time, it elicited little attention, and President Truman aroused only moderate interest in his early attempts to politicize agricultural issues. By late July, however, Brannan had begun to raise the CCC question, and Truman followed his lead. This issue, along with the one Brannan created out of the ill-advised Stassen remark, helped put the administration's campaign on the offensive. The fall campaign officially opened on Labor Day, September 6, and no holds were barred.

The CCC question was a complex one. It was relatively easy for Democrats to turn it into an "us against them" issue. But it was not so easy for Republicans to convince farmers that the Democrats were not telling the whole story, especially since they had dug their own grave on this issue, and the charges contained a substantial amount of undeniable truth. The roots of this damaging controversy could be found in the need to pass a new CCC charter before June 30, 1948. Originally established as a Delaware corporation, the Commodity Credit Corporation had become an integral part of the farm policy apparatus. Postwar changes in the law—passage of the Government Corporations Control Act—required that government corporations be given federal charters, and discussion of this circumstance with regard to the CCC began in 1946. No one questioned the need to make the corporation permanent, but there was some early disagreement,

---

needs of the "family farm" and should not give too much support to (and thus promote) the big producers or farm units. The former Minnesota governor also speculated that his own strong showing among farmers during the primaries might have influenced Truman's decision to make a big effort to capture farm state support during the general election campaign (Harold E. Stassen, telephone interview with author, November 30, 1992, St. Paul, MN).

61. Truman, *Public Papers of the Presidents, 1948,* 400; Donovan, *Conflict and Crisis,* 402; McCoy, *Presidency of Harry S. Truman,* 111.

even within the administration, over the extent of its powers and life of its federal charter.[62]

Secretary Anderson directed efforts in late 1946 and early 1947 to prepare a permanent charter, and Senator Arthur Capper introduced a bill (S. 1322) to this effect in May 1947. Congress needed time to study the issue, though, and the decision was made, with no objection from the administration, to extend the life of CCC for another year pending action on a permanent instrument before June 30, 1948. In 1947 and early 1948 the discussions seem to have been genuinely nonpartisan. Allan Kline, president of the conservative American Farm Bureau Federation, wrote Senator Capper that "the operations of the Commodity Credit Corporation have been of inestimable value to farmers and to the national economy. The Corporation is a cornerstone upon which many of the basic laws of agriculture must depend to make their provisions effective." Kline informed the senator that the AFBF's annual convention had urged that the CCC be made a permanent agency and that Congress "provide adequate lending authority, permitting the operations of the Corporation to remain sufficiently flexible to assure that unforeseen contingencies which arise in agricultural production and distribution may be met." Kline, for the AFBF, endorsed the "objectives and provisions of S. 1322" with only a couple of minor suggestions for modification and opposed efforts to "restrict unduly the operations of the Corporation in carrying out the responsibilities placed upon it by Congress." Senator Capper agreed that "flexibility in operation is essential to the corporation" and informed Kline that he had appointed a subcommittee to consider the issue.[63]

In the lower house, the CCC charter bill was assigned to the budget conscious Banking and Currency Committee. To the chagrin of Congressman Hope, this committee's chairman, Jesse P. Wolcott (R-MI), decided that the new charter should recognize that for some time, on its own volition, the corporation had been liquidating storage space.

---

62. Various reports and letters on the proposed charter act (S. 1322), General Legislation, 1947, Bureau of the Budget, Record Group 51 (hereafter cited as Bureau of the Budget, RG 51), NA; *CR,* 80th Cong., 2nd sess., Senate, April 22, 1948, 94, pt. 4: 4754–64.
63. Kline to Capper, February 25, 1948, and Capper to Kline, March 2, 1948, Agricultural Correspondence, Capper Papers.

Desiring to encourage this trend, thereby reducing its expenditures and limiting its competition with the private sector, Wolcott's committee reported a bill (H.R. 6263) that prohibited the CCC from acquiring or leasing any new "facilities for the physical handling, storage, processing, servicing, and transportation of the agricultural commodities subject to its control."[64] An additional provision, which proved just as objectionable to the USDA and many farm congressmen, changed the composition of the corporation's board of directors, effectively divesting the secretary of agriculture of the general supervisory authority he had traditionally exercised over CCC operations.

Significantly, in light of the partisan advantage gained by the Democrats on this issue during the subsequent campaign, opposition to H.R. 6263 was nonpartisan. In fact, its most vocal critics were Republicans. Congressman Hope told a constituent, "frankly, in its present form it is absolutely unworkable," and on June 18 he reminded his colleagues of the corporation's indispensable role in the effective execution of price supporting operations.[65] The charter bill contained, in Hope's estimation, "two very serious defects in the bill as it now stands. One of them is that the bill prohibits the Corporation from acquiring or leasing any plant or facility for warehousing, transporting, processing, or handling of agricultural commodities, or from acquiring or leasing real property or any interest therein except the rental of office space." The second problem related to the provisions, which provided that

> the Board of Directors shall consist of five members, one of whom shall be the Secretary of Agriculture or his nominee, and the remaining four to be appointed by the President. . . . Not more than one-half of the members of the Board could be employees of the Corporation or any Department or agency of the Government. . . .
>
> This means that three members of the Board of Directors must be appointed from outside the Department of Agriculture and the Federal Government, and that the control of the operations of the Corporation would be in the hands of the appointed members. . . . [Thus] while the Secretary of Agriculture would

64. *CR,* 80th Cong., 2nd sess., House, June 18, 1948, 94, pt. 7: 9001; Donovan, *Conflict and Crisis,* 402–3.
65. Hope to W. E. Bush, June 16, 1948, FF, Hope Papers.

have the responsibility for carrying out the provisions of law relating to support prices, under the terms of this bill he would
lack the authority to do so effectively.

Congressman Hope proceeded to enter into the *Congressional Record*
communications he had received from the National Grange, the National Council of Farmer Cooperatives, and the American Farm Bureau Federation that expressed concerns similar to his own; he then
offered amendments to "cure the serious defects" just discussed.[66]

Unfortunately, as Hope pointed out, the bill had been brought up
under rules that did not allow for amendments from the floor. The
only hope was that the conference committee would make the necessary corrections. This opportunity came on June 19 when Senate and
House conferees met to hammer out the major differences in their
respective bills. With time running out on the Eightieth Congress,
the conference quickly produced a report, which was returned later
that same day. The bill, as finally passed, provided a permanent charter for the CCC and addressed one of the major defects: the five-
member board would consist of three USDA employees and two
people from outside the department. The objectionable section limiting the corporation's ability to provide adequate storage facilities
was left intact.[67]

The administration was understandably concerned, but far from
devastated, by the charter bill's defects. In a June 25 letter to Budget
Director Webb, Secretary Brannan outlined the purpose and the
powers of the corporation. He then focused on what he considered
the most significant problem with the new charter—organization. As
the secretary explained, "Under the present organization of the Corporation, the members of the Board of Directors and the officers of
the Corporation are appointed by the Secretary of Agriculture from
responsible officials within the Department of Agriculture." Only
slightly overstating his case in light of the modest changes made by
the conference committee, Brannan insisted that "under the Federal
charter, the Corporation will not be subject to the direction and super-
vision of the Secretary of Agriculture, although the responsibility for
carrying out the farm program . . . has been vested in the Secretary of

66. *CR,* 80th Cong., 2nd sess., House, June 18, 1948, 94, pt. 7: 8871–72.
67. *CR,* 80th Cong., 2nd sess., Senate, June 19, 1948, 94. pt. 7: 9130–32.

Agriculture by the Congress." Only one sentence of this three-page letter was devoted to the storage issue.

"Despite the objectionable features of the charter," the secretary informed Webb that the USDA was recommending approval of the bill because the existing charter expired on June 30, and "the bill does provide a permanent agency with flexible powers and adequate financial resources."[68] President Truman signed S. 1322 and reiterated his secretary's objections. But the president was not concerned enough to raise the issue with the Turnip session, and there was no indication that this obviously defective bill would become a political boon for the Democratic Party.[69]

In late August and early September, however, circumstances changed; the CCC issue was used to identify Republicans with big grain traders, and Stassen's remarks, made after his meeting with the Republican presidential candidate, were turned into a GOP assault on the entire price support system. Actually, Stassen had merely accused the administration of deliberately keeping consumer prices high on agricultural products with unjustified USDA purchases. He had not even mentioned price supports. In the skillful hands of the agriculture secretary, though, this became a subtle Republican effort to introduce the idea of abandoning price supports altogether. As Matusow explained, "Brannan's accusation was a brilliant stroke that at once relieved the Administration of responsibility for low prices and threw the Republicans on the defensive."[70]

Although Dewey realized that his identification with Stassen's statement was hurting his candidacy in the farm belt, his attempt to console farmers with denials had little impact. After meeting with Senator Aiken and Congressman Hope on September 17, the candidate announced that he favored the support system. But despite the efforts of numerous midwestern Republicans, the governor, according

68. Brannan to Webb, June 25, 1948, and Elmer B. Staats, assistant director, Legislative Reference, to William J. Hopkins, White House, June 28, 1948, General Legislation, 1948, Bureau of the Budget, RG 51, NA .

69. Forsythe, "Clinton P. Anderson," 556; Donovan, *Conflict and Crisis,* 403.

70. Matusow, *Farm Policies and Politics,* 177–78; "The Washington Merry-Go-Round," as printed in *Garden City [Kansas] Telegram,* October 23, 1948; Hamby, *Beyond the New Deal,* 249; Hechler, *Working with Truman,* 90; Abels, *Out of the Jaws of Victory,* 173: Donovan, *Conflict and Crisis,* 416, 420.

to Jules Abels, "failed to understand the urgency of the situation."[71]
He continued to hold a substantial (although slightly diminished)
lead in the polls, and most continued to see his victory as imminent.
The Gallup Poll reported that farmers, questioned during the second
week of September 1948, still gave Dewey a 50 to 44 percent edge.
But a close look at Gallup's projections shows that a slight shift was
under way. In early August, farm opinion, as reported by the pollster,
mirrored national sentiment, giving Dewey a 55 to 43 percent margin.[72] It will be noticed that although Truman's percentage increased
by only one point, a 4 percent increase in the number of undecided
farmers is revealed. In itself, this shift should not be overemphasized,
other indicators (in particular farm prices) were also going against
Republicans, and Truman was now definitely on the offensive.

With some farm prices beginning to fall, Truman picked up on
the Brannan theme in a major farm address at the national plowing
contest near Dexter, Iowa, on September 18. President Truman,
speaking before an enormous noontime crowd, appealed to what he
saw as the common interest of farmers and laborers. He warned his
fellow midwesterners and a national radio audience that Republicans
were mostly concerned with the interests of "Wall Street . . . gluttons
of privilege." Democrats, according to the president, were interested
in all the people and were pursuing a policy that would lead to general prosperity. The "Republican strategy," he insisted, was "to divide
the farmer and the industrial worker. . . . To gain this end, they will stop
at nothing. On the one hand, the Republicans are telling industrial
workers that the high cost of food in the cities is due to this Government's farm policy. On the other hand, the Republicans are telling
the farmers that the high cost of manufactured goods on the farm is
due to this Government's labor policy. That's plain hokum." Accusing
the "Republican Congress" of sticking "a pitchfork in the farmer's
back," Truman proceeded to highlight the grain storage problem and
repeat the Brannan charge that Republicans were now "attacking the
whole structure of price supports for farm products." The farmer
could expect a long period of prosperity, Truman promised, if he was

71. Abels, *Out of the Jaws of Victory,* 231; Forsythe, "Postmortem on the
Election of 1948," 343; Stassen, telephone interview.
72. George H. Gallup, *The Gallup Poll: Public Opinion 1935–1971,* 1:750, 761.

only given "a fair deal." The danger was that "he may be voted out of a fair deal, and into a Republican deal."[73]

Looking only at the Republican and Democratic platforms, it is hard to see how the "Republican deal" for agriculture could be interpreted as the reverse of the "fair deal" promised by the president. Both parties had pledged their support to family farms, cooperatives, farm credit, and soil conservation; and in the words of the Democratic platform, the parties had called for "a permanent system of flexible price supports for agricultural products, to maintain farm income on a parity with farm operating costs."[74] As Walter Wilcox, told the American Farm Economic Association on September 15, 1948, "One can find little difference between the two parties in terms of their promises."[75]

In addition, the major farm organizations were still in basic agreement with the principle of the Agricultural Act of 1948. Stassen's September 2 statement, however, had caused widespread concern, and the administration successfully exploited it for political advantage. While the Farmers Union unfairly blamed Stassen for making the farm price support system a "political football," it nevertheless endorsed "the present bi-partisan agricultural policy and program, including the 90 percent of parity supports, and reiterate our purpose to fight to the limit during this Congress to retain it intact.... If this terrible spiral of inflation can be halted, then we feel that the long-range, flexible program provided in the present law, to become effective in 1950, can safely be put into effect."[76]

73. Truman, *Public Papers of the Presidents, 1948,* 504–6. For a discussion of the delivery and crowd response, see *Time* 52 (September 27, 1948): 23; Underhill, *The Truman Persuasions,* 276–77; Ross, *The Loneliest Campaign,* 182. Ross claimed a crowd of about eighty thousand heard a speech filled with "rhetorical violence" but the reaction was simply polite. *Time* put the crowd at one hundred thousand—"ten acres of people" (23).

74. Kirk H. Porter and Donald Bruce Johnson, comps., *National Party Platforms, 1840–1964,* 434, 452.

75. Unpublished paper sent to Hope by Wilcox, "Additional Legislation Needed," September 18, 1948, General Correspondence, Hope Papers.

76. "Statement of the National Board of Directors of the National Farmers Union Adopted in Denver, Colorado, September 15"; James Patton to Hope, October 1, 1948, Legislative Correspondence, Hope Papers. In his cover letter to the congressman, Patton emphasized the Union's support of the current program and called Hope "a true friend of farmers" (Patton to Brannan, October 13,

It was Stassen who committed the fumble, but it was the administration, and specifically Secretary Brannan, who recovered this political football and carried it for all it was worth. Although Truman
adopted the secretary's themes as his own, he did not fail to recognize
Brannan's campaign contributions. On the day of his boss's Dexter
speech, presidential secretary Charles Ross cabled Brannan to convey
Truman's approval and appreciation of his efforts. "The President,"
wired Ross, "hopes you will crack down on Dewey's Farm Statement
in your usual vigorous and effective fashion." Brannan did just that,
and as the president's "Whistle Stop" campaign rolled through September and October, he too continued to repeat the charges raised by
his agriculture secretary against Stassen and, by implication, against
Dewey.[77]

Press reaction to the president's first tour was mixed. At Dexter,
according to Irwin Ross, many of the journalists present thought
"there was a certain incongruity between the impassioned language
of the orator and the jolly country fair atmosphere of the gathering.
To Joseph Alsop, 'the obviously decent, moderate and flatly unemo-
tional President is almost comically miscast in the role of William
Jennings Bryan.'" Reporters covering the rest of the tour found it
entertaining but had no reason to believe the president was gaining
votes. "Crowds were large, curious, good-natured, but not especially
enthusiastic."[78] While Truman was "entertaining" large crowds with
blistering assaults on the past Congress, Dewey remained silent. His
running mate, Governor Warren, did challenge the president's Dexter speech, but his main emphasis was the need for bipartisanship in
agriculture.[79]

Congressional Republicans tried to counter the president's offensive, but with little cooperation from the Dewey organization, they
experienced limited success. The Republican National Committee

---

1948, Brannan Papers; Wilcox to Hope, September 18, 1948, General Correspondence, Hope Papers; Stassen, telephone interview).
    77. Ross to Brannan, September 18, 1948, OF, Truman Papers; Truman, *Pub-
lic Papers of the Presidents, 1948,* 549, 559, 661.
    78. Ross, *The Loneliest Campaign,* 183, 190.
    79. Yarnell, *Democrats and Progressives,* 607; Forsythe, "Postmortem on the
Election of 1948," 343–44; *Time* (September 27, 1948): 19–22.

reprinted Congressmen Hope's July 7 *Congressional Record* statement entitled "What the Eightieth Congress Has Done for the
Farmer" for distribution to speakers and local party leaders.[80] And
Hope tried to assure fellow Republicans that there was no foundation for the Democratic vendetta. "In view of the record of the 80th
Congress with regard to agricultural matters," Hope wrote Congressman Charles W. Vursell of Illinois, "the Democrats are hard put
to find any campaign material which they can use in the agricultural
sections of the country. Otherwise they would not be forced to manufacture campaign material out of the whole cloth like they are in
this grain storage matter." After quoting the most contemptuous portions of the president's Dexter speech, Hope said that these statements were being repeated by "campaign orators throughout the
country" and "circulated in a whispering sort of way by payrollers all
over the agricultural sections." Although Hope "absolve[d] the President from deliberately misleading the people because he in all prob-
ability does not know the facts," the statements were nevertheless in-
correct.[81] In speeches and statements made throughout the campaign,
Hope and others forcefully defended Dewey and the Republican
Congress and countered the administration's indictment. These efforts,
however, could not make up for the faulty strategy followed by the
candidate himself.[82]

By the time Governor Dewey delivered his own farm address in
mid-October, in which he endorsed the Hope-Aiken Act and insisted
that Democrats were intentionally misleading farmers, a charge that
contained a great deal of truth, the Truman-Brannan effort to raise the
fears of a new farm depression had apparently taken root. Truman
and Brannan could not attack the flexible support features of the
Aiken bill that they had supported, but local Democrats could. With

80. Hope, Extension of Remarks, *CR,* 80th Cong., 2nd sess., House, June
19, 1948, 94, pt. 12, *Appendix:* A4423–28; Hope, "What the Eightieth Congress
Has Done for the Farmer," June 19, 1948, Speech file, Hope Papers.
81. Hope to Vursell, October 5, 1948, Legislative Correspondence, Hope
Papers.
82. Ross, *The Loneliest Campaign,* 218; Smith, *Thomas E. Dewey and His
Times,* 532; Aiken to R. C. Carrick, October 20, 1948, and other items related to
the organization of Dewey Farm Committee, Republican National Committee,
1948, Aiken Papers.

the help of farm leaders and USDA agents in the field, they convinced
many that Hope-Aiken could mean the end of supports. Dewey's
endorsement of flexible supports and his failure to point out the con-
tradictions in the administration's position did nothing to relieve
farmers' fears.[83]

The president's campaign continued at a furious pace through the
last weekend of October. On Saturday, October 30, on his way home
to Independence, Truman delivered a rousing speech in St. Louis. In
what Ken Heckler characterized as "far and away the best political
speech of his entire career, bar none," the president touched all the
familiar bases. When he came to agriculture, Truman told his home-
state audience "that any farmer in these United States who votes
against his own interests, that is who votes the Republican ticket,
ought to have his head examined."[84] Two days later, on election eve,
Truman closed out his campaign with a 9:37 p.m. speech to a nation-
wide radio audience. When the ballots finally were tallied four days
later, the president would know that his tireless efforts had paid off.

The precise implications of the farm vote to Truman's surprising
victory on November 2, 1948, are difficult to assess. Many issues and
constituencies figured prominently in the outcome. In addition to his
success among labor and minority voters, Truman held together the
old Roosevelt coalition, despite the loss of four southern states to
Governor Strom Thurmond of South Carolina. The incumbent president benefited also from the foreign policy situation, particularly the
Berlin Crisis. Ironically, Truman was able to profit from these circumstances only because his policies in this area received bipartisan
support, including unprecedented appropriations from the Republicans of the Do-Nothing Eightieth Congress.[85]

Nevertheless, the president did make significant gains in traditional
Republican farm states. As a result, Dewey was convinced that the

83. Abels, *Out of the Jaws of Victory,* 224–31; Smith, *Thomas E. Dewey and
His Times,* 533; Matusow, *Farm Policies and Politics,* 181–84.
84. Truman, *Public Papers of the Presidents, 1948,* 935; Heckler, *Working
with Truman,* 104.
85. See, for example, Yarnell, *Democrats and Progressives,* xii; Robert A.
Divine, "The Cold War and the Election of 1948," 109; Smith, *Thomas E. Dewey
and His Times,* 530; William E. Pemberton, *Harry S. Truman: Fair Dealer and
Cold Warrior,* 124–25; William C. Pratt, "The Farmers Union and the 1948 Henry
Wallace Campaign," 349.

farm vote he won in 1944 but lost in 1948 cost him the election.[86] Congressman Hope agreed. It happened, he wrote, because the "High Command" was misled by early polls and considered the farm vote "in the bag." Since the party's congressional losses "were mostly in the strong labor Districts," Hope was convinced "that had the proper kind of campaign been carried on in the agricultural areas, Dewey could have carried all the agricultural states with the possible exceptions of Minnesota and Missouri."[87] As for the president, he reportedly gave labor much of the credit, but former Secretary Anderson, who won his senate contest in New Mexico, "was thrilled indeed at this vote of confidence in the farm policies of the Truman Administration and my own three years in the Truman Cabinet." Although Clinton Anderson was justified in taking some of the credit for Harry Truman's 1948 farm support, it was Charles Brannan who had defined the political issues in a "vigorous campaign that literally took him to the barnyards."[88] It was also Brannan who was to give direction to the administration's agricultural policy in 1949. With a restored Democratic majority in Congress, guided by a new secretary of agriculture and a confident president, a renewed search for a long-range program for agricultural appeared inevitable once the Congress convened in January 1949. In what direction would the Truman-Brannan administration steer this search? What did the election results indicate about American attitudes toward farm policy? Had President Truman received a mandate for change? Throughout the winter of 1948–1949, Americans interested in farm policy matters pondered the last two questions and awaited, with some apprehension, an answer to the first.

86. Donovan, *Conflict and Crisis,* 438; Donovan, *Tumultuous Years: The Presidency of Harry S. Truman, 1949–1953,* 13; Thomas G. Ryan, "Farm Prices and the Farm Vote in 1948," 387; Matusow, *Farm Policies and Politics,* 185–88; Soth, *Farm Troubles,* 13; "Why Farmers Swung to Truman," 23.

87. Hope to Gunnell, January 4, 1949, FF, Hope Papers. Stassen's subsequent assessment also emphasized the overconfidence of the candidate's national organization, which ignored contrary warnings (Stassen, telephone interview; *Time* 52 [November 8, 1948]: 21).

88. AP, "Midwest's Farmers Swung to Truman," *Garden City [Kansas] Telegram,* November 4, 1948; Anderson, *Outsider in the Senate,* 93. For Truman's opinion, see Gosnell, *Truman's Crises,* 410; Donovan, *Conflict and Crisis,* 438.

5

THE BRANNAN FARM PLAN
Agricultural Panacea or Political Football?

Coming out of an election that had possibly politicized the farm question more than ever before, many in the Truman administration saw the results as a mandate for change in farm policy. Neither Truman nor Brannan had directly attacked the flexible price support provisions of the Aiken portion of the 1948 act. But their constant hammering at Republican farm legislation had left many interested Americans with that impression, and the new Democratic majority was anxious to try its hand at farm legislation when Congress convened in January 1949. Secretary Brannan, who had never been fully convinced of the wisdom of his predecessor's pricing policies, was also eager to guide the administration's farm policy in a new direction.[1] No one, according to Alonzo Hamby, "had come to the office of secretary of agriculture with clearer credentials as an aggressive liberal" than Charles F. Brannan. His efforts during the campaign had attracted the president's attention and "brought him into the White House inner circle. Brannan had grasped the potential Democratic strength on the farms, had defined the issues, and had stumped the country areas for the administration." Truman's success in these areas "made the secretary one of the major figures of the administration and also

1. Clarence Cannon to Truman, January 7, 1949, OF, Truman Papers. See also "Why Farmers Swung to Truman," 24; Brannan, interview; Saloutos, "Agricultural Organizations and Farm Policy," 390; Soth, *Farm Troubles,* 13.

suggested new political strategies to liberals both inside and outside the government."[2]

Any effort to assign credit for the Democratic victory of 1948 would be precarious at best. A few points, however, can be made with certainty. The Democratic Party's spectacular comeback is the most obvious factor. It regained control of both houses of Congress after only two years in the minority and won a presidential election that even the party faithful had thought hopeless. Truman triumphed with a one million popular vote plurality over the combined totals of his two major opponents (Dewey and Thurmond) in part because of his remarkable farm belt victory. He held many of the midwestern and western states that FDR had carried and recaptured Colorado, Iowa, Ohio, Wisconsin, and Wyoming, which had gone back to Dewey and the Republicans in 1944.[3] The total electoral vote of these five states in 1948 was fifty-six. If these are subtracted from Truman's 303 and added to Dewey's 189, the latter still comes up a loser by a slim two vote margin. But if Truman had received only 247 electoral college votes—all other factors remaining the same—he would have been nearly twenty votes short of a majority, and the House of Representatives would have been called on to choose the next president. Assuming the Eighty-first Congress was controlled by the Democratic Party (which probably can safely be done), Truman would still have been elected.

The president also emerged from the campaign with renewed confidence, ready to push harder for his Fair Deal package. In the farm policy arena, Brannan's contribution to the Truman victory made the president, who had always been inclined to leave such matters in the hands of his secretary of agriculture, more disposed to follow the

2. Hamby, *Beyond the New Deal,* 303; Aiken to Gerald L. Dearing, January 18, 1949, "Farm Bill 1948, Correspondence," Aiken Papers.

3. Bureau of the Census, *Historical Abstracts of the United States, Colonial Times to 1970, Bicentennial Edition, Part 2,* 1075. Henry A. Wallace came in fourth with 1,156,000 votes, just behind Thurmond who polled 1,169,000. There are many different opinions concerning the importance of the farm vote. Abels, *Out of the Jaws of Victory,* 290–92, saw it as pivotal, but more recent scholars have tended to downplay its impact: see, for example, Forsythe, "Clinton P. Anderson," 612; Donovan, *Conflict and Crisis,* 438; Ryan, "Farm Prices and the Farm Vote in 1948," 387.

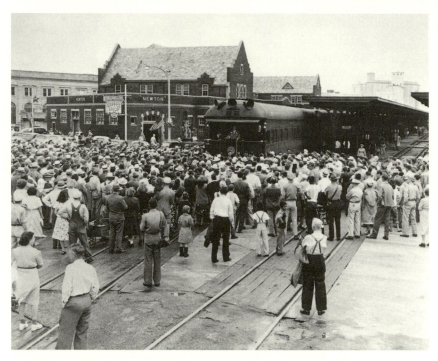

President Truman practiced the campaign techniques that were to carry him to victory in the fall at numerous "whistle stops" from Crestline, Ohio, to Olympia, Washington. The president's special railroad car, the *Ferdinand Magellan,* rolled into Newton, Kansas, on June 16, 1948, where Truman delivered some "rear platform remarks" to a large crowd gathered at the Santa Fe depot. Copyright unknown, photograph courtesy of the Harry S. Truman Library.

secretary's lead. Truman proved to be quite amenable to the suggestions of Charles Brannan, and both men seemed convinced that the election had given them a mandate to change the government's agricultural program. But what did the election results really indicate about farmers' attitudes toward future farm policy, and how would this Democratic victory affect the ongoing search for a long-range program? In this regard, the only thing that can be said with confidence is that no one really knew what the returns meant or in what direction the administration would move.

In its postelection analysis, *U.S. News* cited "alarm over the sliding-scale" provision in the new farm bill as one important reason for Truman's remarkable success in the farm states. Farmers anticipated the end of "good times" and, perhaps, believed the Democrats and "high" (90 percent of parity or more), fixed price supports would be their best insurance against such developments. Apparently, many farmers, and *Time* magazine, counted "full economic support" among the president's numerous campaign promises, when, in fact, as *U.S. News* observed, Truman and Brannan were among the many backers of flexible (or sliding scale) price supports.[4]

This ambiguity served Truman well during the campaign. But the time for a policy decision was at hand. The fact that many farmers expected the administration to offer a generous support plan helped push Truman and Brannan away from the flexible support principle, as did their own instincts. There was little indication of this shift, however, in the months immediately following the election. A high, mandatory support system made sense in a country at war, but to the postwar taxpayer worried about inflation, it seemed wasteful and unnecessary. Secretary Brannan recognized public dissatisfaction with certain facets of the farm policy and insisted that his goal was abundant production and expanded consumption, but he remained consistently vague as to how the administration planned to attain these objectives.[5]

In early December 1948, at a St. Louis Production and Marketing Administration (PMA) conference, the secretary said, "Our price support is extremely important to farmers and to the public. But we must not expect to substitute support prices for fair market prices. Our objective is still for fair market prices, with supports in the role of aiding us in reaching that objective and protecting farmers when they fall short of it." This statement was strongly endorsed by Henry C. Taylor, agricultural economist for the Farm Foundation. On December 14, he wrote Brannan: "You will have rendered a great service if you can provide the leadership that will result in the farm organizations

4. "Why Farmers Swung to Truman," 23, 24; *Time* 52 (November 8, 1948): 21; *Kansas Union Farmer,* December 1948; AP, "Midwest's Farmers Swung to Truman," *Garden City [Kansas] Telegram,* November 4, 1948; *Newsweek* 33 (January 3, 1949): 10; *Newsweek* 33 (January 10, 1949): 12, 16; Ryan, "Farm Prices and the Farm Vote in 1948," 387.

5. Clipping sent to Brannan by James Daniel, *Rocky Mountain News,* November 5, 1948, Meetings 3–3, General Correspondence, 1948, Office of the Secretary of Agriculture, RG 16, NA; Patton to Brannan, November 24, 1948, James G. Patton folders, Subject file, 1938–1988, Brannan Papers.

taking that position. If your position is accepted by them and by Congress, price can continue to be the guide to production."[6]

Responding to a letter from the executive secretary of the California Farm Research and Legislative Committee, Edward J. Overby, an assistant to the secretary of agriculture, explained the so-called Woolley Plan, which was of great interest to his correspondent. This plan, which involved the use of compensatory payments, Overby explained, was one of several proposals discussed by PMA deputy administrator Frank Woolley at the National Farm Bureau Convention. Because relatively high and rigid price supports had proven unsatisfactory for some crops, most notably perishable commodities like potatoes, Woolley had indicated that "thought has been given in some places to the benefit payment idea instead of the present methods of price support. Under such a plan, all farmers would receive the market price for their crop, but an additional amount would be paid the farmer who cooperated with his goal in order to bring his total returns nearer the parity figure." Overby was quick to point out that "the legislative basis for such a program, beginning January 1, 1950, is contained in the Agricultural Act of 1948 which authorizes the Secretary through Commodity Credit Corporation and other means available to him to support prices of agricultural commodities to producers through loans, purchases, payments (underscoring supplied), and other operations." Since farmers preferred "to get their entire income in the market place," however, "the advantages and disadvantages of the payment idea should be weighed carefully."[7]

As the administration weighed these various options, advice and unsolicited election analysis poured in from all quarters. Allan Kline, in a confidential December 18 letter, offered the president some "background" information for use "in the preparation of your statement to the Congress. . . . In the first place," avouched the influential head of

6. Taylor to Brannan, December 14, 1948, Farm Program 6, Office of the Secretary of Agriculture, RG 16, NA. The Brannan statement was quoted in Taylor's letter. See also Jim Daniel, Scripps-Howard Newspaper Alliance, to Brannan, November 5, 1948 (and attached article and reply), Meetings 3–3, Office of the Secretary of Agriculture, RG 16, NA.

7. Grace McDonald to Brannan, December 15, 1948, and Overby to McDonald, January 5, 1949, Farm Program 6, Office of the Secretary of Agriculture, RG 16, NA.

the nation's largest farm organization, "there is a lot of misinformation abroad with regard to the attitude of a number of states on high
rigid price supports, and the regimentation and control involved."
Truman's success in farm states did not mean "that farmers had de-
serted the principles of the long-range farm bill," which had passed
the Senate Agriculture Committee with "vigorous bi-partisan support,"
and the president should not be "misled into the belief" that farmers,
"who had so dramatic a part" in his victory, were for "high rigid price
supports."[8]

While numerous national and state farm bureau officials feared
Truman was reading the election as a mandate to abandon his commitment to the flexible support principle of the new farm law, many
farmers were concerned that the election had had the opposite effect
on the administration. The White House and USDA received a number of letters and telegrams during late December and early January
from farmers throughout the country calling for 90 to 100 percent of
parity. Many of these took exception with the stated positions of their
so-called leaders, especially those of the AFBF. One correspondent
sent Secretary Brannan a copy of a letter he had written to the New
York State Farm Bureau Federation in which he urged the AFBF to
move away from the Republican Party and to begin cooperating with
the administration. Another, who obviously believed Truman had
endorsed the Hope-Aiken Act, pointedly asked: "Does the Democratic Party feel that farmers will not be needed in 1952?"[9]

Obviously, there existed a great deal of consternation regarding
the administration's position on price supports during the weeks following the 1948 election. This situation had not developed by accident.
Truman had successfully manipulated the farm issue to his advantage
during the campaign, distancing himself from the controversial shift
to flexible supports and tagging the GOP as a threat to continued
farm prosperity. Although most farm leaders correctly believed that
the administration had endorsed the principles of the Aiken bill, they

8. Kline to Truman, December 18, 1948, OF, Truman Papers; Curtis Hatch,
president, Wisconsin Farm Bureau, to Brannan, December 30, 1948, Farm Program 6, Office of the Secretary of Agriculture, RG 16, NA.
9. Alfred Barnes, chairman, National Committee for Agriculture, Huron, SD,
to Brannan, telegram, January 7, 1949; Everett Blazey to Brannan, December
18, 1948, Farm Program 6, Office of the Secretary of Agriculture, RG 16, NA.

were not sure how the election would affect this earlier position. In this they were not alone. As Hope aptly observed, "While the Department supported the Aiken bill, there is every reason to believe that it has been influenced considerably by the results of the election, and is now wavering in its position, although I am sure that no definite conclusion has been reached as yet."[10]

On January 2, 1949, Carl Hamilton, the editor and publisher of the *Iowa Falls Citizen* and a former high-level USDA official, expressed his bewilderment in a letter to his friends in the Agricultural Department. "Tell me, kind sirs, what the hell is the pitch on this parity business—is the party line 60 percent, 90 percent, 100 percent or what?" From his vantage point, Hamilton wrote that the answer was indiscernible, "And I'm right here to tell you that some right sharp differences of opinion exist on that subject. The Bureau, the Union and the PMA are going around out here in about as good a three-cornered dog fight as I have seen since leaving the government service! . . . I am pretty well confused on this whole matter. What is the Secy's pitch on it anyway. Is the PMA off the reservation again (or should I say yet?)"[11]

Edward Overby did little by way of providing answers to Hamilton's queries. In a January 19 letter, he wrote that "it is a little bit difficult to answer your questions because as yet, there isn't any 'party line' at '60, 90, 100 or what' percent." Although Secretary Brannan had not "felt particularly obligated to set himself up as a target for everybody to shoot at [yet] . . . he will be as definite as possible when he goes before Congress." Overby offered assurances that Brannan would "certainly not be cataloged as a low support man," but he was vague

10. Hope to Kirk Fox, January 8, 1949, FF, Hope Papers; *Newsweek* 33 (January 3, 1949): 10; *Newsweek* 33 (January 10, 1949): 12, 16. Senator Aiken expressed a similar sentiment: "Of course, we don't know what the President is going to recommend today, but if he advocates tearing down the provisions of the 1948 price support program it would be nothing short of sheer hypocrisy for he and the Department of Agriculture both backed us to the limit last summer" (Aiken to Gerald L. Dearing, January 6, 1949, "Farm Bill 1948, Correspondence," Aiken Papers).

11. Hamilton to "Art and Jerry," January 2, 1948 [1949], Farm Program 6, Office of the Secretary of Agriculture, RG 16, NA; Albertson, *Roosevelt's Farmer*, 158, 226–27. Hamilton was a chief assistant and confidant of Claude Wickard.

as to specifics. He hinted at the possibility of a new emphasis, however, by writing that the secretary "would like to get people to think
about the whole program—the many different ways of maintaining
farm income and living standards—instead of concentrating their
whole attention on the mandatory minimum level of support for a
few commodities." As to the position taken by PMA state commit-
teemen, who had come out in favor of 90 percent supports, Overby's
answer was that they were not "off the reservation" but "neither are
they necessarily speaking for the Secretary. The 'reservation' doesn't
yet have a fence around it."[12]

Although some interest in new policies and approaches can be seen
within the USDA before January 1949, there is no indication that a
major departure was in the offing. The department was clearly on
record in support of flexibility. "The Administration has asked Congress to make flexible its mandate to support prices," read an official
position paper issued soon after the passage of the Hope-Aiken Act.
"The 80th Congress went only part way with this request. The compromise legislation it passed . . . handicaps us seriously by delaying
for another year the flexibility needed and by giving special restrictive treatment to several commodities."[13] Flexibility, as used in this
context and as explained repeatedly by Brannan during the debate
that followed his April 1949 testimony, undoubtedly meant more to
USDA officials than the sliding scale of price supports. But flexible
price supports were a major part of the new law, which the administration had not yet denounced.

In fact, Brannan's remarks at the AFBF annual convention in December 1948 seemed to reaffirm the administration's earlier commitment. On December 30, H. E. Slusher, the Missouri Farm Bureau president, wrote: "It was heartening to have your statement and tentative
approval of the variable price support program, as set out in the present
law." Brannan's reply of January 18 contained no hint that the secretary took exception with Slusher's interpretation. Remaining noncommittal on a specific approach, Secretary Brannan placed his emphasis

12. Overby to Hamilton, January 19, 1949, Farm Program 6, Office of the
Secretary of Agriculture, RG 16, NA.
13. Statement sent to William D. Hassett, secretary to the president, by
Brannan, July 29, 1948, OF, Truman Papers.

on the importance of a fair income and a price support program designed for the farmer. "So long as I am Secretary of Agriculture," he asserted, "like my predecessor, I shall endeavor to have farmer thinking reflected in the formulation and administration of the price support program to the maximum possible extent."[14]

In material prepared for the president's State of the Union address, the secretary suggested that the agricultural portion should begin with a statement on general conditions and the need for a comprehensive program. The emphasis, according to Brannan, should be on "three main program fields: (1) markets, prices, and income, (2) conservation and improvements of natural resources, and (3) rural living, cooperatives, and farm credit." The secretary attached a preliminary draft of the proposed presidential statement that stressed conservation needs and that encouraged the president to "consider a special message dealing with the need for additional general farm legislation." Although the USDA believed Congress should reexamine the entire farm program and improve the existing price support structure, there was no indication that a radical new approach should be advanced.[15]

Ready to begin his new term of office and confident that he had received a mandate for change, the president delivered his State of the Union address on January 5, 1949.[16] Truman was careful not to commit himself or the USDA to a specific approach to the plight of the American farmer, and he spoke in general terms about the many needs of rural America. He called for improvements in the national farm program and insisted, "our goals should be abundant farm production and parity income for agriculture." Noticeably absent was his previous endorsement of a flexible price support system. He still believed farm supports must be an "essential part of our program." They should be used, Truman explained, "to prevent farm price declines which are out of line with general price levels, to facilitate

14. Slusher to Brannan, December 30, 1948, and Brannan to Slusher, January 18, 1949, Public Relations 10–3; Curtis Hatch to Brannan, December 28, 1948, Public Relations 2, Office of the Secretary of Agriculture, RG 16, NA.

15. Brannan to Truman, November 29, 1948, and other materials, in Public Relations 10–2, Office of the Secretary of Agriculture, RG 16, NA.

16. The president enjoyed a 69 percent approval rating in January 1949. This dropped to a still strong 57 percent by March, with farmer approval at 56 percent, 24 percent disapproving of his performance (Gallup, *Gallup Poll,* 2:784).

adjustment in production to consumer demands, and to promote good land use." But the president left the door open for a new approach.[17]

While the administration procrastinated, there were signs indicating that it was a hot time for agricultural policy in the Eighty-first Congress. First, the new majority party was eager to fix the damage wrought by the Republicans during the previous term. Just what this meant with respect to policy was not yet clear, but in agricultural matters the Congress was to be led by southerners who favored "high-level price supports for farm products."[18]

Second, the injection of partisanship during the previous campaign had set the stage for a lively debate. Congressman Hope believed the USDA was "going to be run on a pretty political basis during the next four years" and feared "that whatever policies are adopted will be based upon the question of what is conceded to be good politics."[19] The Farm Bureau also was concerned about this trend. On January 18, Roger Fleming, the director of the Washington office of the AFBF, insisted that the flexible support principle of the Agricultural Act of 1948 had enjoyed bipartisan support. He was especially afraid that the policy debate was becoming too politicized and insisted that it was the duty of private farm organizations to make "certain that the employees of the various Government farm program agencies stay out of the field of partisan and policy politics."[20]

17. Truman, *Public Papers of the Presidents, 1949,* 4. The president's inaugural address, delivered two weeks later, focused exclusively on foreign policy and is remembered for its "Point Four" program (112). Senator Aiken, for one, noticed that Truman did not take a position on support levels in his speech and wrote: "His best advisers are telling him to let my program alone. It may be he will do so" (Aiken to George A. Ellis, January 7, 1949, "Farm Bill 1948, Correspondence, 1949," Aiken Papers).

18. Benedict, *Farm Policies of the United States,* 478. In the House, Representative Harold D. Cooley of North Carolina replaced Hope as the chairman of the agriculture committee, and Senator Elmer Thomas of Oklahoma replaced Arthur Capper as chairman of the corresponding Senate committee.

19. Hope to George Carmichael, New York, January 12, 1949, FF, Hope Papers.

20. Quoted in memo to "The Secretary" from Nathan Koenig, February 2, 1949, Public Relations 10, Office of the Secretary of Agriculture, RG 16, NA; Fleming to Brannan, January 21, 1948, and copy of Fleming's January 18 talk to the Minnesota FBF, Farm Credit Administration and Farm Program, Correspondence, Brannan Papers.

During this period of uncertainty it is not surprising that the farm press began to speculate about possibility of farm policy change. In its January issue, for example, *Successful Farming* predicted that agriculture, "especially price supports," would be a contentious issue during this session of Congress. In "back of the oncoming battle," according to editor Kirk Fox, "is the wide disagreement among new agricultural leaders in Congress, U.S.D.A. officials, and major farm organizations." He correctly indicated that among the major players, southern congressional leaders generally favored holding support levels at 90 percent of parity and that the Farmers Union had moved toward higher supports. Interestingly enough, the editor had not yet detected a shift in Secretary Brannan's position, and he grouped him with the National Grange and the Farm Bureau as the backers of flexible supports similar to those contained in the current law.[21]

Congressman Hope, who had not only lost his chairmanship but also a shot at the top job in the USDA as a result of the election, saw little possibility that the new Congress would decide to support prices at full parity but continued to believe that some changes were needed. As he wrote the president of the Pratt County Farm Bureau, "it was distinctly understood on the part of all conferees [on June 19, 1948], and I so stated in the report which I made to the House, that there would be some revision of the Aiken bill in this Congress." Hope believed this would happen even though the Democrats had taken the majority and despite the fact that the AFBF, the leading supporter of the long-range program, was "insisting on retaining the Aiken bill with its flexible price supports."[22]

From the halls of Congress, early signs that the partisanship of the past campaign was not easily forgotten emerged during debate on a bill (S. 900) to amend the Commodity Credit Corporation (CCC) Charter Act. Many members of Congress agreed with a January 1949 article in *Successful Farming,* that indicated that Democratic charges

21. See clipping sent to Hope by Fox, January 6, 1949, and John M. Collins to Hope, January 29, 1949, Legislative Correspondence; Hope to J. W. Morgan, January 21, 1949, FF, Hope Papers. For the NFU position, see "NFU to Seek Full Action," *Kansas Union Farmer,* January 1949; M. W. Thatcher to Aiken, February 2, 1949, and to Edward J. Thye, February 3, 1949, "Farm Bill 1948, Correspondence, 1949," Aiken Papers.

22. Hope to Merle E. Lambert, January 4, 1949, FF, Hope Papers.

with regard to this issue had been "nothing short of political propaganda."[23] Congressman Hope, no admirer of the charter bill himself, nevertheless agreed that "with respect to the matter of farm storage, the misrepresentations made by the Democrats were colossal. . . . The whole thing was pure political hooey."[24] Beginning in early February and continuing throughout the first session of the Eighty-first Congress, debate on the House and Senate floors, and in committee hearings, reflected the partisanship that had engulfed the CCC issue and the Republican belief that, months after the election, Brannan was continuing to blame the Eightieth Congress for all of agriculture's problems.[25]

As political tensions built during the first weeks and months of the session, the administration appeared to be in no hurry to give direction to the farm policy debate. When asked at his January 8 news conference if he was in favor of amending the flexible support provision of the current legislation, Truman insisted that it was up to Congress. Asked specifically if he favored flexible price supports, the president said he had not "given the matter thought," but that "if they [Congress] like it, I will sign it."[26] A month later, Truman informed the White House press corps that the secretary would announce the administration's policy on price supports as soon as the congressional committee was ready to hear from him. Truman would give no details, however, and when asked on March 3 if he would urge rigid 90 percent parity support, he had no comment.[27]

In light of the increasing public concern with price supports at a time of general inflationary problems, and skepticism from farmers

23. See clipping sent by Kirk Fox to Hope, January 6, 1949, Legislative Correspondence, Hope Papers; Bills Proposed by the Department of Agriculture, Legislation 1, Office of the Secretary of Agriculture, RG 16, NA.

24. Hope to E. J. Ferguson, January 10, 1949, FF, Hope Papers.

25. *CR,* 81st Cong., 1st sess., Senate, February 10, 1949, 95, pt. 1: 1127; *CR* (House), May 10, 1949, pt. 5: 5992–6002; *CR* (House), June 7, 1949, pt. 6: 7355–56; *CR* (Senate), June 13, 1949, pt. 6: 7590. See also House Committee on Agriculture, *General Farm Program: Hearings before a Special Subcommittee,* 81st Cong., 1st sess., pt. 1, 1949, 82.

26. Truman, *Public Papers of the Presidents, 1949,* 38.

27. Ibid., 130, 156. Actually, Senator Thomas had already invited the secretary to appear before his Committee on Agricultural and Forestry at Brannan's earliest convenience (Thomas to Brannan, January 12, 1949, Farm Program 5–6, Office of the Secretary of Agriculture, RG 16, NA; M. W. Thatcher to Aiken, February 12, 1949, "Farm Bill 1948, Correspondence, 1949," Aiken Papers).

and their spokespeople about the flexible support plan scheduled to take effect the following year, Truman's insistence that he had not thought about this feature of the agriculture program appears less than candid. Whether or not he was personally contemplating price support policy, his secretary of agriculture had given the matter plenty of consideration in the wake of the 1948 election. Planning had, in fact, been under way for some time. As Truman explained in his *Memoirs,* their goal was to devise "a permanent system of price supports for agriculture commodities" and to take much-needed action in the areas of soil conservation, marketing, and distribution. "In order to provide answers to these and other problems," wrote the former president, "I asked Charles F. Brannan, the Secretary of Agriculture, to make an over-all study of the farm situation and to draw up specific proposals, as Brannan and I had discussed various plans and ideas on three or four different occasions."[28]

To help him complete the study, Brannan asked O. V. Wells, head of the Bureau of Agricultural Economics, to chair a series of "departmental seminars." The secretary attended these meetings but, in the early stages, acted more as an observer; his primary interest was in providing a forum for the free discussion of ideas among the various top USDA officials. In his 1959 study of the Brannan plan, Reo Christenson wrote that of the many issues discussed during the eight sessions, which concluded on March 3, "Probably no subject was more fully explored than compensatory payments, that is, the use of direct federal payments as a substitute for price supports."[29] This is not surprising. Many agricultural economists had been heralding the benefits of this concept for some years, and a provision for limited use of such payments had been included in the long-range portion of the Agricultural Act of 1948. Brannan himself had endorsed the same approach two years before while working under Secretary Anderson.

Thus, as the secretary's thinking crystallized during the seminars of early 1949, it followed naturally that compensatory payments would become the cornerstone for the department's new farm policy recommendations. The seminars produced no policy consensus, but, toward the end of February, a skeletal Brannan plan was taking shape. In

28. Truman, *Memoirs,* vol. 2, 263–64; Matusow, *Farm Policies and Politics,* 190.
29. Christenson, *The Brannan Plan: Farm Politics and Policy,* 26, 28.

early March, the secretary assembled a smaller group of five men to work out specific policies and his congressional testimony: O. V. Wells; Wesley McCune, an executive assistant to the secretary; Ralph S. Trigg, an administrator of the PMA; John Baker, an expert in federal agricultural programs; and Maurice DuMars, an administrative officer in the office of the secretary, with considerable professional writing experience.[30]

On March 1, 1949, Brannan wrote Edwin G. Nourse, chairman of the Council of Economic Advisors (CEA), to explain the ongoing process and the reasons the department had been slow to announce administration policy. "I have organized a small group within the Department that is reviewing this whole question of agricultural price policy." They had reached no fixed conclusions, and Brannan was not ready to announce the USDA's policy recommendations. "I do think, however, that the Agricultural Act of 1948 as now drawn is too narrow. It concerns itself almost exclusively with price policy and one of the things which bothers me most about the current discussion is the emphasis which is placed on 60 percent versus 90 percent of parity." The department's "efforts," Brannan explained, had been "directed toward developing some other or new approach to this whole question of farm-nonfarm parity relationships."[31]

As the secretary pointed out, it would not be easy to devise a plan that would meet the needs of farmers and that would be acceptable to a public increasingly apprehensive about costly farm programs. Department efforts to draft a new approach were sincere, and USDA officials may have been working with all deliberate speed. But if Brannan gave any thought to the patience of Congress, he misjudged its ability to be long-suffering. The secretary had been holding an open invitation from the agricultural committees for nearly two months, and the delay, warranted or not, was causing considerable anxiety and apprehension.

Like most of his colleagues, freshman congressman Harold O. Lovre (R-SD) was "interested in seeing that the family sized farmer is assured a program which will provide him with economic assurance and

30. Ibid., 30–31.
31. Brannan to Nourse, March 1, 1949, Public Relations, Office of the Secretary of Agriculture, RG 16, NA; Edward S. Flash Jr., *Economic Advice and Presidential Leadership: The Council of Economic Advisers,* 20–21.

a solvent economy." He agreed with the administration that some revision was needed in the current law and believed "the family sized
farmer should be assured of full parity of income." Lovre was anxious
to see the legislative process move forward on this problem, and he
let the secretary know that his patience was wearing thin. As he pointed
out, the president had long since "outlined a broad legislative program," and Congress had "already begun consideration on a good
many of these proposals." But,

> on the question of farm price supports, little has been done.
> This is of grave concern to me and a good many of the farmers I
> represent because of the recent sharp break in commodity prices.
> It is the feeling of a good many members of Congress that action
> should be deferred on this vital subject until recommendations
> have been submitted by the Secretary of Agriculture as they feel
> that you are in a position to be intimately aware of the farmer's
> problems and the provisions which a fair, workable program
> should contain. While the Congress might not necessarily agree
> with your recommendations they should serve as an excellent
> guide in its deliberations.

Time was "drawing short" and the committees needed to hear from
many other persons, so Lovre urged the secretary to "make known
your feelings on the question of long range farm legislation."

> Farmers are wondering what program will be in effect [in
> 1950] . . . so that they can make plans for the future. Therefore, I
> believe that, out of fairness to an important part of our popula-
> tion, the Department of Agriculture, members of Congress and
> farm organizations should join hands in working out a program
> to provide for the future welfare and security of the American
> farmer.
>   This problem is too broad in scope to allow partisan politics
> to interfere in any way. It is too vital to the national welfare
> and to the future of America to be the subject of bickering or
> haranguing.[32]

Partisan "bickering" and "haranguing" had already commenced, however, and administration delays only allowed the situation to grow worse.

32. Lovre to Brannan, March 5, 1949, Farm Program, Office of the Secretary of Agriculture, RG 16, NA.

Nearly forty years later, Brannan recalled that when Congress asked him to open the hearings with his testimony on farm policy he "tried a slight maneuver. I said why don't you call the farm organizations first? Because, I said, we want to rework our views and get them in good shape and so on." Whether or not Brannan's recollection of these now distant events was entirely clear, he most certainly was on the mark when he concluded: "they [Congress] would have none of that!"[33] Republicans simply interpreted the delay as a sign of the administration's continued political maneuvering, and even the Democratic leadership was becoming increasingly frustrated.

On March 14, Stephen Pace, chairman of a special subcommittee of the House Committee on Agriculture, informed Brannan that his subcommittee was nearly finished with its study of the Agricultural Act of 1948 and was about ready to look at "price supports and related subjects." Since it would be best to hear first from the secretary, the congressman hoped Brannan was ready to present the USDA's recommendations. "I assure you," Brannan wrote in reply, "that my staff and I are working intensively to have a well-prepared and well-rounded program to present to Congress in the very near future."[34]

The administration's tactic (if indeed that is what it was) was also receiving less than flattering press coverage. During the first week of March, a newswire story informed the nation that in Washington "Farm State Congressman" had moved to "smoke out the administration views on farm price supports." Representative Charles Hoeven (R-IA) reportedly told the press "he intends to 'Force a showdown' on the Price Support issue if Brannan appears before a House Agriculture Subcommittee Hearing scheduled this week." Hoeven insisted that Brannan was "stalling in order to test the Political Wind. But this question is too important for political bickering. The Farmers are getting impatient."[35]

33. Brannan, interview.
34. Brannan to Pace, March 17, 1949, Hearings, Office of the Secretary of Agriculture, RG 16, NA; Pace to Hope, February 18, 1949, Agricultural Committee—Notice of Hearings and Meetings, Hope Papers.
35. Lovre to Brannan, March 5, 1949, Farm Program, Office of the Secretary of Agriculture, RG 16, NA. The document that contained this quote was attached to the Lovre letter to Brannan and Brannan's reply of March 11. The wire story also mentioned Lovre's letter to the secretary.

With its apparent procrastination, the administration was not only trying the patience of farmers and allowing political differences to crystallize but also losing what momentum it may have gained from the past election and, most significantly, sacrificing what little chance it had to acquire bipartisan support for a new proposal. Is it possible, for example, that someone like Clifford Hope would have supported the administration's new plan had Secretary Brannan seized the initiative earlier in the new session and at least made the pretense of pursuing a more traditional course in the formulation of policy? Congressman Hope had previously expressed support for production payments; although his mail was running in all directions, after the first of the year, he had come to the conclusion that farmers were willing to accept more controls in exchange for high-level support. He was upset with the AFBF's intransigence, and he was definitely committed to change in the Aiken bill.[36]

In February, Hope understandably was disturbed by the situation on the farm policy front. He did not find it surprising that farmers had come to believe that "they should have 90% or 100% of parity" because "that is what everyone has been telling them for many years past. As a result of this the principal question with most farmers is not whether they are entitled to 90% of parity, but the method to be used in giving it to them." Farmers had come to view this as "a matter of right."

> The sad part of the whole thing is that the Farm Bureau insisted last year that Congress pass the Aiken bill, which is a hastily gotten up concoction, full of contradictions and weak spots. Now they think they have to defend it and there really isn't much in it that can be successfully defended. My notion last year was that under all the circumstances we shouldn't try to pass a long range bill. That was the decision we reached in the House Committee and was the original decision of the Farm Bureau . . .
>
> Later on for some reason they changed their position and very largely wrote the Aiken bill. They used all the political pressure which they could bring to bear to get it enacted in the Sen-

36. Hope to J. W. Morgan, January 21, 1949; to Browne, February 4, 1949; to J. N. Tincher Sr., February 7, 1949; and to M. W. Thatcher, February 5, 1949, Legislative Correspondence, Hope Papers.

ate and then to get the House to accept it without any hearings or consideration whatever.

Hope was still upset that passage of the Aiken bill had hurt Republicans in the 1948 election by giving "the Democrats a chance to say the Republicans were for only 60% and they were for 90%. This notwithstanding the fact that the President signed the bill and its principles were endorsed by both Brannan and Anderson."[37]

The congressman would have expected as much from the Democrats, but he was "terribly disappointed in Allan Kline" who was forcing his position on the entire AFBF. "To an extent that is difficult to believe," Hope lamented, "he is becoming more like John L. Lewis every day and I am really very much disturbed about the situation. It isn't simply a question of what the support levels will be but it is a question of whether a little group of leaders who are entirely out of touch with the thinking of people on the farms are going to dictate farm legislation." Hope was not sure what should be done with regard to price policy. "But if we are going to have all the controls that are contained in the Aiken bill," he said, "we might just as well have 90% of parity price supports and let the farmer be getting something out of it."[38]

Hope's letter, written in "confidence," reveals considerable common ground between the former chairman of the House Committee on Agriculture and the secretary of agriculture. Fundamental differences remained, but, despite the partisanship of the past campaign, Hope respected Brannan and expressed considerable confidence in his efforts to find a solution for the price support problem. "I know that Secretary Brannan is giving a great deal of though[t] and study to the matter," he wrote on February 3, "and that he has the best brains in the Department working on it now. I am sure he wants to do everything possible to work out a solution to the question."[39] Hope would have been a valuable ally in the fight for the Brannan plan. Realistically, it probably would have taken more compromise on the part

37. Hope to Don L. Berry, February 12, 1949, FF, Hope Papers.
38. Hope to Berry, February 12, 1949, FF, Hope Papers. See also Hope to Roy Schrock, February 15, 1949, and to Herb W. Hoover, February 16, 1949, FF, Hope Papers.
39. Hope to Ed T. Hackney, February 3, 1949, FF, Hope Papers. See also Christenson, *The Brannan Plan,* 158–59.

of the secretary to win Hope's support than he was willing to make. Any chance he might have had, however, was lost as positions crystallized during the weeks of waiting for the USDA to provide direction.

Meanwhile, interested individuals and organizations, inside and outside the Congress, formulated their own plans. The longer they had to wait for the department's guidance, the less apt they were to accept it. Representing the position of his state's farm bureau, a little-known Republican senator from Wisconsin, Joseph R. McCarthy, argued that the Agricultural Act of 1948, with its provision for flexible price supports, should be given a fair trial. "Our farmers fear not only the regimentation and the restriction of opportunity which would follow rigidly supported prices," he warned his Senate colleagues, "but they also recognize that such a program, universally applied, could alienate the good will of the public, and impose an excessive burden on the Federal Treasury."[40]

Just a week before, the senior senator from Wisconsin, Alexander Wiley, had registered the opposite view on behalf of his state's Farmers Union. It focused on the small portion of the food dollar that was received by the farmer and called for 100 percent of parity and a modernized parity formula. The *Dakota Farmer* agreed. In "Whose Freedom Is It?" the editor argued that people who criticized high supports because the resulting restrictions limited the producer's freedom did not know what farmers were thinking. Reflecting attitudes similar to those found by Congressman Hope among Kansas wheat growers, the North Dakota editor insisted farmers were willing to accept limits in the form of acreage controls, in exchange for fairer prices.[41]

This heightened interest in farm policy during the first months of 1949 can be partially attributed to the belief that the period of abnormally high farm prices had come to an end. According to a *Washington Post* editorial from February 19, 1949, the farm economy had experienced sharp drops in the prices of two principal farm commodities since the previous year. Since early in 1947, the price per bushel

40. *CR,* 81st Cong., 1st sess., Senate, March 8, 1949, 95, pt. 2: 1963.
41. *CR,* 81st Cong., 1st sess., Senate, February, 25 1949, 95, pt. 2: 1547–48; *CR* (Senate), March 1, 1949, 95, pt. 2: 1629. The editorial was entered into the *Congressional Record* by Senator William Langer (R-ND).

of wheat had declined to $2.08 from a high of $3.10, and corn had dropped from $2.83 to $1.19 in one year. Farm production, according to the *Post,* had by this point exceeded demand, and the period of high prices had past. But as Senator Milton Young (R-ND) pointed out, while farm prices were falling, the prices of things farmers bought continued to rise.[42]

Shortly before the introduction of the Brannan plan, Lauren Soth, a columnist with the *Des Moines Register* and a former USDA and OPA economist, lucidly discussed current attitudes regarding farm policy. Most farm leaders, he explained, supported the new method of figuring parity and agreed that surplus problems could eventually lead to a loss of public support. On the question of support levels, though, there was real controversy. Most notably, the AFBF favored the flexible support approach while southern farmers and the NFU backed fixed, high-level supports. A third group, made up of many of the nation's agricultural economists, was advocating the elimination of direct price supports, and the American Farm Economic Association had endorsed "the principle of government payments to farmers, rather than support of prices through the marketplace. They would allow price to go free, so as to clear the market, and then pay farmers the difference between the free price and the guaranteed price when necessary." Repelled by the whole idea of accepting a subsidy, however, the AFBF and National Grange opposed direct payments, ostensibly because they felt it would be "easier to go to Congress for appropriations to make crop loans and purchases than for direct benefit payments."[43]

As concern with the farm situation increased and patience with the USDA wore thin, Brannan received policy advice from many quarters. But it was the NFU, which had abandoned its earlier commitment to flexible supports, that had the most influence. The secretary's philosophical commitment to the New Deal, his background in the Farm Security Administration, and his friendship with fellow Coloradoan

42. *CR,* 81st Cong., 1st sess., Senate, February 25, 1948, 95, pt. 2: 1548. Senator Young entered the *Post* article into the *Congressional Record.*

43. Soth, "Conflicts in Farm-Price Policy," 64. For more on Soth, see biographical introduction by Richard S. Kirkendall in Lauren Soth, *The Farm Policy Game Play by Play.*

Jim Patton probably made further lobby efforts unnecessary at this point. The similarity between the NFU's new farm policy position and the secretary's final statement to Congress is remarkable.

On February 17, 1949, Patton sent Wesley McCune a copy of a Farmers Union memo entitled "Fundamentals of a Federal Agricultural Program as of early 1949" for his "confidential reading." Although the document specifically addressed the situation in New York and was "particularly" related to milk, its implications had a much broader application. First, the policy statement demanded an end to those federal programs or practices that allowed "reactionary elements to dominate and control political and economic farm thinking." The document indicated several ways in which the "farm mind" was being "dominated and controlled in its political and economic thinking by Republican reactionaries," but its primary focus was "the existing Extension Service-Farm Bureau hookup" that was then being addressed by Congress. It was the NFU's opinion that this nearly thirty-year-old "connection" enhanced the "prestige" of its reactionary, rival farm organization and furnished it with an unfair political advantage.[44]

Second, "a positive federal farm program," according to the memo, should move away from the current price support approach that was simply "a stop gap and a dead end road." In its stead, the NFU sought a system that would complement both "production and consumption to optimum limits." "The subsidy should be paid on production, graduated to promote family type operations and not scientifically designed to teeter the farm price level just above the desperation point but rather to place producers on a parity of income level with the rest of the nation's folks."[45]

44. Patton to McCune, February 17, 1949, Farm Program 6, Office of the Secretary of Agriculture, RG 16, NA; E. H. Teagarden to Hope, February 28, 1949, and Hope to Teagarden, March 4, 1949, Legislative Correspondence, Hope Papers; "Divorce of Extension from The FB," *Kansas Union Farmer,* February 1949, and March and April issues. The controversy over the Brannan plan would put this issue on hold, but the Thomas bill (S. 1078) and a similar House bill were introduced in February 1949 for the purpose of divorcing the Farm Bureau and the Extension Service.

45. Patton to McCune, February 17, Farm Program 6, Office of the Secretary of Agriculture, RG 16, NA; M. W. Thatcher to Edward J. Thye, February 3, 1949, "Farm Bill 1948, Correspondence, 1949," Aiken Papers.

Interest in farm policy reform, in all quarters, continued at a high-level during the month of March. Nevertheless, the USDA remained remarkably tight-lipped as to its forthcoming recommendations, and the secretary and his subordinates refused to discuss the emerging details even with the party faithful.[46] On March 21, 1949, McCune sent Aubrey Williams, an old New Deal liberal, who was the editor of the *Southern Farmer,* some material on the president's economic stabilization proposals. With regard to farm policy recommendations, however, McCune told Williams, who maintained close ties with the administration, that hearings were to begin soon, with the secretary as the opening witness. "Charlie's recommendations on a price support program are shaping up as rapidly as possible and should be ready around the first of the month. I know that you will be very interested in them and I think you are going to like them."[47]

By the end of the month, Brannan was "putting the finishing touches" on his price support recommendations, and he sent the president a draft of his proposed remarks. Truman responded with a memorandum in which he noted only a few minor points for additional consideration or alteration. In some marginal notes on his draft copy of the Brannan plan, the president expressed concern with regard to the potential cost of the program, correctly pointing out a few of the questions that would arise in this area during the debate. He asked Brannan to seriously consider the provision for "an allowance for economic growth after 1948 at the rate of two percent a year" since "labor and industry are not assured increases." Truman's most significant comments, however, had to do with the use of a particular descriptive phrase. Revealing his desire to create a definite identity for his "Fair Deal" apart from FDR's "New Deal," as well as his dislike for Roosevelt's first secretary of agriculture, Truman informed his agriculture secretary that he would "like to get rid of that expression,

46. See, for example, Brannan to Harry S. Dole, March 18, 1949, Farm Program 6, Office of the Secretary of Agriculture, RG 16, NA.

47. McCune to Williams, March 21, 1949, Farm Program 6, Office of the Secretary of Agriculture, RG 16, NA. For more on Williams, see Otis L. Graham Jr. and Meghan Robinson Wander, eds., *Franklin D. Roosevelt: His Life and Times, An Encyclopedic View,* 455, and John A. Salmond, *A Southern Rebel: The Life and Times of Aubrey Willis Williams, 1890–1965.*

'ever-normal granary.' That is a Henry Wallace slogan and I hope we won't have to use it."[48]

Five days later, on the eve of his appearance before the Senate and House committees, Brannan sent the president a final draft. The secretary's proposal reflected the administration's desire for a farm program designed to encourage abundant production, to promote realistic adjustments in farm production decisions, to ensure the farm family an equitable living standard, and to help maintain high levels of employment and stability in the general economy. To accomplish these objectives, Brannan suggested an income support standard based on a more recent and realistic base period, a new list of basic commodities to be guaranteed full parity support, a system of production payments to be used for perishable commodities, and a limit on the amount of a farmer's production eligible for price support. "I believe," the secretary wrote in a brief cover letter, "the views are consistent with our many statements to farmers during the campaign and at the same time will help advance the best interests of all the people— farmers, consumers and processors. I sincerely hope that the statement will bring credit to your administration."[49]

Brannan knew that he had a difficult sales job ahead. Indeed, the marketing task had begun within the administration, without complete success. Although most executive branch officials loyally fell in line behind the Truman-Brannan proposal for agriculture, several Bureau of the Budget (BOB) officials shared their concerns with the White House. E. Fenton Shepard and Lee Dashier understood that Brannan had discussed the various aspects of his proposal with the president, nevertheless, they informed the White House, "good budgetary practice would require" an estimate of costs before the proposal was accepted. Without this, the BOB could only "hazard a guess" as to its "budgetary implications and economic effects." Their guess was that the cost would be high. Although the justification for this outlay was the disparity of farm income, Shepard and Dashier pointed out that the disparity had always existed and would probably continue

48. Truman to Brannan, April 1, 1949, PSF, Truman Papers.
49. Brannan to Truman, April 6, 1949, PSF, Truman Papers; *Congressional Digest* 29 (March 1950): 79.

to exist because of the excess population in rural areas—shifts were needed out of agriculture and into more stable and lucrative nonfarm occupations. Production payments were a desirable feature, but these benefited mainly commercial farmers.[50]

The most notable administration intransigent, however, was Edwin Nourse, the relatively conservative chairman of the president's Council of Economic Advisers. Nourse had been a highly respected economist and was the former president of the American Farm Economic Association. At the time of his appointment as the first chairman of the CEA in 1946, he was the vice president of the Brookings Institution. As far as the administration's farm policy was concerned, Nourse was a hard sell.[51] On April 4, 1949, attached to a note stamped "confidential," Brannan sent Chairman Nourse an outline of the farm program he was about to present to Congress, followed the next day by a copy of the complete statement. In the initial two-page summary Brannan emphasized that his proposal did not break sharply with past legislation. If there was anything "new" in his recommendations, the secretary reasoned, it was the idea of starting "computations with an income [rather than commodity price] criterion as the base on which price supports are determined." This principle had existed in previous laws but only as "decoration," and Brannan believed it was time to actually implement this concept because income was what really mattered. Anticipating some of the criticism that was to follow, Brannan pointed out that the production payment feature was nothing new. In explaining how this approach would be used for nonstorables, the secretary admitted that one objective was increased consumption. He was convinced, for example, that some city people had cut down their consumption of milk because they believed it was too expensive.[52]

In drawing this early sales effort to a close, Brannan summed up

50. Shepard and Dashier to Richard Neustadt, memo, White House, April 5, 1949, Agricultural Adjustment Act of 1949, Bureau of the Budget, RG 51, NA.

51. Flash, *Economic Advice and Presidential Leadership,* 20–21. In fact, Nourse remained unconverted. His well-publicized differences with the administration and his two CEA colleagues (Leon H. Keyserling and John D. Clark) over a range of policy choices led to his resignation, under fire, late in 1949.

52. Brannan to Nourse, April 4, 1949, "Brannan Plan," microfilm copy, reel 3, Edwin G. Nourse Papers, Harry S. Truman Library (hereafter cited as Nourse Papers).

the pros and cons and admitted that the present program would "not go very far toward closing the gap between farm and nonfarm income. It offers a realistic beginning but eventually we will have to go much further if we are to have parity of living conditions." He also confessed that it did nothing for the poor farmer who would have to turn to the Farm Home Administration for assistance. A complete farm program would have to recognize the declining opportunity in farming and provide job training programs and placement for those leaving agriculture for work in town. In addition, there was still a need to expand soil conservation and many other programs, much like those put forth in the 1947 proposal. "Price support is not the only matter that requires our attention," the secretary concluded. "However, it is the most immediate, pressing problem. And I would say, further, that it must be the heart of our policy, for it will determine to quite an extent how successful the rest of our program can be."[53]

Nourse remained unconvinced, but the long awaited administration proposal was unveiled shortly after 10 a.m., April 7, 1949. Congressman Harold Cooley, chairman of the House Committee on Agriculture, called the joint committee session to order and then introduced the secretary of agriculture. Brannan began his testimony by thanking the members for the opportunity to discuss some of the administration's "views and recommendations" with regard to price supports, "the heart of our farm policy."[54] The preliminary version of Brannan's plan that followed did not include the expression *ever-normal granary,* so disagreeable to the president. But it did contain several proposals that proved to be very disagreeable to a variety of organizations and individuals outside the administration.

Secretary Brannan expressed his commitment to price supports as "the most effective method yet suggested" for helping farmers "maintain a reasonably stable income at a fair level." He acknowledged the differences of opinion that had developed around the issue but insisted that it was an "oversimplification" to characterize this as a simple clash between proponents of "rigid support of prices at 90 percent of

53. Ibid.
54. House Committee on Agriculture, *General Farm Program, including Joint Hearings with the Senate Committee on Agriculture and Forestry,* 81st Cong., 1st sess., pt. 2, 1949, 138. A copy of Brannan testimony also can be found in Farm Program, Brannan Papers.

parity" and advocates of "flexible supports ranging from 60 to 90 percent."[55] The issues involved were anything but simple, and recent bumper crops, increased plantings, continued surpluses, and price declines had begun to clarify the postwar farm situation. Agriculture was reaching the "point where we seriously need some shifts in farm production if we are to avoid surpluses. . . . In short," Brannan continued,

> some additional problems have come out of the realm of theory into the here-and-now. Hence, the preparation of my first recommendations to the Congress on the important matter of price supports has required me to make a rather complete review of objectives, legislation, and alternative programs. In addition to considering simple revisions in present legislation, we have taken a new look at various ways of measuring parity and just about all of the program suggestions that have been seriously considered in the past. . . .
>
> The result of all this study is not likely to startle anyone; I have no revolutionary ideas to present to you. But I do have some definite recommendations for your consideration.

The secretary's recommendations were designed to build on "the firm foundation" of farm programs that had existed for nearly twenty years. From this experience, Brannan explained, certain "realistic criteria" could be established by which to "judge" and "guide" new programs. The secretary then proceeded to outline four of the more prominent "criteria and requirements" that should be followed. First, any basic farm program had to help the farmer cope with those "circumstances beyond his control" that often kept him from recouping even his costs of production. Second, a program that effectively serves farmers also "should be fair to consumers and business people" and thus had to ensure "plentiful and steady supplies" of farm commodities. Third, the program had to be operated efficiently at a cost "commensurate with the benefits to the Nation." And fourth, "It must serve general policy objectives, including national security, the maintenance of high-level employment, and cooperation with other

55. The secretary was obviously referring to remarks made by Senator George Aiken (see Aiken's Farm Forum speech, Minneapolis, MN, March 10, 1949, printed in *CR,* 81st Cong., 1st sess., Senate, April 7, 1949, 95, pt. 3: 4033).

nations in the interests of peace and prosperity." "It can do this," Brannan argued, "by conserving and strengthening our basic productive resources, providing reserves against national emergencies, and encouraging free-flowing world trade by reasonably assuring sufficient products for export."[56]

Because he believed too many people still considered the farm program "class legislation," Brannan next listed six "ways in which we can expect effective farm-production and price-stabilization programs to serve the interests of all the people." These were points that agrarians had been making for decades in their efforts to justify federal aid to agriculture. First, since most depressions had been "farm-led and farm-fed," a program that maintained a healthy agricultural economy would "help prevent depression." Second, a healthy rural economy would contribute substantially to increased markets for manufactured goods and thus help maintain full employment. Despite the progress of recent years, Brannan believed "rural people [still] represented a vast untapped market for all sorts of goods," and "a program that helps to stabilize farm prices and incomes will help to stabilize markets for factory goods and will keep thousands and thousands of 'Main Streets' busy."

Third, stable commodity prices and farm incomes encouraged abundant production, which was "the greatest assurance of reasonable prices to consumers." Fourth, adequate farm income contributed to the maintenance of the country's agricultural resources, by making it possible for farmers to implement good conservation practices. "The depression," Brannan explained, "taught us that hard times make poor farmers and poor land." Price supports could also be used to encourage conservation and a shift to more livestock production. Fifth, "An effective farm program is essential to our national security, will provide a reservoir of goods which protects the Nation against crop failure, and will assure supplies for an even flow of world trade." Far from being a liability, "reserves of storable commodities" were "an aim as well as a result of the farm program" and served as "insurance which the public buys with the funds it invests in maintaining a healthy agriculture."

56. House Committee, *General Farm Program* (pt. 2), 138–39.

With his sixth and final point, Brannan struck a cord that came from the heart of traditional agrarian fundamentalism. "A price-support program which safeguards our rural economic strength can help stabilize the rural community and help maintain individual opportunity in our free-enterprise system." According to the secretary, "One bulwark of democracy may be found in the prosperous rural community mainly composed of economically strong families farming in the traditional American pattern. It is an ever-present answer to communism." Brannan ended this portion of his statement by pointing out the potential threat posed by the "steady increase in the number of large-scale, industrialized type farming units" and insisting that price supports were "the farmer's equivalent of the laboring man's minimum wage, social security, and collective-bargaining agreements."[57]

Following these rather lengthy introductory remarks, the secretary moved to specific recommendations, concentrating on a program for "production and price adjustment with a definite income objective" that he believed had to be the "core" of any sound, overall program for agriculture. The heart of Brannan's proposal contained four basic elements: (1) a new standard of support based on income rather than on price criteria, which represented "a realistic minimum below which it is not in the interest of farmers or consumers to allow farm prices to fall"; (2) a more recent, realistic, moving ten-year base period (initially 1939 through 1948) for computing the new income support standard; (3) support accomplished through the use of loans, purchase agreements, production payments, and direct purchases; and (4) eligibility for price support limited to producers who practiced good soil conservation, complied with acreage allotments and marketing quotas and agreements, and who did not exceed the predetermined volume of production—"a volume high enough to benefit most farms but one which will not encourage the development of extremely large, industrialized farming."[58]

Brannan pointed out repeatedly that, in principle, there was very little new in this proposal. As he explained the specifics of how it was to operate, however, it became obvious that the administration's plan

57. Ibid., 140–43.
58. Ibid., 145.

for agriculture was a significant departure from previous programs in terms of emphasis and scope. The new standard was to be used to support a much longer list of commodities, and, for the first time, these crops were to be supported at what amounted to 100 percent of parity. Abandoning the old "basic commodity" classification, Brannan recommended that certain farm products be designated as "first-priority, or group 1" commodities. At minimum, Brannan believed this list should include corn, cotton, wheat, tobacco, whole milk, eggs, farm chickens, hogs, beef cattle, and lambs. These commodities would "have first priority on the funds available for price-support purposes" and would be "maintained at not less than the full-support standard." If possible, all other commodities "should be supported in line with or in relation to group one commodities," and the secretary should have the authority to "support any commodity at whatever level is required to increase supplies or meet national emergencies."

With regard to price support methods, Brannan believed commodity loans and purchase agreements were well suited for storable commodities, which accounted for "roughly 25 percent of our annual cash receipts from farm marketings." As for the other 75 percent, the so-called "nonstorables—products which are either highly perishable or which can be stored only at heavy expense," the secretary recommended reliance on "production payments," defined as "a payment to the farmer to go on producing to meet genuine consumer needs, rather than restricting output short of that need."

Secretary Brannan believed his system of production payments offered several advantages. "Under this system," he explained,

> the farmer would be paid in cash the difference between the support standard for commodities which he produced and the average selling price for those commodities in the market place. Because the payment would go directly to the farmer it would be an efficient support operation.
>
> Another big advantage is that the system would induce efficient production and marketing, because any farmer who could exceed the average market price by quality of product or good bargaining would benefit to the extent that his selling price exceeded the average market price.
>
> A third advantage of this system is that it would allow farm income to remain at a high enough level to sustain abundant production while retail prices sought their supply and demand level

in the market place. This level is bound to be reasonable for consumers because of the larger supplies brought out.

Brannan was so convinced of the benefits to be derived from the production payment approach, which was a secondary feature of the
Aiken Act, that he encouraged Congress to give him the authority to
use it to support hogs and milk before January 1, 1950.[59]

Most of the secretary's suggestions with regard to conditions and
limits on eligibility were based on tried-and-true methods and thus
were not particularly controversial. His final recommendation in this
area, though, was new and caused immediate consternation and controversy. Brannan believed it was necessary to further limit the extent
of support to ensure that the public was not "providing financial
encouragement for the continued development of extremely large-
scale, industrial farming." Although efficiency was essential, he maintained that efforts to achieve this goal should not be allowed to undermine the traditional family farm. It would be "wrong to allow our
programs to operate in such a way as to encourage the concentration
of our farm land into fewer and fewer hands," Brannan insisted. To
help avoid this undesirable development, the secretary recommended
"that the production of a farm in excess of a predetermined amount
be not eligible for price support." He suggested that to determine
per farm eligibility a "common unit of measurement" be established.
"I am suggesting a 'comparative unit,' which would be equal to 10
bushels of corn, almost 8 bushels of wheat, or a little more than 50
pounds of cotton." Brannan preferred "that not more than 1,800 comparative units per farm be eligible for support. The effect," he explained, "would be about as follows: The operators of all farms, no
matter how large, would receive benefits of the price-support program
to the extent of 1,800 units of the commodities grown on that farm.

59. Ibid., 148. Initially, the idea was to push for early authority to use this
method for all Steagall commodities; by the time it was actually proposed (April
27, 1949), the amendment only covered hogs. The administration's apparent
strategy was to illustrate the viability of the Brannan principles to facilitate the
plan's passage (Brannan to Alben W. Barkley, president of the Senate, and to
Sam Rayburn, Speaker of the House, April 27, 1949, and other documents
related to proposal to amend the Agricultural Act of 1948, Legislation 1, Office
of the Secretary of Agriculture, RG 16, NA; General Legislation, Bureau of the
Budget, RG 51, NA; *New York Times,* April 17, 1949, 36).

Farms which produce in excess of 1,800 units would not enjoy support on the excess. This would exclude part of the production on approximately 2 percent of the farms of the Nation."

Secretary Brannan concluded his prepared statement with a summary of his program recommendations and called "attention to some of its shortcomings." As he had told Chairman Nourse, the proposed program did not "close the gap between farm and nonfarm income" and did not meet the needs of the poorest farmers. It was simply a beginning. Programs for job training and placement were needed, and existing soil conservation, school lunch, and crop insurance programs should be expanded. There was still work to be done in the areas of rural services, research and education, and cooperative credit. "In general," the secretary concluded, "I would reemphasize the recommendations made by the Department of Agriculture in 1947"— recommendations for which Charles Brannan, then assistant secretary of agriculture, was primarily responsible.[60]

During the brief period of questioning that followed Brannan's testimony, most of the issues that would be the focus of the battle over the Brannan plan were raised. Senator Spessard L. Holland (D-FL) questioned production payments, Senators Milton Young and Clinton Anderson (D-NM) asked about the eighteen hundred-unit limitation on production eligible for support, and Senator Elmer Thomas (D-OK) inquired about the costs involved in such an extensive program. But, in his first response, Secretary Brannan's answers were brief, only hinting at the controversy that was to follow.[61]

Although he may not have anticipated the intensity of the opposition that surfaced almost immediately after the plan's unveiling, Brannan had already initiated efforts to educate the public and to sell his proposals. He had been booked for an interview with Walter Cronkite on April 8, a speech on CBS's *Farm Journal* on April 9, and a live ABC radio broadcast on April 11.[62] The administration's new farm program also received immediate press coverage. On page three

60. House Committee, *General Farm Program* (pt. 2), 151–52, 154.
61. Ibid., 157–67.
62. Kenneth D. Fry to McCune, April 6, 1949, Public Relations, Office of the Secretary of Agriculture, RG 16, NA. Fry was associate director of Publicity and radio director for the Democratic National Committee, which helped keep the secretary extremely busy in April, May, and June.

of his April 7 broadcast script, Edward R. Murrow gave a brief explanation of how the plan would work and concluded by saying that the executive vice president of the Chicago Board of Trade called it "a step toward socialism. . . . The American Farm Bureau Federation thinks the plan looks pretty good and worthy of a fair trial. The National Farmers Union agrees," and the Congress would be taking a closer look.[63]

Congress began examining the program immediately. Shortly after the conclusion of Brannan's prepared testimony, Senator George Aiken seized the opportunity to inform his colleagues of his opposition to "the Department of Agriculture's recommendations for a farm price-support program." The senator stated, for the record, that he regarded the secretary "as a sincere, conscientious public servant" and "a personal friend." He "would resent any implication" that Secretary Brannan should be categorized as "socialistic." "But this morning I find that I have to be critical of some of the recommendations which he made before the joint meeting of the Committees on Agriculture." There could be little demurral with the secretary's objectives, but the Congress, Aiken said, would want to carefully study the means recommended for obtaining these laudable goals.

"Most of the recommendations of the Secretary," the senator continued, "appear to be simply the provisions of the Agricultural Act of 1948 in a new dress." Aiken, however, found "four radical departures" from the provisions of the current law that carried his name. First, eligibility for support was dependent upon a farmer's compliance with "minimum and sound soil-conservation practices." The second "radical departure" was the eighteen hundred-unit limitation, and the third was that the ten major farm products (Group 1 commodities) would be supported at "what amounts to 100 percent of parity." Aiken's final objection was with the new income support standard, which "veers somewhat from the parity concept as we have known it." Aiken was convinced that, if adopted as a package, the Brannan

63. Copy of Murrow transcript, Public Relations, Office of the Secretary of Agriculture, RG 16, NA. Murrow obviously misrepresented the AFBF position, as did the *New York Times* on April 10. On April 18, however, the paper printed a correction and reported that the bureau was actually very much opposed to the Brannan plan, the basic principles of which the AFBF characterized as "a startling reversal of policy... revolutionary in their effect."

recommendations would mean "far-reaching Government control over the Nation's agriculture."[64]

"In spite of all the camouflage and avoidance of customary phrases and wording," Aiken insisted "that the recommendations of Secretary Brannan in the final analysis follow closely the high rigid support levels for the more important agricultural commodities and provide for far more rigid Federal controls over our farms than we have ever had up to this time." The senator considered this a "very high price to pay for a guaranteed income," insisting that when the entire program was in place "it would be a controlled economy with a vengeance." The question of support levels was "a fundamental issue not only of economics, but of philosophy of government as well" for the Vermont senator. "A program to assure a high fixed standard of income could not stop on the farm," he insisted. "If government undertakes to guarantee a satisfactory income to the producers of farm commodities, can we, with a clear conscience, deny the same guarantee of satisfactory income to other groups of our population? Where can we stop?" No matter how noble the goals, Senator Aiken simply could not "agree that such objectives should be obtained at the price of a governmental guardianship over the 6,000,000 farm families of America."[65]

The following day, in a brief statement that clearly expressed the Republican animosity that had arisen during the previous election year, New York representative Kenneth B. Keating reminded the House that it had

> heard much in the last campaign about raising prices for everybody that produces, and lowering prices for everybody who consumes. We thought that could not be done, but, lo and behold, the administration has come out with a bill that is supposed to do that very thing. This feat of legerdemain is the fantastic brain child of Secretary of Agriculture Brannan, and we are told it has the blessing of the President. We are told that by the President himself.

Keating represented a point of view that was not particularly fond of any price support program, but his objections to this particular "two-

64. *CR,* 81st Cong., 1st sess., Senate, April 7, 1949, 95, pt. 3: 4031–32; Aiken to editor, *New York Herald Tribune,* April 9, 1949, "Farm Bill 1948, Correspondence, 1949," Aiken Papers.
65. *CR,* 81st Cong., 1st sess., Senate, April 7, 1949, 95, pt. 3: 4032.

price system" were shared by many of agriculture's most faithful friends. From this perspective, the administration's recommendations amounted to "sleight-of-hand proposals" under which the "producer and consumer turn back in the form of higher taxes the illusory gains they have reaped during the dual system of prices."[66]

In his first piece of correspondence after Secretary Brannan's presentation, Hope commented on the production payment feature of the proposed plan. "Farmers generally," the former agricultural committee chairman believed, would "oppose the cash subsidy plan because they will feel there is no certainty of it being put in operation." It would be wholly dependent on annual appropriations, and farmers would have no way of knowing, at planting time, if payments actually would be forthcoming. "Furthermore, most farmers consider a payment of that kind a consumer subsidy rather than a farm subsidy." Nevertheless, Hope assured his correspondent that the committee would give all the secretary's recommendations careful consideration.[67]

Reaction to the Brannan plan was registered quickly outside of Washington as well. Although the administration eventually had considerable mass media support, a *New York Times* editorial called the administration plan a "political maneuver," and other news agencies began claiming that its real author was Jim Patton of the National Farmers Union. A steady stream (during some periods it might have been characterized as a flood) of letters and telegrams began arriving at the USDA and the White House on the day following Brannan's committee appearance. Frederick Thompson of the *Belington [WV] Central-State News* expressed a sentiment that was typical in many of the opposition letters the USDA received. Thompson asked the secretary, why not subsidize "my" industry, too? The subscribers to his paper would appreciate a reduction from two dollars to one dollar, and the government could make up the difference.[68]

Within hours of the secretary's initial presentation, the battle lines

66. *CR,* 81st Cong., 1st sess., Senate, April 8, 1949, 95, pt. 3: 4154–55.
67. Hope to C. N. Hiebert, April 8, 1949, and to John D. Murray, April 13, 1949, FF, Hope Papers. Hope also had been critical of the Aiken Act, see "Long-Range Program for Agriculture," March 21, 1949, Columbus, Ohio, Speech file, Hope Papers.
68. B. S. Bercovici to Brannan, April 10, 1949, and Thompson to Brannan, April 9, 1949, Farm Program, Office of the Secretary of Agriculture, RG 16, NA.

had been drawn. Although the debate intensified as lawmakers and the general public began to focus on specific legislation, the pros and cons remained surprisingly constant. Truman and Brannan endeavored to convince the nation that the Brannan plan was not a new approach, but in many ways the administration's proposed program was in fact a sharp departure from previous policy. With regard to basic principles, the administration was speaking the truth. The plan contained little that was not present in existing legislation. Even the controversial production payments were a feature of the Aiken Act. In the Brannan plan, however, they were a centerpiece. The big difference was in emphasis, unprecedented high levels of support, and mandatory supports for many perishable commodities. As Congressman Hope explained to the president of the Oklahoma Farm Bureau, "It is the slant which the Secretary has put on the matter that disturbs me."[69] It was this "slant" that disturbed many, and the road ahead of the administration promised to be extremely rough, if not impassable.

The president, Secretary Brannan, and many other farm leaders were favorably disposed toward a generous farm bill because of the 1948 farm vote. While Truman continued to endorse flexible supports for several months after the election, the secretary of agriculture and his advisers were moving in another direction, and many administration officials, PMA committees, and the NFU began pushing for 90 or even 100 percent of parity. Out of this diversity, and at times uncertainty, emerged the Brannan plan for agriculture, which, in the words of historian Harvard Sitkoff, "promised farmers continued prosperity and consumers lower prices but did nothing to aid the sharecroppers, tenants, and migrants who desperately needed a minimal fair deal."[70]

More important to the ultimate success or failure of Brannan's plan, however, were two tactical errors committed by the administration during the weeks before April 7, 1949. The first was its failure to consult with key members of the congressional farm bloc and the leadership of the major farm organizations before introducing the

69. Hope to John I. Taylor, April 16, 1949; to Russell Wilkins, April 14, 1949; and to H. K. Thatcher, May 20, 1949, FF, Hope Papers; Truman, *Memoirs*, vol. 2, 264; House Committee, *General Farm Program* (pt. 2), 139.

70. Sitkoff, "Years of the Locust," 97; Gosnell, *Truman's Crises*, 442; *Newsweek* 33 (January 3, 10, and 24, 1949).

new farm bill. This immediately alienated many congressmen of both parties and the powerful Farm Bureau, contributing significantly to the plan's demise.[71] The second error was the department's seemingly inexplicable tardiness in preparing a plan for presentation to Congress. This delay seems to have caused the administration to lose the initiative. It allowed time for the crystallization of firmer opposing viewpoints and made Republicans even more suspicious of administration motives. The negative consequences of both actions are relatively clear, but the historical record is murky regarding motivation.

It can only be assumed that the explanation for the delay lies somewhere between the Republican charge that the administration was simply jockeying for political advantage and the department line that it was working as quickly as possible to iron out the details of a complex policy proposal. There seems to be no reason to doubt Brannan's 1985 explanation that he was trying "a slight maneuver."[72] The secretary hoped this tactic would force Congress to proceed with the testimony of the farm organizations. He then would have had the advantage of being able to tailor his testimony to theirs, addressing their objections to his plan and denying them the opportunity for such a visible platform for direct assault. By implication, this maneuver was political. As many Republicans contended at the time, Brannan was also testing the political wind. To have done otherwise would have been a sign of political naiveté, something that definitely was not characteristic of the Truman administration.

The president and the secretary of agriculture believed they had been issued a mandate in the election of 1948. But what was it a mandate for? By the end of March 1949, Brannan was convinced it included the enactment of a generous price support program for farmers, which at the same time gave consumers the benefit of lower grocery bills. Guided by the belief that he could muster popular support for his plan, the secretary, who knew conservative farm leaders would object, seems to have decided that it would serve no purpose to make them a part of the original discussions; if compromise was to come it was best to start from one's optimum position. In retrospect,

71. Sitkoff, "Years of the Locust," 97; Theodore W. Schultz, "That Turbulent Brannan Plan," 5.
72. Brannan, interview.

it is clear that Brannan's failure to consult the Farm Bureau, National Grange, and the congressional leadership was, in the words of Reo Christenson, "a first-class blunder."[73]

Brannan had charted an aggressive liberal course for administration farm policy. But the man who had so effectively played the political game with agriculture during the previous fall seemed unwilling to play by the political rules of the game in formulating farm policy. Many Republicans had not yet forgiven the administration for its 1948 tactics, and Brannan's failure to play according to the rules in 1949 alienated conservative farm organizations. In addition, his plan contained principles that, under the best of circumstances, would have been difficult for conservatives to swallow. The administration also had to contend with conservative Democrats, mostly from the South, who were frequently aligned with Republicans on Fair Deal issues. The road ahead looked rough, but Secretary Brannan was confident that his plan would carry the day—if not in 1949, certainly in 1950.

73. Christenson, *The Brannan Plan,* 173.

6

Reaction to the Brannan Plan

Political success for the administration and the Democratic Party in 1948 did not translate into legislative success for the Fair Deal in 1949. The administration had garnered substantial support for its new farm proposal, but the political powers that be had been locked out of the process early on and were not easily converted. Republican farm leaders, many of whom were philosophically opposed to the liberal implications of the new proposal, also were motivated by the conviction that their expected control of the White House and Congress had been stolen by the use of blatant misrepresentation and falsehood. Congressman August Andresen (R-MN) insisted that "farmers [would] not be fooled again by political trickery."[1] Andresen's Grand Old Party intended to do all it could to ensure the correctness of his prophesy. The immediate result was a contentious debate and the passage of a 1949 farm package by the Democrat-controlled Eighty-first Congress in which USDA leadership was totally ignored.

In the wake of Secretary Brannan's April 7 testimony, it was apparent that the most controversial aspect of the Brannan farm plan would be the secretary's scheme for offering relief to both consumers and producers. Nonperishable or storable commodities were to be supported in much the same way as they had been under existing legislation, but perishable commodities would be supported under a new system of production or income payments.[2] In practice, the secretary

1. Andresen quoted in *CR,* 81st Cong., 1st sess., Senate, June 9, 1949, 95, pt. 6: 7514.
2. House Committee, *General Farm Program* (pt. 2), 145.

would determine a support standard, and a direct payment would be made to the producer to make up the difference between the standard and the market price of that commodity. This meant an undisguised government subsidy to the farmer, which in itself was a hard pill for many inside and outside farm circles to swallow, and a consumer subsidy, which was anathema to most conservatives.

A second provision, which also proved quite controversial, was designed to encourage the "family-sized farm" by denying government support beyond a certain level of production. In an effort to co-opt those groups most likely to oppose this particular concept, Brannan wrapped his explanation of this point in a cloak of American idealism and agrarian fundamentalism. Prosperous rural communities and strong farm families were "one bulwark of democracy" and "an ever-present answer to communism," according to the secretary. By limiting "eligibility for price support to a defined volume of production on each farm," Brannan believed the government could avoid encouraging "large, industrial farming" and still help most farmers who were relatively small-scale producers.[3]

Reaction to the Brannan plan was quick and vigorous. A few hours after the secretary unveiled the administration's policy recommendations, President Truman told White House reporters: "I know exactly what is in it, and it's all right."[4] But it was not acceptable to everyone, and the administration immediately faced stiff opposition from three of the nation's four major farm organizations—the American Farm Bureau Federation, the National Grange, and the National Council of Farm Cooperatives. Only the National Farmers Union, with its special ties to the administration through Secretary Brannan, endorsed the new farm plan. Before looking at this opposition and support in some detail, however, we turn first to reaction not directly linked to these powerful farm lobbies: the print media, the general public, and non-farm organizations.

The press reaction to the Brannan plan, as measured by editorial positions, was mixed, and it followed fairly typical liberal and conservative lines. Basing his conclusions almost entirely on the opinions

3. Ibid., 143, 145.
4. Truman, *Public Papers of the Presidents, 1949,* 203.

At the National Plowing Match near Dexter, Iowa, on September 18, 1948, President Truman met with some defending champions from Iowa, Missouri, and Nebraska, and told his farm audience that the "Republican Congress has already stuck a pitchfork in the farmer's back." Ernest L. Johnson, Story City, Iowa, courtesy of the Truman Library.

expressed in the *New York Times,* historian Allen Matusow insisted that the "general response of the nation's newspapers and magazines was almost as hostile as that of the Republicans."[5] But when reaction beyond the East Coast is taken into consideration, this generalization is questionable. Even in the East, journalists did not exhibit unanimity.

On April 16, 1949, for example, *The Nation* prodded "everybody who does not grow his own food ... to spend all his spare time urging Congress to enact Secretary Brannan's proposed new agricultural program." The liberal journal insisted that the Brannan plan would be good for farmers and consumers, and that it would "allow market

5. Matusow, *Farm Policies and Politics,* 201.

forces to take effect" and emphasize soil conservation. "It all sounds so good that our chief fear is Congress will kill it."[6]

The Nation, however, did not give the Brannan plan its unqualified endorsement. By late spring the editors of the magazine were taking the position that the new plan might be trying to do too much for farmers. The government, by basing the guaranteed income of perishable commodity producers on the previous ten-year period, was supporting prices at inflated wartime levels, and people would be encouraged to stay in farming who actually should be leaving the industry. The main problem with the old system was the antiquated parity formula, and, at the very least, "the public would benefit as consumers" from the new approach. But the failure to apply the new plan to staples such as wheat and cotton meant "the major evils of the old system would remain." "The farm organizations are courting disaster," the writer insisted, "if they think American consumers will indefinitely subsidize farmers to produce crops which the consumer cannot buy."[7]

In the East, generally, press reaction was not favorable and in some cases could have been characterized as hostile. Elsewhere, the administration enjoyed more support from farm and nonfarm publications. Counted among the former was the *Breeder's Gazette,* edited and published by Samuel Guard of Louisville, Kentucky. Guard placed his publication, which reached "two hundred and ten thousand subscribers, squarely behind" the secretary, and his "Sam Guard's Roundup" focused on the Brannan plan's emphasis on livestock production. Aubrey Williams's *Southern Farmer* also supported the new farm plan and ran an interview with Secretary Brannan "to secure understanding of and support for the [secretary's] proposals."[8] Both Williams and Guard had been, and would continue to be, frequent correspondents and persistent supporters of Brannan and the USDA.

6. *The Nation* 168 (April 16, 1949): 430.
7. "New Farm Plan Needed," 649–50; Jerry Tallmer, assistant editor of *The Nation,* to Brannan, June 7, 1949, and Brannan to Tallmer, June 10, 1949, Farm Program 6, General Correspondence, 1949, Office of the Secretary of Agriculture, RG 16, NA.
8. Williams to Wesley McCune, May 8, 1949, and Guard to Brannan, (letter accompanying an advance copy of this May editorial), April 13, 1949, Farm Program 6, Office of the Secretary of Agriculture, RG 16, NA.

Within a month of his initial endorsement, Guard wrote: "I am taking a beating from my subscribers, and advertisers too, right now," but he continued to support the administration because of his confidence that "we are right"—farmers would come around in time.[9]

Although the administration enjoyed considerable, if at times qualified, support from the country's print media, it also faced some powerful opponents. Both the president and the secretary recognized the significance of this opposition and seized every opportunity to favorably influence or counter damaging stories and editorials, including those that frequently appeared in two Washington, D.C., newspapers, the *Post* and the *Daily News*. In typical Truman fashion, the president advised his secretary of agriculture on the necessity of dealing with negative publicity. Truman insisted that the unfavorable "propaganda" that had begun to appear in the *Daily News* should be countered immediately. "This no doubt is the start of propaganda by Roy Howard in all his lousy sheets. I'd suggest that you get right after it."[10]

Despite the administration's efforts, newspapers and magazines outside the nation's capital continued to join the rising tide of opposition. *Commonweal* recognized that farmers' unique situations and problems "entitled [them] to a special status and to special benefits." Nevertheless, it labeled the administration's proposal "a radical new farm program" and leveled its major criticisms at the plan's potential costs and the likelihood that its adoption would ultimately lead to increased "statism." The *Christian Science Monitor,* the *Dallas Morning News,* and the *Nation's Business* can also be counted in the ranks of the opposition. Among farm journals that took editorial positions

9. Guard to Brannan, May 11, 1949, Farm Program 6, Office of the Secretary of Agriculture, RG 16, NA. See also J. S. Russell, *Des Moines Register* and *Des Moines Tribune,* to McCune, June 20, 1949, and Louis Levand, *Wichita Beacon,* to Brannan, June 3, 1949, Public Relations, Office of the Secretary of Agriculture, RG 16, NA; Brannan to Barnet Nover, *Denver Post,* June 10, 1949, Farm Program 6, Office of the Secretary of Agriculture, RG 16, NA.

10. Truman to Brannan, April 15, 1949, PSF, Truman. For Brannan's efforts to influence the *Post,* see correspondence with Herbert Ellison, editor, June 27 and July 12, 1949, Farm Program 6, Office of the Secretary of Agriculture, RG 16, NA. Roy Howard headed Scripps-Howard Newspapers, one of several chains that were consistently on Truman's black list, which included the McCormick and Hearst newspapers (Ferrell, ed., *Off the Record,* 268; Donovan, *Tumultuous Years,* 305).

against the Brannan proposals were the *Farm Journal,* a Philadelphia publication, and the *Farm News,* of Indianapolis, Indiana.[11]

Public opinion with regard to the Brannan plan was also mixed. Among the hundreds of letters received by the USDA in the weeks following the secretary's April 7 testimony, comments ranged from expressions of enthusiastic support to bitter condemnation. Some correspondents praised Brannan as a savior and as the only man in Washington who cared about their problems; others were convinced the villainous secretary and his contemptuous plan threatened every-thing that was good about America.[12] In terms of volume, during the first few weeks the department's mail was weighted fairly heavily in favor of the opposition. But by May, the pros and cons appear to have been nearly balanced. Although the secretary received comments from all over the nation, cards and letters of support came primarily from the upper Midwest and the northern plains states: Wisconsin, Minnesota, and the Dakotas. Negative reaction originated in urban areas, the old Midwest (Ohio Valley states), and the South.

A few brief examples will suffice to convey the tone and substance of this flood, and later steady flow, of public opposition and support. Many who opposed the administration's proposal reacted with bitter-ness, fear, and disbelief. A mining engineer from Colorado Springs asked: "Just what kind of a blankety blank jackass do you take John Q. Public to be?" Likewise, a Wisconsin stock grower could hardly be-lieve America was considering such a "communistic agriculture pro-gram." "Surely a man in your position," he wrote to Brannan, "realizes that totalitarianism destroys the people, particularly farm people." He insisted that farmers did "not want to be supported at somebody else's expense" and would "not stand for regimentation inevitable in your proposal. I only wish that you could read what some unbiased

11. *Commonweal* 50 (April 22, 1949): 29; George Ericson to Brannan, April 19, 1949, and William F. Farrell to Brannan, May 11, 1949, Farm Program 6, Office of the Secretary of Agriculture, RG 16, NA; Edith Hirsch, "Uncle Sam's Indigestion," 25; Wheeler McMillen to Brannan, May 5, 1949, and McCune to Oscar W. Cooley, August 8, 1949, Farm Program 6, Office of the Secretary of Agriculture, RG 16, NA.

12. This general assessment is based on hundreds of cards and letters from all types of people in Farm Program 6, Office of the Secretary of Agriculture, RG 16, NA.

historian will write one hundred years hence, about how you and your kind witlessly lead a great people into decadence."[13]

Others were even more sardonic. "I could only believe in your farm program if and when I should join the communist party," wrote an Ohio farmer who "still believe[d] in free enterprise." Still others considered the secretary's proposal just more of the same old "New Deal Communist bunk," and a Michigan "housewife" saw the plan as a "scheme for socializing farming" that would "lead our country only into the degradation of the English 'one pork chop a week' and on to eventual totalitarianism."[14] Many critics also expressed sentiments similar to those penned by the president of the Patrician Knitting Company of Syracuse, New York, who would have supported the farm program in full if the reasoning were applied to his industry as well. "I would be most in favor of someone such as the Federal Govt. guaranteeing me against any operating loss regardless of the market conditions or any error I may make in my business management."[15]

The mail supporting the Brannan proposals, unlike the letters of opposition, which had poured into the secretary's office immediately after the plan's unveiling, was somewhat slower in materializing. On May 4, a correspondent informed the secretary that Allan Kline and the Farm Bureau were under the influence of the 2 percent of big farmers "that has least to benefit from the [new] program." A plains state farm woman agreed: "We have always paid Our Dues to the Farm Bureau but cant see any benefit in it for us: the way I see that other plan [Aiken Act?] is to help the rich wheat farmer while it makes it harder every day for the little man to have a Job or money to buy his groceries. . . . I know all the little people are left holding the bag again: the rich are always protected." She wanted to hear more about the Brannan plan "in plain language" but already "thought it

13. Carl Taylor to Brannan, April 14, 1949, and J. D. Fisher to Brannan, April 17, 1949, Farm Program 6, Office of the Secretary of Agriculture, RG 16, NA.

14. Howard Bouden to Brannan, April 20, 1949; Chemical Attraction Oil Corp. (San Antonio, TX) to Brannan, May 6, 1949; and Mrs. I. E. Ingraham to Brannan, April 19, 1949, Farm Program 6, Office of the Secretary of Agriculture, RG 16, NA.

15. David W. Hosmer to Brannan, April 20, 1949, Farm Program 6, Office of the Secretary of Agriculture, RG 16, NA.

was much better than the one we got: the meat counters are all full now: but many a working man has not the money to buy it." Another farmer encouraged the secretary to "keep on working" and assured him that "we're for your farm program. We want security on the farm, even if we have to control production and have less freedom. A man in the middle of the ocean has a world of freedom but no security."[16]

It is interesting to note the department's response to this outpouring of public concern and interest. During the last weeks of April, most of the critical mail was simply marked "No Reply." Although sometimes delayed for several weeks, letters of support were gratefully answered, almost without exception. And in some instances, where there seemed to be a chance for a "conversion," critical mail was answered with the enclosure of additional information. In these cases, Secretary Brannan (or Wesley McCune and other members of the secretary's staff for their boss) repeatedly expressed the belief that the public, especially the farmers, would support his program if they only understood the issue a little better.

One such convert was D. H. Richert of North Newton, Kansas. On April 18, Richert wrote the secretary expressing the commonly held concern that the new plan would lead to excessive regimentation or government control of America's farms. In his reply, Secretary Brannan thanked Richert for this "opportunity to discuss . . . the bogey of regimentation." The secretary assured him that the USDA "did not propose to the Congress that farmers should be pushed around and regimented a lot" and made some general remarks about his recommended program. Brannan insisted that the regimentation issue was just a smoke screen, designed "to arouse opposition." "We must not allow ourselves to be stampeded by these alarmist cries into a failure to make full use of the tools of economic self-help which farmers have fashioned for themselves over the past 16 years. . . . Our great depressions have been farm-led and farm-fed," warned Brannan. "This time we must prevent a depression." In this case the depart-

16. J. A. Meyer to Brannan, May 4, 1949; Mrs. Thomas Williams to Brannan, July 28, 1949; and Theodore J. Regier to Brannan, June 16, 1949, Farm Program 6, Office of the Secretary of Agriculture, RG 16, NA.

ment's efforts paid off. Richert had been convinced that this was "a fine program" and only wished "there would be some way of bringing the truth to the farmers."[17]

This particular instance undoubtedly reinforced the department's belief that education was the key to success. Brannan and his subordinates let it be known that additional information was available for the asking, and they filled numerous requests throughout the spring of 1949. Whether or not USDA officials were correct in assuming that the more people knew, the more likely they were to support the Brannan plan, polls seem to indicate that there was a definite need for more information.

Toward the end of May, a *New York Times* poll revealed that the Democrats had not yet made the farmer understand the Brannan plan. Nevertheless, the USDA seemed to be making some progress. The Republicans had lost out with the farmer, according to correspondent Will Lissner, because Truman and Brannan had "seized the initiative on the issue of farm price supports"; since farmers were coming to accept crop controls as necessary, GOP warnings about regimentation and socialism had had little effect. Many were not convinced that the administration plan would work but supported the president for making good on his promises. Lissner, however, detected no real shift in farm opinion: "In general, the American farmer is sitting on the fence," skeptical of the Hope-Aiken Act and the Brannan plan. Both parties considered the farm vote critical to their political futures, but "Republicans have not yet succeeded in convincing the farmer who votes out of economic interest that the party as a whole is conscious of the farmer's need for a positive farm program and determined to get it for him."[18]

On May 22, pollster Elmo Roper told his CBS radio audience: "For the past six weeks in Washington, one of the most discussed and debated issues has been the new farm program of the Administration."

17. Brannan to Richert, April 28, 1949, and Richert to Brannan, April 18, 1949 and May 2, 1949, Farm Program 6, Office of the Secretary of Agriculture, RG 16, NA. A staffer's note attached to the latter reads: "No reply seems required. Looks like we made a convert."
18. "Survey Shows Both Parties Fail to Clinch Farm Vote," *New York Times,* May 22, 1949.

Although Roper said it was "still too early to test public opinion on the new Brannan-Truman farm proposals," his survey indicated increasing farm concern with "declining farm income," which was "due partly to the drop in prices."[19] At about the same time, George Gallup reported that 61 percent of America's farmers believed the Democratic Party best served their interests and gave Truman a 50 percent approval rating. But a month later, the pollster found that only 43 percent of the midwestern farmers contacted were following the discussions surrounding the Brannan plan, and they were evenly divided on the issue, with 7 percent expressing no opinion. Sixty-two percent of those surveyed by *Wallaces' Farmer* in June had heard of the Brannan farm plan. Within this group, 24 percent responded, "Looks like it might be all right," while 18 percent did not "like the sound of it," and 60 percent were "Not sure."[20]

Toward the end of the first session of the Eighty-first Congress, despite repeated setbacks for the Brannan plan on Capitol Hill, USDA officials had reason for optimism. There was little chance of passage in 1949, but it appeared that their educational and promotional efforts were slowly paying off. Maybe 1950 would be their year.[21]

Public opinion, especially that of the individual farmer, slowly came around for the administration, but organizational opinion remained surprisingly constant. Labor and consumer groups supported the secretary's proposals from the beginning, as did the Americans for Democratic Action (ADA) and the NFU, but the other major farm

19. Roper to Brannan, June 2, 1949, Farm Program 6, Office of the Secretary of Agriculture, RG 16, NA. Roper enclosed a transcript of his May 22 broadcast.

20. Donald R. Murphy to Wesley McCune, July 19, 1949, Farm Program 6, Office of the Secretary of Agriculture, RG 16, NA; Gallup, *Gallup Poll,* 2: 837. The first poll referred to was published on June 13; questioning for the second took place from July 2 to July 7, and the results were reported on July 31, 1949.

21. Hubert H. Humphrey to Brannan, September 14, 1949, and McCune to Donald Murphy and Merrill Gregory, September 27, 1949, Farm Program 6, Office of the Secretary of Agriculture, RG 16, NA. Humphrey sent results from a Minnesota State Fair poll that showed approval of the Brannan plan at 63 to 37 percent. See also Alonzo L. Hamby, "The Vital Center, the Fair Deal, and the Quest for a Liberal Political Economy," in Hamby, ed., *Harry S. Truman and the Fair Deal,* 152.

organizations, and most leading agricultural economists, remained opposed to the plan. The business community, often represented by the Chamber of Commerce, also raised strenuous objections from the outset.[22]

The secretary's plan was endorsed by a number of state and local farm organizations whose national leadership opposed the Brannan plan, but support among major farm organizations was confined primarily to the Farmers Union.[23] "You and Charlie Brannan," Jim Patton wrote President Truman on April 18, "have hit the nail on the head again in the new program for agriculture and consumers." More specifically, Archie Wright, president of the Farmers Union, Northeastern Division, told the secretary, "the more I study [the new agricultural program] the better I like it." "I believe that if this program can be adopted," Wright continued, "historians will hold it to be one of the great points of departure in our national and agricultural development."[24]

Secretary Brannan also received many hearty letters of endorsement from state and local farmers unions throughout the country, especially from the upper plains states, where the NFU enjoyed its greatest support. A typical example came from the editor of the *Kansas Union Farmer,* the official publication of the Kansas Farmers Union. C. E. Perkins took exception only with Brannan's proposal to limit benefits to the farmer's first twenty-five thousand dollars of income (eighteen hundred units). He believed this maximum was too high

22. An example of the latter group's vigorous opposition can be found in the position of the San Francisco Chamber: Henry E. North to Senator William F. Knowland (R-CA), May 16, 1949, Farm Program 6, Office of the Secretary of Agriculture, RG 16, NA. For agribusiness's position, see A. W. Carpenter, executive director, Eastern Federation of Feed Merchants, to J. Howard McGrath, July 11, 1949, Proposed Legislation, 1947–1950, J. Howard McGrath Papers, Truman Library (hereafter cited as McGrath Papers). ADA support and cooperation is reflected in Patton to Brannan, June 10, 1949, James G. Patton folders, Subject file, 1938–1988, Brannan Papers.

23. For contrary views, see Joseph W. Fichter, Ohio State Grange, to Brannan, April 22, 1949, and Hugh Craig, AFBF member, to Brannan, May 6, 1949, Farm Program 6, Office of the Secretary of Agriculture, RG 16, NA.

24. Patton to Truman, April 18, 1949, OF, Truman Papers; Wright to Brannan, April 20, 1949, Farm Program 6, Office of the Secretary of Agriculture, RG 16, NA.

but saw the Brannan plan as the first "family type farm proposal."[25]
"You have so much heat from the Big Gun's in Agriculture," wrote
John T. Robertson of Palacios, Texas, "that I am sure your Plan is
O.K. for We little people. More Power to you." Actually, the "Big
Gun's" were just beginning to turn up the heat. A few weeks later, the
director of public relations for the Farmers Union Grain Terminal
Association in St. Paul, Minnesota, wrote to inform Brannan that his
state's farm bureau was "tagging all of us as Anglophiles, calling your
plan the 'British' Farm Program. We're steeping a cup of hot water
in case there's another tea party."[26]

In a telegram to Illinois senator Scott W. Lucas, Glenn Talbott,
chairman of the NFU's executive committee, reacted to press reports
that the Democratic floor leader had "decided to drop the new farm
bill embodying the Brannan proposals from the list of 'must legislation.'" He summarized the reasons for his organization's strong
support and maintained that "the Brannan plan should be given top
priority."

> The need for it is most urgent. Farm income is presently down
> to a critical point. Further farm deflation means certain disaster.
> Surpluses of many farm commodities seem certain and without
> assurance of parity income the economic condition of millions of
> farmers will be irreparably impaired. More than this, the nation's
> general economy is presently in no position to withstand the
> shock of a severe farm depression. The absence of any adequate
> farm program would have far-reaching and disastrous effects
> upon our entire economy. We are convinced that Title II of the
> 1948 Farm Act is totally inadequate to cope with the urgency of
> the problems now facing agriculture.

At the very least, Talbott insisted that Congress should extend Title I's
90 percent of parity price support provisions for another year. He re-

---

25. Perkins to Brannan, April 28, 1949, Farm Program 6, Office of the Secretary of Agriculture, RG 16, NA. While a good many of state and local bureaus
and granges took exception with their national leadership, from top to bottom,
the NFU was virtually unanimous in its endorsement.

26. Gordon Roth to Brannan, June 7, 1949, and Robertson to Brannan, May
12, 1949, Farm Program 6, Office of the Secretary of Agriculture, RG 16, NA.
The many letters of support, especially from the Dakotas, Wisconsin, Montana
and Minnesota, can also be found among this group of papers.

minded Senator Lucas that it would be "politically disastrous for this administration" to allow the Aiken portion (Title II) of the 1948 law to take effect, and he wrote: "Aside from the economic necessity of formulating and passing a new farm bill immediately, guaranteeing farm families parity income, the 81st Congress and this administration is morally committed, by the campaign pledges and the results of the election, to enact new farm legislation to replace the 1948 Farm Act which was clearly repudiated by the farmers of the nation on November 2, 1948."[27]

As for the opposition, some, in particular the leadership of the AFBF, were predisposed toward their posture at least partly because the administration had failed to play the game according to the peculiar rules of agricultural politics. Rather than allowing the agriculture committees in close contact with the major farm interest groups to work out the details of the farm program, by the end of 1949 Brannan and the USDA had presented Congress a fully developed plan that merely needed approval. This disregard for accepted procedure was disturbing to many farm leaders inside and outside Congress. William F. Groves, a Wisconsin dairy leader, found several redeeming qualities in the administration's proposal. He was troubled, however, by the secretary's failure to consult "practical farm leaders or farm operators ... while drafting the plan," and he lamented the fact that the Brannan plan was, as a result, "the brain child of swivel chair economists and cloistered theorists."[28]

The farm groups and organizations that opposed the Brannan plan also did so for specific policy reasons. The National Association of Commissioners, Secretaries and Directors of Agriculture assured Secretary Brannan that it was not supporting or opposing his proposal at that time. The association's April 28 letter to the secretary of agriculture, however, constituted a notice of rejection. The executive committee had unanimously agreed not to "endorse the [Brannan] plan" because members believed it would require extensive controls

27. Talbott et al. to Lucas, telegram, May 26, 1949, Farm Program 6, Office of the Secretary of Agriculture, RG 16, NA.

28. *CR,* 81st Cong., 1st sess., Senate, June 16, 1949, 95, pt. 6: 7788–89. Groves's comments appeared in a *Dairyland News* (Madison, WI) article, May 9, 1949, and were entered into the *Congressional Record* by Senator Alexander Wiley (R-WI). See also Hardin, "Politics of Agriculture in the United States," 576.

and excessive outlays from the federal treasury and increase in the number of federal employees needed to administer the farm program. These state agricultural officials doubted that farmers were "ready to scrap" existing methods "for an untried" program of "complete Federal control" and feared that the Brannan plan "would become a 'potato program' for each and all of the agricultural crops." They thought the new proposal would most likely result in a demand from all segments of the economy that they too be guaranteed "parity of income." Thus, the commissioners, secretaries, and directors concluded that the Aiken bill should be given a fair trial; if that was amiss the old McNary-Haugen plan could be tried; and, if both proved unsatisfactory, they might then be ready to support the Brannan plan.[29]

In the weeks immediately following the plan's unveiling, a steady stream of letters expressing similar sentiments was delivered to the USDA and the White House. The Los Angeles County Farm Bureau was "definitely opposed to the New Farm Program," and the National Independent Meat Packers Association went "on record as opposed to the said program in its entirety" because it contained at least six "serious defects and weaknesses."[30] The association insisted that the plan was "un-American" and "highly discriminatory," as well as misleading to consumers because it held "out to them apparent savings in food prices, whereas much of the heavy cost of the program would have to be paid in taxes by the same consumers." It also would contribute to the already serious problem of "national indebtedness" and "cost untold billions," and it proposed a regimentation of agricultural that threatened to destroy the traditional "freedom" and "independence" of America's farmers.

In a "Letter to Congress," an angry Oscar Bledsoe, president of the Staple Cotton Cooperative Association of Greenwood, Mississippi, wrote that a "Judas Iscariot" had appeared on the "political scene"

29. National Association of Commissioners, Secretaries and Directors of Agriculture to Brannan, April 28, 1949, Farm Program 6, Office of the Secretary of Agriculture, RG 16, NA.

30. Robert G. Platt, executive secretary of the Los Angeles County Farm Bureau to Truman, April 29, 1949, and resolution adopted by the National Independent Meat Packers Association, April 12, 1949, Farm Program 6, Office of the Secretary of Agriculture, RG 16, NA. The former, like many letters pertaining to the Brannan plan received at the White House, was referred to the USDA for response.

proposing "a most clever vote buying scheme. He [Secretary Brannan?] proposes that the Federal Government pay part of the grocery bill of the 80% urban dwellers by encouraging and reimbursing the 20% farm group to grow five times as much as they need so as to feed the 80% urban group." The underlying objective was the establishment of "an artificial price structure within our nation." Bledsoe insisted that "the Statesmen within our Congress will turn down this proposition with disdain, but the politicians...will rub their hands with glee and sell their souls and our nation into a Socialistic State."[31]

Of all Brannan's many farm organization opponents, however, Allan Kline, president of the AFBF, undoubtedly proved the most formidable. Although there was never any question as to Kline's position on the Brannan proposals, during the first few weeks of the debate, the disagreement remained relatively civil. In an April 15 letter devoted primarily to other "monetary and fiscal matters," Kline told Brannan that he was "truly sorry that we had no opportunity to visit with you during the development of your farm program proposals. I do regret being in opposition."[32] Kline may have been sincere in his regret, but he left little doubt where he stood regarding the plan in his April 28 testimony before the House Committee on Agriculture. Brannan wrote a wavering Ohio Farm Bureau official that after reading "Kline's statement and especially his replies to the Committee's interrogatories, I assume that any grounds for a consolidation of his and my views is rather remote."[33]

As congressional consideration of the Brannan plan intensified during the late spring and summer of 1949, so did the dispute between the secretary of agriculture and the president of the nation's largest farm organization. Although Brannan and Albert Goss, master of the National Grange, were also at odds on farm policy, their

31. Copy of letter forwarded to E. D. White, assistant to the Secretary of Agriculture, April 15, 1949, Farm Program 6, Office of the Secretary of Agriculture, RG 16, NA.

32. Kline to Brannan, April 15, 1949, Meetings 3–3, Office of the Secretary of Agriculture, RG 16, NA. In light of the later acrimony between these two principals, it is quite possible that this seemingly innocuous passage was laced with sarcasm.

33. Brannan to H. W. Culbreth, May 2, 1949, Farm Program 6, Office of the Secretary of Agriculture, RG 16, NA. For Kline's committee testimony, see House Committee, *General Farm Program* (pt. 2), 431–42.

differences were in no way as intense or personal as those that developed between the secretary and the AFBF president. In a letter dated June 14, Brannan "respectfully" drew Goss's attention to the June 4 issue of the Grange's *Washington Farm Reporter* and specifically repudiated a statement that read, "Brannan has made certain that both Grange master Albert Goss and Farm Bureau president Allan Kline know he considers their opposition an unfriendly act." "I wish to assure you," Brannan wrote, "that I have not intended to convey that impression to you nor do I entertain that attitude.... On the contrary, I have repeatedly stated that my proposals were made as part of our comprehensive effort toward the best possible farm program. I have at no time maintained that our recommendations were the final word. I have expected and will continue to welcome constructive criticism."[34]

While Brannan may have been sincere when making this statement, his actions and words during the weeks and months that followed often belie this sentiment, especially as they related to Kline. The two men remained relatively cordial in their correspondence during the month of June, but Brannan wrote at least two letters complaining about statements made by other AFBF officials and articles printed in bureau publications. In some of the cases he cited, the secretary was probably correct in his interpretation that his proposals were being misrepresented. In others, however, it is hard not to conclude that Brannan was overreacting and taking the criticism too personally. With regard to one such article, which he admitted could be interpreted in different ways, Brannan insisted it did "not meet the standards of objectivity which I had hoped might be followed in discussing my proposals on their merits rather than smearing by innuendo a program which, whatever the faults, was recommended in good faith."[35]

By early summer, the AFBF position had been made quite clear, and it had been given wide circulation. As outlined by Congressman Kenneth Keating (R-NY), who insisted that farmers in his area "do not want to sell their birth right," the bureau's opposition boiled down to six main objections. The Brannan plan would: (1) make farmers

34. Brannan to Goss, June 14, 1949, Farm Program 6, Office of the Secretary of Agriculture, RG 16, NA.
35. Brannan to Kline, June 27, 1949, and June 10, 1949, Farm Program 6, Office of the Secretary of Agriculture, RG 16, NA; Brannan to Clark M. Clifford, June 8, 1949, Farm Program, Brannan Papers.

dependent on a government handout; (2) be staggeringly expensive to administer; (3) lead to rigid controls and extreme regimentation, because of the high price goals it established; (4) result in low farm and high consumer prices, despite the promises made by the administration; (5) amount to the abandonment of the "fair exchange concept of parity"; and (6) further plunge the farm program into the partisan arena.[36]

Although coming at the issue from a somewhat different perspective, most of the nation's leading agricultural economists agreed with some of the positions taken by the AFBF. This group of experts, which included a number of officials within the administration itself (members of the BOB and the CEA), did not join in the popular outcry against production payments and the eighteen hundred-unit limitation feature. Farm economists, however, faulted the Brannan plan for its failure to make provision for the adjustment of support levels in light of demand and supply (flexible supports) and for setting these levels at an excessive 100 percent of parity. Most favored Brannan's complete break with the obsolete 1910–1914 base period, the new parity formula, the income support standard, and the increased use of direct payments; but they generally feared that the Brannan proposals would "require either huge payments from the Treasury or detailed and severe controls over agricultural production and marketing."[37] "Most leading agricultural economists, including progressives," wrote Alonzo Hamby, "were convinced that the plan would be unworkable and prohibitively expensive. Some progressive economists especially deplored its failure to give the rural poor at least as much aid as the middle-class family farm."[38]

Members of the State Department's Office of International Trade Policy agreed with D. Gale Johnson, a professor of economics at the

36. *CR,* 81st Cong., 1st sess., House, July 6, 1949, 95, pt. 7: 8948.

37. F. V. Waugh and Herman Southworth to CEA, memorandum, April 21, 1949, Nourse Papers; undated memo for the president from the director of BOB, regarding "Draft Bill, Submitted by Secretary Brannan, Amending the Agricultural Act of 1948"; J. Weldon Jones to director (BOB), memorandum, May 4, 1949; and "Confidential" memo, May 10, 1949, Agricultural Adjustment Act of 1949 (Brannan Plan), Bureau of the Budget, RG 51, NA.

38. Hamby, *Beyond the New Deal,* 309; Donovan, *Tumultuous Years,* 123. Russell Smith, legislative secretary for the NFU, also recognized the extent of this formidable opposition group ("The Brannan Plan: Counterattack in Favor," 62).

University of Chicago, who believed, "On the whole," that the Brannan plan was "inferior to the Agricultural Act of 1948 in almost every respect." "This is particularly true," Johnson wrote on May 17, "of the impact the program would have upon international trade in agricultural products."[39] According to Johnson, Brannan had "shown himself to be a politician of the first rank," not because he had proposed anything new, but because he had "taken the offensive in a persuasive manner. . . . The combination of his astuteness and frankness has given his proposal a wide hearing; a hearing wider than it deserves, in my opinion." Johnson gave the secretary credit for his positive proposals; but the economist insisted that under Brannan's plan "it will not only be necessary to control domestic production and trade, but extensive controls over international trade will be required to buttress the domestic controls. Brannan's proposals are a real threat to obtaining the advantages from freer trade."

Johnson and many other economists also believed that under the administration's plan most of the benefits "would accrue to the large farmers." "The small family-size, commercial farm would receive little benefit, while the subsistence farmer whose position is the weakest of all, would receive even less."[40] In August Johnson wrote: "Not only does a high-level support price program fail to meet the needs of low-income families, but the cost of the program is likely to be so great that it will preclude Congress' taking any action to meet the problems presented by low incomes in agriculture."[41]

Always the outsider on the inside of the administration, CEA chair-

39. Johnson to Joseph D. Coppock, May 17, 1949, Agricultural Adjustment Act of 1949 (Brannan Plan), Bureau of the Budget, RG 51, NA.

40. Johnson to Coppock, May 17, 1949, Agricultural Adjustment Act of 1949 (Brannan Plan), Bureau of the Budget, RG 51, NA. Quotations from a radio speech, "The Brannan Program," a copy of which was sent to Coppock. The White House was informed that Johnson was not only "a particularly competent agricultural economist" but also a State Department consultant as well, who "deserves attention" (J. R. Schaetzel to Richard Neustadt, "Confidential" memo, May 25, 1949, Agricultural Act of 1948 (Brannan Plan), Bureau of the Budget, RG 51, NA). See also Christenson, *The Brannan Plan,* 109.

41. D. Gale Johnson, "High Level Support Prices and Corn Belt Agriculture," 519; Geoffrey P. Collins, "Agricultural Policy and the General Economy," 191; Clay L. Cochrane, "Price Supports and the Distribution of Agricultural Income," 330; William O. Jones, "Current Farm Price-Support Proposals in the United States," 253.

man Edwin Nourse resisted pressure coming from the budget bureau for quick council action, preferring to remain in touch with the USDA on possible changes. As he wrote Harvard economist John D. Black, "We are continuing our parleys with Brannan and his staff people in the hope that useful modifications may be suggested."[42] On May 11, Chairman Nourse communicated his concerns to Secretary Brannan, quoting at length from the council's May 6 letter to the BOB and its memorandum to the president. Nourse and the CEA were especially interested in seeing "a law developed that would bring about adjustments in support levels that would assure farmers an adequate and stable income, that would not require excessive expenses to the Government, and that would require a minimum use of acreage allotments and marketing quotas."[43] On these broad objectives there was undoubtedly little disagreement, but Nourse was convinced that the Brannan proposals, as currently constituted, did not provide an adequate means to these ends.

Chairman Nourse, a frequent dissenting voice on the three-member board, had signed on to the council's statements, but he believed it was his duty to be more forthright in the communication of his "belief that your bill in its present form definitely fails to attain the stated objectives or the soundest compromise between them." The chairman appreciated Brannan's effort to move away from the obsolete pre–World War I base period. He also "thoroughly approve[d]" of the switch to an income parity concept and agreed with the inclusion of meat, dairy, and poultry products in the support program as a way to encourage appropriate production shifts. Despite these positive features, Nourse outlined four "major difficulties," which, as he pointed out, were reflected in the comments of many other economists of the day: "cost; adverse effect of arbitrary corrections; production and market controls; and administrative burden." In summarizing his more detailed discussion of these perceived problems, Nourse wrote:

42. Nourse to Black, May 6, 1949, Nourse Papers; Nourse to Roger W. Jones, assistant director, legislative reference, BOB, May 6, 1949, Agricultural Adjustment Act of 1949 (Brannan Plan), Bureau of the Budget, RG 51, NA. Black became well known for his opposition to the Brannan plan and was the target of Smith's "The Brannan Plan: Counterattack in Favor."

43. Nourse to Brannan, May 11, 1949, Agricultural Act of 1949 (Brannan Plan), Bureau of the Budget, RG 51, NA.

"you will see that my recommendations would point to the setting of lower support levels and the adjustment of support prices of individual commodities in line with particular supply and demand conditions as they develop."[44]

In the face of this rather heavy criticism, and despite his oft repeated willingness to compromise and discuss all the complex issues involved, including price or income support levels, Brannan remained steadfast in his commitment to the original proposals.[45] When he responded to Professor O. B. Jesness's suggestion "that the level of support should be 75 percent rather than 100 percent of the price support standards," Brannan insisted that he was "still open-minded as to the precise level of price supports," but he believed that his proposed income support standard was "a reasonable one." The secretary knew that "Dr. [Theodore] Schultz and a considerable number of other economists feel that the price support level which I have recommended tends to 'overvalue' farm products and that they also have the further feeling that the farmers' acceptance of lower prices might somehow or other alleviate the control problem." Although he claimed not to consider himself "the final authority on farm product prices," Brannan maintained that "in view of the general inflation in incomes which has developed during and following the war,... the burden of proof lies upon those who would recommend a considerable further deflation in farm incomes."[46]

Apparently, the secretary's standard of proof was never met. Although his frequent contacts with this coterie of distinguished critics remained cordial, Brannan was doggedly committed to his original plan and was willing to suffer early setbacks in the belief that its merits would eventually lead to victory.[47]

44. Nourse to Brannan, May 11, 1949, Agricultural Act of 1949 (Brannan Plan), Bureau of the Budget, RG 51, NA (see also unattributed position paper on the advantages and disadvantages of the Brannan plan, May 13, 1949).

45. Brannan to Black, May 2, 1949, Farm Program 6, Office of the Secretary of Agriculture, RG 16, NA.

46. Brannan to Jesness, chief, Division of Agricultural Economics, University of Minnesota, June 22, 1949, Farm Program 6, Office of the Secretary of Agriculture, RG 16, NA. See also O. B. Jesness, "What Do We Expect from a Farm Program," 5.

47. With regard to the conviviality of this relationship, see Schultz to Brannan, June 9, 1949, and Brannan to Schultz, June 20, 1949, Public Relations, Office of

In retrospect, the administration's failure to seek out common ground in 1949 appears unfortunate. An accord with the professional economics community would not have guaranteed passage of even a modified administration proposal, but it could not have hurt. At the very least, it would have partially disarmed some of Brannan's other critics and possibly allowed the debate to focus on the areas of agreement—most notably, the benefits of production payments and the need to assist the rural poor, who even Brannan admitted would not be helped by the administration's proposal.[48]

Although his numerous critics benefited immensely from their ability to call attention to this high level dispute, the areas of agreement between Brannan and the professional economists were actually quite extensive.[49] Willard W. Cochrane of Pennsylvania State College, for example, found himself in basic agreement with the secretary's proposal for agriculture. On June 28 he wrote, "And perhaps of more importance, I find that most of the younger agricultural economists, who are concerned with the price-income problem in agriculture are also sympathetic to your proposal." "We have argued for some time," Cochrane continued,

> that rigid support prices imposed to enhance farm incomes set in motion undesirable consequences, and to some degree needless

the Secretary of Agriculture, RG 16, NA; Black to Brannan, July 29, 1949, and Brannan to Black, August 18, 1949, Farm Program 6, Office of the Secretary of Agriculture, RG 16, NA. In addition to Professors Black and Schultz, the group referred to here included: Walter W. Wilcox, Department of Agricultural Economics, University of Wisconsin, and Willard W. Cochrane, Department of Agricultural Economics and Rural Sociology, Pennsylvania State College (see Wilcox to Brannan, September 3, 1949, and Cochrane to Brannan, June 28, 1949, Farm Program 6, Office of the Secretary of Agriculture, RG 16, NA).

48. Schultz to Brannan, June 9, 1949, and Brannan to Schultz, June 20, 1949, Public Relations, Office of the Secretary of Agriculture, RG 16, NA. This particular exchange followed a joint appearance (which also included Senator George Aiken) on a "Round Table" sponsored by the University of Chicago and broadcast by NBC on May 29. See also Varden Fuller, "Political Pressures and Income Distribution in Agriculture," in Vernon W. Ruttan, Arley D. Waldo, and James P. Houck, eds., *Agricultural Policy in an Affluent Society,* 255–56.

49. Schultz, *Agriculture in an Unstable Economy.* Indeed, the secretary's proposals were so similar to those previously suggested by Schultz, Brannan repeatedly had to fend off charges that the professor was the author of the Brannan plan (*New York Times,* April 12, 1949, 4; Smith, "The Brannan Plan: Counterattack in Favor," 70).

consequences, since better ways of aiding farmers with their income problems exist. Your proposal, which would permit the price of animal and perishable products to seek their own level but which would supplement the return to producers by production or compensatory payments, is representative of one of those better ways. And in light of the current fixation of certain farm groups with fixed prices you are to be commended for taking a courageous step, but which in the longer run I suspect will be heralded as one of great political acumen. The pursuit of a price and income policy such as you have proposed *enjoins the interests of the city worker and the farmer;* that is its great significance; that is what the fuss is all about.[50]

Cochrane was concerned, however, about what he called "a fallacious type of reasoning" that was too prevalent within the USDA. He sought to focus the secretary's attention on the "surplus problem." "You may say—we will not have surpluses when animal and perishable product prices are permitted to seek their own levels; increased consumption will eliminate surpluses. I can only reply that we had surpluses in 1932–33 when farm prices were at ruinously low levels, that the size of the collective stomach of the United States has limits, but that advancing technology would seem to have none." Cochrane believed the traditional tools of production control (acreage allotments and marketing quotas) could be effective when dealing with one or two surplus commodities. But in the likely circumstance that all or most farm product areas were experiencing low prices and surpluses, they could not work. He outlined the essence of the farm problem and the policy dilemma facing the nation during this second agricultural revolution, when he pointed out that farmers had no place to shift their resources except to other commodities and to increased production.

> We get little or no variation in total farm output in response to the fluctuating farm price level for the reason that agriculture is somewhat like a water-tight compartment. We get a free flow of human and capital resource between potatoes and sugar beets, between corn and soybeans and between many other types of

50. Cochrane to Brannan, June 28, 1949, Farm Program 6, Office of the Secretary of Agriculture, RG 16, NA.

farm enterprises in response to a change in prices, but not between farming and banking or farming and retailing. Productive
resources in agriculture are largely fixed—sunk—in the individual farm enterprise, and in the short-run they stay on the farm
no matter what happens to the farm price level. If farm prices
rise the farmer and his family work harder with fixed amounts of
machinery, buildings, land and livestock to expand output and
so reap greater profits. If farm prices drop the farmer and his
family make every effort to expand output and so minimize the
loss of income. Thus, we have a flow of production *at or near
maximum capacity for every individual farm at all times.* In the
longer run we get the following result: if prices (incomes) remain
high farmers will invest in new technologies and increase their
output, but if prices are low, farmers just keep on producing so
that the flow of production is sustained.[51]

In the short run, Cochrane saw production payments as a "good
temporary solution, to the price-income problem in agriculture," but
over the long haul they would be another factor contributing to
ruinous farm surpluses. Cochrane recognized that the "answer to this
aggregate supply problem is not an easy one," and he did not claim
to have the solution; but he was giving more attention to the efficacy
of "a systematic program of migration off the farm"—a necessity
recognized and discussed by Schultz in 1945. Specifically, Cochrane
closed his rather lengthy, but he hoped constructive, letter with three
specific criticisms: (1) the "calculated prices" that emerged from Brannan's plan were too high; (2) the mechanics of the new parity formula
were "unnecessarily complex"; and (3) the proposal lacked a "positive technique for expanding consumption."

The secretary's detractors represented a wide social, political, and
economic spectrum. Surprisingly, when attention is confined to the
rational objections to the Brannan plan, it becomes evident that there
was considerable agreement that it contained certain basic problems.

51. Cochrane to Brannan, June 28, 1949, Farm Program 6, Office of the
Secretary of Agriculture, RG 16, NA. It is interesting (and significant) to note
that the fundamental points Cochrane made in this 1949 letter to Secretary
Brannan remained the focus of much of the economist's scholarly attention for
several decades thereafter (see Cochrane, *Farm Prices: Myth and Reality;* Cochrane,
"The Need to Rethink Agricultural Policy in General and to Perform Some
Radical Surgery on Commodity Programs in Particular," 1002).

Many were willing to give Brannan credit for helping to focus attention on the farm problem and for at least suggesting a new approach.[52] Most agreed, however, that the plan pegged farm prices at unrealistically high levels, placed serious demands on the federal treasury (the taxpayer), worsened the surplus problem, and required severe governmental control ("regimentation") of agricultural production. When the politically motivated protests and the irrational fears, such as creeping socialism or communism, are added in, it is little wonder that the Brannan plan faced rough sledding on Capitol Hill.

52. See, for example, Hope to William H. Nicholls, May 28, 1949, FF, Hope Papers; Robert H. Estabrook, "The Bogey in the Brannan Plan," 77. Estabrook was a *Washington Post* editorial writer; Nicholls was a professor of agricultural economics at Vanderbilt University.

7

THE BRANNAN PLAN IN CONGRESS

Under the best of circumstances, the controversial Brannan plan for agriculture would have had a difficult journey through Congress. These were not the best of circumstances, and the administration's innovative approach to the farm problem was down for the count within four months of its unveiling. There were many contributing factors, but there can be little doubt that partisanship, introduced so effectively by the administration during the 1948 presidential campaign, played a major role. Republicans believed that Truman had been playing "politics with the welfare of the farmers of the Nation" for more than a year. Senator George Aiken, who had been so gracious in his expression of appreciation for the USDA's cooperativeness just a year earlier, became involved in a public feud with Brannan after the senator accused the department of distributing propaganda to "promote a political plan of prosperity for farmers." "The men in the Agriculture Department," echoed Congressman Arthur L. Miller (R-NE), "are making a political football out of the farmers production."[1]

There was ample partisanship on both sides of the aisle, but the new majority and the administration desperately wanted to claim credit for a Democratic farm law. As was the case on so many Fair Deal issues, however, the majority party could hardly count on a united front. Many southern Democrats joined Republicans and the AFBF in vigorously opposing certain aspects of the administration's proposal. They

1. Aiken, *CR,* 81st Cong., 1st sess., Senate, June 13, 1949, 95, pt. 6: 7590; Miller, *CR* (House), June 30, 1949, 95, pt. 7: 8748; *New York Times,* June 14, 1949, 3; Christenson, *The Brannan Plan,* 114–42.

objected to unit limitations, which would have denied large producers the benefit of government support prices, feared the prospects of increased regimentation in the agricultural sector, and worried that the farm program proposed by the administration would be prohibitively expensive. Unlike the national Farm Bureau and its president Allan Kline, southerners opposed flexible supports. But in the South, the bureau made no effort to stop southern members of Congress from advocating 90 percent of parity, and the major sponsors of legislation opposing the Brannan plan were from that region.[2]

On April 13, the *New York Times* reported that one key southerner, Congressman Stephen Pace, was concerned about the potentially "stupendous cost" of the Brannan plan. Secretary Brannan was unable to assuage these fears, but less than a week after the initial introduction of his farm program, the secretary moved to ward off southern opposition to another feature of the plan—the unit limitation provision. During questioning before the House Committee on Agriculture, Brannan explained that this provision would not be applied to crops already under acreage limitations and marketing quotas. Unfortunately for the administration, this maneuver did not satisfy its southern critics. Republican congressman Clifford Hope also protested, claiming that the eighteen hundred-unit limitation provision would hardly be worth the red tape if it were not applied to all crops. Although Brannan continually argued that he had not abandoned this principle, Hope believed "that the Secretary very largely eliminated that proposal . . . when he stated that this limitation should not be in effect as to commodities upon which acreage allotment and marketing quotas were in effect."[3]

After hearing from Secretary Brannan in April, Congress anxiously awaited the preparation and introduction of an administration bill. This was by no means a period of inactivity, and by the time the USDA measure was introduced in May, the nature of the congressional opposition was quite clear. "I think the matter should be carefully studied in Congress," wrote Hope, "but frankly I am dubious about any farm

2. "Brannan Outlines Limits to New Plan," *New York Times,* April 13, 1949, 58; Saloutos, "Agricultural Organizations and Farm Policy," 390; Hamby, *Beyond the New Deal,* 306; Benedict, *Farm Policies of the United States,* 480.

3. Hope to Russell Wilkins, April 14, 1949, FF, Hope Papers. See also House Committee, *General Farm Program* (pt. 2); "The Elusive Cost Factor," 78.

plan which has to be carried out by means of payments to producers." The Kansas congressman was apprehensive about a proposal that so closely resembled the "program which they had in England." "It is in effect a subsidy to the consumer and apparently in England the consumers have gotten so fond of the subsidy that any talk about raising prices brings a threat of a political revolt.... The thing that bothers me is that if we start such a program here and consumers adjust themselves to the subsidized prices, the chances are we will never get rid of them." A week later Hope argued that the Brannan plan "would in the end, in my opinion, bring about a situation very much the same as the farmers in England are confronted with at the present time, which is total control of their farming operations."[4]

Congressman Hope did not oppose the principle of production payments, and he recognized that the Aiken bill contained such a provision. But, he reasoned, "until Secretary Brannan came along with his proposal, no one ever had any idea that payments would be used to the extent that he suggests." He objected because "farmers consider such payments a handout or dole." Hope's greatest fear was that the Brannan plan would undermine past efforts to convince consumers that parity prices were fair prices.[5]

Lawmakers also renewed efforts to legislate their positions. On April 22 Democratic senator Olin Johnston, a former governor of South Carolina, introduced a bill (S. 1671) "to continue price support of agricultural commodities at current levels for two years." Its purpose, the senator explained in a prepared statement entered into the record, was to delay the effective date of the Aiken farm bill so that further study of the effects of flexible price supports could be completed. Efforts of this type had begun earlier in the year and would continue throughout the session.[6]

4. Hope to Samuel R. Guard, May 14, 1949, and to Mrs. Hermie Kastens, May 23, 1949, FF, Hope Papers. See also Brannan to F. S. N. Williams, May 26, 1949, Farm Program 6, Office of the Secretary of Agriculture, RG 16, NA.

5. Hope to Samuel R. Guard, May 14 and May 20, 1949, and to Robert I. Lupfer, April 21, 1949, FF, Hope Papers.

6. *CR,* 81st Cong., 1st sess., Senate, April 22, 1949, 95, pt. 4: 4908; General Legislation, S. 1671, 1949; General Legislation, S. 367, 1949, 2124, 2276, Bureau of the Budget, RG 16, NA. Senator Richard B. Russell (D-GA) introduced S. 367 to support basics for cooperators at 90 percent of parity on January 13; Senator Karl E. Mundt (R-SD) proposed S. 2124 "to extend indefinitely the period in

Although the Brannan plan generated a great deal of interest, many did not expect the plan to pass during the current session. In fact, Congressman Hope was sure that Brannan himself did not expect his plan to be enacted in 1949; if he had, he would have presented it to Congress earlier. Republicans like Hope were convinced that, just months after the last election and more than a year and a half before the next, the administration was already involved in political posturing. "I think it would be a terrible mistake for the Republicans to stand on the Aiken bill," Hope declared in a May 14 letter. The congressman was convinced that it would not be effective and that Brannan would not try very hard to make it work. If Aiken failed, the administration would make a grand campaign for the Brannan plan, and it would "be a big issue in the 1950 Congressional campaigns. Frankly, there is hardly anyone in Congress from farm sections who favors the bill, but it has plenty of political appeal, and if we go into 1950 with a plan that will not work, the Brannan plan can probably be sold to farmers, although they are very skeptical of it at the present time."[7]

Despite the gloomy prognosis that was generally accepted by early June 1949, many liberals and administration officials believed the Brannan plan could be revived with the proper educational and promotional efforts. To this end, the secretary campaigned tirelessly, the administration sponsored conferences throughout the country, and the CIO and NFU worked hard to keep the plan alive and to build a labor-farmer coalition.[8]

Congressman Hope was among those who did not believe that the Brannan plan had gained enough farm support to pass, but he was concerned about the political implications and especially the active involvement of organized labor. "Most of the support," he argued, "is coming from the CIO and there is no doubt but what it is a CIO

which Title I of the Agricultural Adjustment Act of 1948 shall be applicable" on June 22; and Senator Milton R. Young (R-ND) introduced S. 2276, "To continue price support of agricultural commodities at current levels for one year and to require price support for oats, barley, and rye" on July 18 (Young, *CR*, 81st Cong., 1st sess., Senate, July 18, 1949, 95, pt. 7: 9607).

7. Hope to James P. Selvage, May 14, 1949, FF, Hope Papers. See also *New York Times,* June 17, 1949, 19, and *New York Times,* June 19, 1949, sec. 4, 7.

8. Hamby, *Beyond the New Deal,* 306; Christenson, *The Brannan Plan,* 119.

bill from start to finish. This very fact I am sure is going to make most farmers suspicious."[9] Two weeks later he called the administration's proposal the "CIO Plan" and criticized the "so-called Farm Conference" held by the Democrats in Des Moines the previous week. It was "mostly a rally by the Democrats and Labor leaders trying to get farmers to support the repeal of the Taft-Hartley bill, and incidentally to support the Brannan Farm Plan." Because of labor's substantial influence, Hope believed the Brannan plan gave more to consumers than to farmers. "I have always tried to keep farm legislation out of politics and I think most people have," he wrote on June 25, "but Secretary Brannan and the labor politicians have now gotten it into politics up to its neck."[10]

Speaking of this same conference, Congressman Arthur Miller insisted that it had been designed to court farm support, and that it was "called for the purpose of selling the fantastic Brannan program to the farmers." The meeting had been promoted through the USDA's public relations division and was attended by twenty to twenty-five high government officials at the taxpayers expense. With regard to the Brannan plan itself, Miller reiterated many of the well-known criticisms and tagged it "an amazing sleight-of-hand performance—a political Christmas tree—a pandora's box, with a Mortimer Snerd philosophy." He insisted that it was a political program, not a farm program, that introduced a "cheap food philosophy," with the taxpayer sharing the nation's grocery bills and the government controlling prices and income, land and livestock. Congressman Miller admonished the Des Moines conferees to junk the Brannan plan and to give the Agricultural Act of 1948, which had been supported by the Democrats and the USDA when passed, "a fair trial."[11]

During the extended debate on the new Commodity Credit Corporation Charter Act, many of the political wounds inflicted during the

9. Hope to Mrs. Hermie Kastens, June 4, 1949, FF, Hope Papers.

10. Hope to Dale Richardson, June 25, 1949; to A. H. Couch, June 18, 1949, FF, Hope Papers. At the same time, Hope admitted to Richardson that the Aiken bill was "too much of a United States Chamber of Commerce program."

11. Miller, "The Brannan Farm Program and Politics," in *CR,* 81st Cong., 2nd sess., House, June 9, 1949, 95, pt. 6: 7507, 7508; Hamby, *Beyond the New Deal,* 307; *New York Times,* June 13, 1949, 27, and *New York Times,* June 14, 1949, 3. The latter article appeared under the headline, "New Farm Plan Set as '50 Voting Issue."

previous campaign were reopened.[12] In the midst of this often-heated debate, Congressman George H. Christopher (D-MO) defended the Des Moines meeting, insisting that it was not designed for political purposes but to discuss the new farm legislation so that farmers would not experience "that piece of iniquitous legislation known as the Aiken bill." Addressing the CCC issue, he charged, as he had on at least one previous occasion, that the Eightieth Congress had "tied the hands of the Commodity Credit Corporation so that it could not buy, lease, or build storage." This action had led to the current storage crisis. In a brief exchange with Congressman August Andresen, Christopher almost admitted that the secretary's decision not to lend on ground-stored wheat in 1948 was "political expediency." But he closed by complimenting the Brannan plan and by calling for the passage of the entire Fair Deal program to avoid the situation that developed as a result of Republican policy in the 1920s and early 1930s.[13]

Meanwhile, the department had put the Brannan plan into legislative form, forwarding a "final draft of a bill to express in legislative terms the recommendations previously made by the Department with respect to farm price support legislation" to the Senate and the House leadership on May 17. This proposed revision of "the Agricultural Adjustment Act of 1938, as Amended by the Agricultural Act of 1948," contained all the basic elements suggested by the secretary on April 7, including the controversial eighteen hundred-unit limitation. Brannan was able to support the bill (H.R. 4753) introduced by Congressman Harold Cooley, even though it omitted the "'1800 unit' provision" and added wool and peanuts to the list of "priority" commodities, because during the weeks since his testimony he had softened his commitment to this proposal.[14]

12. Debate on this measure occupied considerable House and Senate time during May and June (*CR,* 81st Cong., 1st sess., 95, pt. 4–6, 4964–93, 5992–6856, 7355–7594, passim).

13. *CR,* 81st Cong., 1st sess., House, June 9, 1949, 95, pt. 6: 7514, 7515, 7355–56.

14. Separate letters and copies of draft legislation from Brannan to Alben Barkley, president of the Senate, Speaker Sam Rayburn, Senator Elmer Thomas, and Representative Cooley, May 17, 1949, and Brannan to Rayburn and Barkley, May 27, 1949, Legislation 1–1, Office of the Secretary of Agriculture, RG 16, NA; *New York Times,* May 18, 1949, 24.

Despite the continued weakening of the original USDA proposal, key segments of the executive branch remained skeptical of its provisions. Frank Pace Jr., the director of the Bureau of the Budget, informed the secretary that his agency had "no objection to the legislation from the standpoint of the program of the President." He thought the income standard of the bill should be a goal for 1950, but he believed "fiscal considerations" made it necessary for individual commodity price supports to be held as low as possible. In what amounted to a reaffirmation of the BOB's continued commitment to "flexible supports," Pace wrote: "There is some apprehension in this office that the support standard for the priority or Group I commodities is higher than necessary to assist farmers to earn the objective income. Therefore, the Secretary of Agriculture should be given additional discretion to vary the level of support for individual commodities in the event that this apprehension should prove correct."[15]

Many in Congress shared the bureau's apprehensions, and further compromise on some of the administration's proposals proved necessary. In mid-June, a subcommittee chaired by Congressman Pace introduced H.R. 5345, which provided for Brannan's income support standard and 100 percent supports for Group 1 commodities but limited the application of production payments as a means of price support to no more than three commodities—a so-called trial run.[16] Secretary Brannan was understandably disappointed that the House Committee on Agriculture had chosen this approach over the USDA's recommendation, but in a letter to Congressman August Andresen, he insisted that he only "offered the proposals in an effort to be help-

15. Pace to Brannan, June 21, 1949, Legislation 1–1, Office of the Secretary of Agriculture, RG 16, NA.
16. Benedict, *Farm Policies of the United States,* 480; Brannan to Frank Pace, June 21, 1949, Legislation 2, Office of the Secretary of Agriculture, RG 16, NA. According to Representative Charles B. Hoeven (R-IA), "before the Brannan meeting in Des Moines, there was unanimous agreement in the subcommittee that we would not consider the so-called Brannan bill, but that in lieu thereof, we would extend the 90-percent parity program for 1 year, and suspend the Aiken bill for 1 year." It would seem, if the veracity of this account is accepted, Democratic leaders were affected by the June rally, and Pace subsequently introduced his modified version of the Brannan plan (*CR,* 81st Cong., 1st sess., House, July 20, 1949, 95, pt. 7: 9852; Matusow, *Farm Policies and Politics,* 208–9).

ful to the Congress in its consideration of price-support legislation."
Trying at least to appear somewhat deferential and conciliatory toward
his Republican antagonist, Brannan commended the committee for its
careful study of the issue and for its many recommendations for
addressing the price support problem. "It has reported a bill," Brannan continued, "which embodies most of the basic viewpoints which
I expressed during the hearings. . . . I am glad to give my support to
this bill."[17] On June 27, the "Pace-Brannan" bill, "a rather pale version of the Brannan plan," passed the full committee on a straight party
vote and was formally introduced to the Committee of the Whole
House on July 7.[18]

It appeared for a moment as if this modified Brannan plan had a
real chance. Congressman Hope continued to object in principle to a
plan that "could lead to a farm program based entirely on payments"
and to favor a simple extension of the current legislation. He was not
satisfied with the Pace bill but indicated that he might "vote for it in
the House in order to get some bill over to the Senate which will result in a repeal or postponement of the Aiken bill."[19] This tactic
proved unnecessary, however, because Democratic solidarity behind
even this "pale version" was fleeting. Most of the southern Democrats
renewed their support for a one-year extension of the Title I provisions, and it was decided that an extension alternative, similar to that
previously offered by Congressman Hope, should be introduced by a
southerner.

This role ultimately fell to Representative Albert A. Gore (D-TN),
who proposed a bill (H.R. 5617) on July 13 to extend 90 percent
supports on basics and to provide 60 to 90 percent support for the
Steagall commodities. Speaking in favor of the Pace bill and against
the Gore substitute, Congressman Adolph Sabath (D-IL) explained
that he had carefully considered this bill, in conjunction with Brannan's original proposal, and found that the laudable objectives of the
administration's plan were maintained in H.R. 5345. He insisted that

17. Brannan to Andresen, June 30, 1949, Legislation 1, Office of the Secretary of Agriculture, RG 16, NA. This letter was precipitated by Andresen's June
28 request for a USDA report on H.R. 5345.
18. Hope to A. J. Beck, July 15, 1949, FF, Hope Papers; Cooley, *CR*, 81st
Cong., 1st sess., House, July 7, 1949, 95, pt. 7: 9078.
19. Hope to Herb Hoover, June 28, 1949, FF, Hope Papers.

there was nothing wrong with a program that tried to benefit both consumers and producers. Although the Pace bill significantly modified the Brannan plan, it contained the basic elements "needed to get started on this new approach to farm-income stability." Two days later during floor debate, Sabath reminded his House colleagues that the Pace bill had been endorsed by the Committee on Agriculture by a two to one margin. As for the Gore bill, the congressman saw it as "merely a Republican move to thwart the efforts of the Democrats to continue legislation in the interest of the farmers and to some extent, also, the consumers of the country."[20]

The favorable committee report notwithstanding, administration supporters had already lost the fight. The rather lengthy House consideration of the Pace bill was a rehash of the many weeks of debate that had transpired since Brannan's April 7 testimony, and it probably changed few, if any, minds. Many tried to portray the situation as a choice between the Brannan plan and the much-maligned Aiken bill. According to Congressman William R. Poage (D-TX), "this Aiken bill, which was passed in darkness and perpetuated in darkness, is based upon the philosophy that you should control the farmers' production, not by having a referendum among the farmers . . . [but] by lowering his support prices. It assumes that as production goes up, support prices will drop until you starve the farmer into submission and bring him in line with the views of the bureaucracy in Washington."[21] Farmers had expressed views (during the committee hearings of the previous years) to the effect that the present program worked well for storables but was a disaster for perishables. Poage reasoned that the approach taken in the Pace bill addressed the issue by keeping the good (old system for supporting storables) and by confronting the problem areas with a new method of support for perishables.

But Congressman Hope and most of his Republican colleagues, supported by a large block of southern Democrats, had more than enough votes to carry the day, and they now supported the Gore substitute. According to Hope, the latter legislation did give the Congress a choice that was not confined to "the Pace-Brannan bill or the

20. Sabath, *CR,* 81st Cong., 1st sess., House, July 18 and 20, 1949, 95, pt. 7: 9690, 9837.

21. *CR,* 81st Cong., 1st sess., House, July 21, 1949, 95, pt. 8: 9925–26.

Aiken bill." It was a "reenactment of legislation now in effect, which," he insisted, "is working as successfully as I think any farm legislation can work in a period of a changing economy—a law which has behind it several years of successful operation."[22]

The following day, July 21, 1949, despite the renewed efforts of Brannan supporters and a final plea from Congressman Pace and Speaker Rayburn, the Gore bill was substituted for the Pace bill and passed by a vote of 239 to 170.[23] This favorable vote came after the acceptance of a friendly amendment offered by Representative Pat Sutton (D-TN) that repealed Titles II and III of the Agricultural Act of 1948. The majority apparently agreed with Representative Reid Murray who had found it "pretty difficult these days to keep cool with COOLEY or to keep pace with PACE." As for Murray, his "particular interest [was] to keep the livestock people of this country from going broke with Brannan."[24]

Even before the House dealt its deathblow to the Brannan plan, Senate action seemed to clearly indicate that it had little chance of passing. According to Congressman Hope, the "final outcome" remained very much in doubt, however, as there were "about as many different ideas of farm legislation in the Senate as there are Senators."[25] In the upper chamber, the administration's proposals were most closely reflected by S. 1971, introduced by Senator Elmer Thomas (D-OK) on May 31. But support in the Senate was even harder to muster than it was in the House; and, to the administration's chagrin, the opposition benefited from the leadership of former Secretary of Agriculture Clinton Anderson, who had moved into a position on the Senate Agriculture and Forestry Committee. Anderson, who was decidedly

22. *CR,* 81st Cong., 1st sess., House, July 20, 1949, 95, pt. 7: 9838–70, 9844–45; *CR* (House), July 21, 1949, 95, pt. 8: 9930, 9934. Both sides had valid positions, as the Gore bill simply preserved "the status quo for another year."

23. Pace, *CR,* 81st Cong., 1st sess., House, July 21, 1949, 95, pt. 8: 9931–32, (Rayburn) 9955. Rich, *U.S. Agricultural Policy in the Postwar Years,* 30; Schapsmeier and Schapsmeier, "Farm Policy from FDR to Eisenhower," 366; Matusow, *Farm Policies and Politics,* 209. A yea vote was, in effect, a vote to kill the Brannan plan. The party breakdown was as follows: Democrats, 79 to 165; Republicans, 160 to 4; with one Independent voting nay.

24. Sutton called the Aiken Act "a monstrosity"; "one of the most damnable things that was ever forced upon the American farmers" (*CR,* 81st Cong., 1st sess., House, July 21, 1949, 95, pt. 8: 9929, 9936).

25. Hope to Joe Starnes, July 23, 1949, FF, Hope Papers.

more conservative than Brannan, remained committed to the principle of flexibility. According to historian James L. Forsythe, Anderson "was shocked by Brannan's plan" and claimed to have been the "most surprised man in America" when Brannan discarded the flexible support concept. Although he probably did regret this break with the administration, the senator exerted considerable influence in the move toward a congressional alternative and became the principal author of the substitute plan.[26]

Anderson purposefully remained somewhat low-key during the initial debate, but the break was becoming clear by late June. On June 30, Brannan expressed his disappointment and dismay with the "almost one hundred percent rejection" of the "Administration's proposal" by Anderson's Senate subcommittee, even "before the Committee has had an opportunity to hear witnesses or critically examine our proposals." The "only apparent area of agreement" was Anderson's support for the "trial run on hogs." "I most respectfully say to you," wrote a disheartened Brannan, "that your letter seems to me to coincide exactly with the Allan Kline line except for slightly increasing levels of support."[27]

Facing some considerable pressure from pro-Brannan groups throughout the country, Senate hearings were finally initiated on July 7. In his opening statement, and in his answers to the committee members' questions, the secretary defended his proposals but sought to underscore their similarities with the Aiken bill. Senator Aiken accepted most of Brannan's comparison and, at the end of the daylong session, indicated that he was "willing to be convinced" on the proposed price support standard. "In our discussion of parity income and related questions," Aiken concluded,

> there are only three basic differences of opinion. One is the limitation on production, the provision for compliance with minimum soil-conservation practices, and the principal difference, the level of support which the Secretary would have at 100 percent

26. Forsythe, "Clinton P. Anderson," 629; Anderson, *Outsider in the Senate,* 98.

27. Brannan to Anderson, June 30, 1949, Farm Program 6, Office of the Secretary of Agriculture, RG 16, NA; Anderson to Brannan, June 30, 1949, Farm Program—Correspondence, Brannan Papers.

and which I would have at 90 percent down to a minimum provided for in the act.

Those are not irreconcilable differences, with the possible
exception of whether we shall guarantee 100 percent support.
That comes pretty near to being a different philosophy. As far as
I am concerned, we can make a few minor amendments to title
II of the Agricultural Act of 1948 and let it go into effect on January 1, and say that three-quarters of the Brannan plan is now in
operation inasmuch as a considerable part of the Brannan plan
was taken from title II of the 1948 act.[28]

Brannan was "gratified" by Aiken's "objective and cooperative attitude" and was "now hopeful that some legislation of real value may
yet be passed by this Congress."[29]

In spite of these conciliatory overtures, all sides had too much at
stake politically for a compromise to be consummated. Some members of Congress sincerely wanted a nonpartisan approach, but politics
as usual carried the season. Many Senate Democrats were committed
to the passage of a Democratic farm law, but to the administration's
chagrin, this did not mean the passage of its plan. In addition, the
Farm Bureau, which continued its relentless campaign against the
Truman administration in general and the Brannan plan in particular,
had considerable influence in the upper house.[30]

Despite the strength and persistence of the opposition, Brannan
stumped the country for his program, with Truman's blessing. The
president had high praise for Brannan's work and believed they were
making some real progress on the farm program. On July 9, Truman
wrote, "Keep up the good work and if you need any boost from me
I am available."[31] Although scholars have argued that Truman really

28. Senate Committee on Agricultural and Forestry Committee, *Hearings
before the Subcommittee on the Agricultural Adjustment Act of 1949,* 81st Cong.,
1st sess., July 7–19, 1949, 113; Brannan's Senate Subcommittee statement, July
7, 1949, Price Supports folder, Brannan Papers.

29. Brannan to Homer Duff, president, Oklahoma State Farmers Union, July
12, 1949, Farm Program 6, Office of the Secretary of Agriculture, RG 16, NA.

30. Hope to Joseph W. Martin Jr., Republican floor leader, July 16, 1949, FF,
Hope Papers; Aubrey Williams, *Southern Farmer,* to Wesley McCune, July 28,
1949, Farm Program 6, Office of the Secretary of Agriculture, RG 16, NA.

31. Truman to Brannan, July 9, 1949, PSF, Truman Papers; Truman, *Public
Papers of the Presidents, 1949,* 427.

did not put up much of a fight for the Brannan plan, the secretary apparently never held this opinion. When interviewed nearly four decades after the fight, Brannan had nothing but praise for the former president, saying that Truman "was a great guy to work for." He insisted that President Truman made every effort to show his support for and commitment to the department's recommendations—a position born out by Clifford Hope's comment to the president of the Kansas Farm Bureau that "the Administration is using every weapon in its arsenal to hook the Democratic Members into line [behind the Pace-Brannan bill]."[32]

By the end of the month, it became all too obvious that the Brannan plan had no chance of passage in 1949. But the fight was still important, as the secretary and his supporters looked toward 1950. Proponents and opponents expected the administration's plan to be a major issue in the next congressional campaign, and pro-Brannan forces continued to believe that educating farmers and the general public was the key to ultimate success. The Republican opposition had long been of the opinion that the Brannan plan was designed more for the 1950 election than for passage in 1949. As Hope argued on August 5, "I think the Brannan plan is dead for the time being, but we can't be too sure that it won't be an issue in the next campaign. Brannan and the CIO will use it if possible." The GOP, he cautioned, must be ready to "meet it as an issue."[33]

After the conclusion of its hearings, Senator Anderson's subcommittee began working on a new bill. Despite his obvious disappointment and continued efforts for the Brannan plan, the secretary insisted that he was ready and willing to assist the Congress in any way he could. Therefore, he was quite disturbed by a wire service report that Democratic and Republican senators had agreed to work out compromise legislation "minus the help of Secretary Brannan." The statement

32. Hope to H. A. Praeger, July 16, 1949, FF, Hope Papers; Brannan, interview. For an example of Brannan's efforts, see Speech to Farmers Coop Picnic, Juneau, WI, July 31, 1949, Public Relations 10–3, Office of the Secretary of Agriculture, RG 16, NA.

33. Hope to Dale Richardson, and to Herman W. Cramer, August 5, 1949, FF, Hope Papers; Hubert H. Humphrey to Brannan, July 28, 1949; Brannan to Cooley and to Stephen Pace, July 22, 1949; and Brannan to Leonard Denholm, South Dakota Farmers Union, July 22, 1949, Farm Program 6, Office of the Secretary of Agriculture, RG 16, NA.

had not been attributed to a member of Senator Thomas's agricultural committee, but Brannan asked Thomas to help clear up the "unfortunate inference... that I or any of the members of my staff are unwilling to aid the committee in any way possible." The reverse was actually the truth, Brannan insisted: "in fact we are at this moment undertaking to put some of Senator Anderson's views with respect to price supports in legislative language at his request."[34]

Secretary Brannan, who had so effectively used agricultural policy in the politically charged campaign of 1948 and who had frequently taken to the stump and the airwaves to promote his particular policy for agriculture, also repeatedly insisted that the USDA was just a servant of the Congress. Typical of this apparent contradictory attitude and approach was the following paragraph in his July 27 letter to Thomas:

> I wonder if I might also impose upon you to help me clarify the term "compromise" which has been used frequently lately in connection with the efforts to formulate a farm price support program. I am not aware that there is any position of the Department to be compromised. We have simply offered our suggestions and recommendations for an effective price support program at the request of both you and Chairman Cooley of the House Agricultural Committee. Obviously, your committees are at liberty to accept or reject our suggestions in whole or in part. Such of the suggestions as are accepted by either committee and find their way into legislation will be carried out to the best of our ability. And, with equal certainty, I assure you that any other legislation in this or any other field which becomes law will be diligently, earnestly and gladly put in force and effect.[35]

Did Brannan fail to see the inconsistency between his words and deeds? Or was this just his way of trying to have the best of both worlds?

34. Brannan to Thomas, July 27, 1949, Farm Program 6, Office of the Secretary of Agriculture, RG 16, NA. Wire service story quoted in this letter.

35. Brannan to Thomas, July 27, 1949, Farm Program 6, Office of the Secretary of Agriculture, RG 16, NA. On that very same day, Senator Aiken wrote University of Illinois economist H. C. M. Case: "Secretary Brannan came before our Senate Committee yesterday and gave a perfect demonstration of complete uncooperativeness. He insisted it was the Brannan plan or nothing.... At one time I had strong hopes that Charlie Brannan would be a good Secretary, but those hopes have pretty well faded now" (Aiken to Case, July 27, 1949, Farm Bill 1948, Correspondence 1949, Aiken Papers).

Whatever the answers to these questions, Brannan's paradoxical behavior did not go unnoticed. As early as March 22, 1949, Brannan had been called to task on this very point. During his testimony before a special subcommittee of the House agricultural committee that was holding hearings on marketing quotas for corn, the secretary insisted that policy decisions were the province of the committee and Congress. The department would make recommendations and provide any assistance requested of it, but the rest "is your business, because we cannot tell the Congress that it has to pass anything." Congressman Andresen, still bitter, as were many Republicans, about the administration's conduct during the past election, admitted to being "a little confused" about Brannan's present attitude.

> I recall that the Eightieth Congress was castigated by certain people because we did pass certain farm legislation and other legislation. I am wondering if the Secretary has in mind that it is now up to the Congress and the committee to formulate a piece of agricultural legislation, or if we are going to listen to the recommendations of the Department later on?
>
> ... If we do not follow your recommendations, will certain people who administer the laws go out and give the Eighty-first Congress the same kind of tongue lashing that the Eightieth Congress got? You have done that, you know.[36]

Whether his deportment during the great farm policy debate of 1949 was inconsistent, contradictory, overly partisan, or (at worst) hypocritical, Brannan was invariable with regard to his commitment to the principles enunciated by his department. He persisted to the end in his efforts to influence farm legislation in this preferred direction. In a formal statement of his views on the Anderson subcommittee's recommended price support bill, the secretary clearly stated his objections. Although Brannan was "gratified" that the subcommittee had "incorporated many of the suggestions made during our discussions," in reality the fundamental differences remained. The most significant difference between the Brannan plan and the subcommittee's

---

36. House Committee, *General Farm Program* (pt. 1), 82. Brannan had no chance to respond to this interrogatory because Senator Pace adjourned the session.

proposal was the subcommittee bill's "failure to provide any effective
and efficient method of support for perishable commodities.... I
refer, of course, to the complete lack of authority in the bill for the
use of production payments or the provision of any substitute device
to accomplish this very desirable end." In conclusion, Brannan declared: "I have indicated in the foregoing a belief in the inadequacy of
the proposed bill to meet the highly complex and difficult problems
with which the Department will be faced in the coming years. Nevertheless, I wish to assure the Congress that once this or any modification or variation of this bill becomes law, every possible effort of the
Department will be exerted, without reservation, to make it work as
successfully and effectively as possible."[37]

By this time, Anderson's subcommittee had rejected the legislative
expressions of the Brannan plan, and the secretary's final efforts to
influence the new bill (S. 2522) were of no avail. To salvage his party's
chances for passing its own farm measure, Truman began late in August
to support compromise efforts. On the afternoon of August 31, the
president and Secretary Brannan met at the White House with congressional leaders to discuss a solution to the farm program impasse
in the Senate agricultural committee. To his cousin Ethel Nolan, Truman wrote:

> [the meeting] was to be behind closed doors and not publicly
> advertised. But the old senator from Oklahoma who is chair-
> man of the Agri. Committee in the Senate whose name is Elmer
> [Thomas] immediately called in reporters and told them that he
> had a date with me to tell me what my farm policy should be. Of
> course all the other gentlemen were as mad as D.A.R. committee
> women when the chairwoman gets her picture in the paper with-
> out them and my conference started off in ice cold atmosphere
> (not air conditioned). But by a few "well turned phrases" and
> some conversation about Democrats getting elected next year—
> my conference was a success.[38]

37. Brannan to Anderson, August 12, 1949, Farm Program 6, Office of the
Secretary of Agriculture, RG 16, NA.
38. Ferrell, ed., *Off the Record,* 163; "File memo," September 1, 1949, regarding presidential meeting with Brannan, Lucas, Thomas, Anderson, Pace, and
Cooley, August 31, 3 p.m., OF, Truman Papers; Anderson, *Outsider in the Senate,*
99; Truman, *Public Papers of the Presidents, 1949,* 459; Brannan to Truman, August 31, 1949, Farm Program 6, Office of the Secretary of Agriculture, RG 16, NA.

The conference did nothing, however, for the administration's program, and as the *New York Times* reported the next morning, the farm bill "sent to the Senate by its Agricultural Committee [after the White House conference] bore no resemblance . . . to the plan of Secretary Brennan." According to the *New Republic,* Truman had "conceded defeat of a major part of his Fair Deal program—the Brannan farm plan."[39]

The Anderson bill enjoyed strong Farm Bureau backing, largely because it managed to incorporate the principle of flexible price supports.[40] It also had received the endorsement of Senator Aiken. In a statement designed to clarify and to defend the provisions of Title II of the existing law, the Republican senator explained that the Anderson bill "would have the effect of strengthening the Agricultural Act of 1948 and of making its provisions less susceptible to misinterpretation. . . . With some modification, the over-all effect of the Anderson proposal, which does not repeal the 1948 act, is to strengthen the means of attaining the objectives of that act." But even if it did not pass, Aiken insisted, "we will still have after January 1, 1950, the strongest, most workable permanent farm support price program ever placed on the statute books, and which will be, from the standpoint of the farmer, the consumer or the taxpayer vastly superior to either the House passed Gore bill or the Brannan plan."[41]

Congressman Hope agreed: "It is not too different from the Hope-Aiken bill and I think it is an improvement in some ways." He predicted the Anderson bill would pass the Senate and believed it was the best they could do at this time. Although Hope maintained a good personal relationship with the secretary, he shared the concerns of some of his Republican colleagues and was afraid that if the Hope-Aiken Act were left alone it would not be administered effectively.

39. *New York Times,* September 1, 1949, 3; "Defeat of the Farm Plan," 7.

40. The secretary and the president received a number of letters and telegrams from state bureaus throughout the country urging support for the Anderson approach (see, for example, Missouri Farm Bureau to Truman, August 30, 1949, OF, Truman Papers; E. Howard Hill, Iowa Farm Bureau, to Brannan, August 30, 1949, Farm Program 6, Office of the Secretary of Agriculture, RG 16, NA).

41. *CR,* 81st Cong., 1st sess., Senate, September 13, 1949, 95, pt. 10: 12775–76; Aiken to H. C. M. Case, July 27, 1949, Farm Bill 1948, Correspondence 1949, Aiken Papers.

"Everything indicates," he wrote, "that Secretary Brannan is so sold on his own plan and so opposed to the Hope-Aiken bill that his administration of the latter will be such as to discredit it. On the other hand he cannot very well do that with the Anderson bill if it is passed by this Congress."[42]

President Truman, like his secretary of agriculture, continued his appeal for a new support program and attacked the critics of the Brannan plan. He also continued to endorse "production payments" as the "most promising method yet suggested" for supporting "perishables." However, in a fiery Labor Day speech in Des Moines, Iowa, that was reminiscent of his Dexter campaign speech a year earlier, Truman left himself room for later support of a congressional alternative if, as he explained, it accomplished the same basic objectives.

Publicly, Truman remained noncommittal with respect to the subcommittee's bill, keeping his criticism low-key, and the USDA helped work out some of the technical problems.[43] Some Brannan plan supporters, however, did not feel so inclined toward circumspection. Jim Patton, the NFU president who was never accused of being too discreet, remained on the offensive and continued to call for passage of the Brannan plan. He claimed the Anderson bill would keep "farmers at the head of the march toward another depression" and charged that the AFBF and the food processors were the main supporters and lobbyists for S. 2522. Samuel Guard, editor of the *Breeders Gazette* and another die-hard administration supporter, planned to "take Clint Anderson apart" in his October issue. He accused the Senate subcommittee of bringing "forth a mouse" after all its labors and told his subscribers that rather "than the silly Anderson Compromise, we'd a heap better stick to the Aiken Law.... Or we'd better take Albert

42. Hope to Pete A. Steffens, September 17, 1949, FF, Hope Papers.
43. Truman, *Public Papers of the Presidents, 1949,* 466–69, 511, 520, 525. USDA efforts were less strident for a time after the White House conference, but the cause was by no means abandoned. Brannan himself continued to take every opportunity to plug his proposals (Brannan to Senator Thomas, report on S. 2482, September 29, 1949, Legislation 1; "The City Dweller's Stake in a Sound Farm Program," Brannan speech to Executives' Club of Chicago, September 30, 1949, Public Relations 7, Office of the Secretary of Agriculture, RG 16, NA).

Gore's bill even and stay right where we are on price supports for another year."[44]

Many senators also were not yet convinced that the Anderson subcommittee bill was the best thing for the country or, at least, for their constituencies. The floor debate, which raged during the first two weeks of October, underscored the lack of consensus among Democrats in the upper chamber. Anderson led the charge for his bill that, as he pointed out, was based on the principle of flexible price supports that had been endorsed by the USDA and the political platforms of both parties in 1948.[45] Strong commitment for 90 percent of parity supports, however, made the battle difficult.

Southern and western congressmen, led by Milton Young and Richard B. Russell (D-GA), tried to replace the Anderson bill with, what amounted to, a permanent 90 percent plan.[46] Anderson spoke out forcefully against the Russell-Young amendment, pointing out that the potato program came under heavy fire because of rigid 90 percent support. He argued that this should not be allowed to happen to the entire farm program for basics. The senators should heed what the Farm Bureau (and all other farm organizations except the NFU) had come to realize. Anderson contended "that high, rigid supports are bound to be the rocks on which the whole farm program will be scuttled, if it shall be scuttled in our generation." Senator Aiken agreed that consumers might rise up against an agricultural program that included this amendment and warned the Senate that it must not try to "get too much in the name of the farmer." He reminded his colleagues that farmers had "political power far out of proportion to our [farmers] numbers." Senator Russell countered that flexible supports should apply only to perishables and insisted that farmers would consider rejection of this amendment a step backward. He claimed that all he was doing was arguing for the equal treatment of

44. Guard to Brannan and Wesley McCune, September 8 and 20, 1949, and editorial, Farm Program 6, Office of the Secretary of Agriculture, RG 16, NA; Patton quoted in *New York Times,* September 4, 1949, 18.

45. *CR,* 81st Cong., 1st sess., Senate, October 3, 1949, 95, pt. 10: 13614.

46. *CR,* 81st Cong., 1st sess., Senate, October 4, 1949, 95, pt. 10: 13742–73. This was an effort to substitute the Gore bill for the Anderson bill (Schapsmeier and Schapsmeier, "Farm Policy from FDR to Eisenhower," 366).

all basic commodities; but the amendment was blocked by a vote of 37 to 38.[47] Moments later, however, a move to reconsider resulted in another vote. This time, on roll call, the vote was a 37 to 37 tie, and the president of the Senate, Vice President Alben Barkley, who favored the 90 percent support idea, broke the deadlock.[48]

Immediately, Senator Aiken gained the floor and exclaimed: "Mr. President, the Senate has now 'out-Brannaned' the Brannan plan." He insisted that the cost of this 90 percent program, which he estimated at five billion dollars, would be more than the administration's plan and accused wheat and cotton growers of ganging "up successfully on the rest of agriculture in the United States."[49] Later that evening, with the help of Majority Leader Scott Lucas, an advocate of the flexible approach, Anderson was able to have the bill recommitted. With a few minor concessions, specifically the inclusion of pulled wool on the list of commodities to receive mandatory supports, Anderson won the necessary votes. He reinstated the sliding scale by deleting the Russell-Young language and reported the revised bill on October 6.[50]

At his "200th press conference" that morning, President Truman fielded only one question related to agriculture: "Mr. President, which is the Democratic Party's position on the farm bill, Barkley's or Senator Lucas's?" The president responded with an ambiguous directive

47. Anderson, *CR,* 81st Cong., 1st sess., Senate, October 4, 1949, 95, pt. 10: 13754, (Aiken) 13755, (Russell) 13756, (amendment vote) 13759. Twenty-seven Democrats and ten Republicans voted yea; seventeen Democrats and twenty-one Republicans voted nay (Rich, *U.S. Agricultural Policy in the Postwar Years,* 29).

48. *CR,* 81st Cong., 1st sess., Senate, October 4, 1949, 95, pt. 10: 13773; Matusow, *Farm Policies and Politics,* 216. Representative Gore reportedly convinced Senator Garrett L. Withers, who had been appointed to Barkley's vacant seat in January 1949 (and did not stand for election in November), that if the move for 90 percent were defeated the House would kill tobacco's special privileges. Although he had initially voted with Anderson, Withers made the motion to reconsider and voted yea (for Russell-Young) upon reconsideration. Several other changes occurred on the second roll call, but the South remained firm, and the yeas were able to hold their original tally. Although the nays got three converts, they lost three to the not voting group.

49. *CR,* 81st Cong., 1st sess., Senate, October 4, 1949, 95, pt. 10: 13774.

50. Rich, *U.S. Agricultural Policy in the Postwar Years,* 29; *CR,* 81st Cong., 1st sess., October 6, 1949, 95, pt. 18, *Daily Digest:* D681; *CR* (Senate), October 6, 1949, 95, pt. 11: 13984. The Russell-Young amendment was offered again on October 7 but rejected 27 to 45 (*CR* [Senate], October 6, 1949, 95, pt. 11: 14115).

to "read my message on it . . . and you will get all the information."[51] The administration, which had stayed out of the Senate fray to this point, according to Allen Matusow, reacted to the "appearance of the strengthened Anderson bill" and tried to "exert leadership." "Brannan wrote a public letter to make clear his opposition to flexible supports, and by implication, the Anderson bill."[52] Brannan also had been contacting senators to line up support for Russell-Young.

Unfortunately, the secretary's influence could not always stand up to counter pressures from back home. On October 8 Senator Lester C. Hunt (D-WY) wrote to apologize for voting "contrary to [the] commitment I had made to you on the phone." Subsequently, Hunt explained, the secretary of the Wyoming Farm Bureau who had insisted that he oppose the 90 percent parity amendment had contacted him. Since the Farm Bureau represented nearly all the farmers in his state, he voted nay. Brannan's reply was empathetic, but he informed the senator that the leadership of the Farm Bureau in many states was not reflective of its membership. He had no specific information on Wyoming, but "everywhere farm sentiment has been gauged it has shown the Farm Bureau leadership to be misrepresenting the sentiments."[53]

Anderson reacted to this increased USDA involvement by telling the press that the department was as "anxious as it can be" to defeat his bill, "because if it doesn't there won't be such a case for the Brannan Plan." Another White House meeting was held on October 11, but presidential pressure for high supports (since the Brannan plan was dead) did not sway the Senate leaders; both Anderson and Lucas openly disagreed with Truman at the conference. Despite these provocations, Truman avoided a public airing of his differences with the

51. Truman, *Public Papers of the Presidents, 1949,* 501, 503. See also Brannan to Truman, October 6, PSF, Truman Papers.

52. Matusow, *Farm Policies and Politics,* 217. For the public letter, see Brannan to Thomas, October 7, 1949, Farm Program 6, Office of the Secretary of Agriculture, RG 16, NA; *CR,* 81st Cong., 1st sess., Senate, October 7, 1949, 95, pt. 10: 14126.

53. Hunt to Brannan, October 8, 1949, and Brannan to Hunt, October 28, 1949, Farm Program 6, Office of the Secretary of Agriculture, RG 16, NA; Allan Kline to Aiken, telegram, October 6, 1949 (and others from various farm bureaus congratulating Aiken for his opposition to the Russell-Young Amendment and support for the Anderson bill), "Farm Bill 1948, Correspondence 1949, Aiken Papers.

former cabinet secretary. On October 12, the Anderson bill passed
the Senate and was sent to conference. At his press conference the
next day, the president cut short a questioner, who was asking about
a report that he opposed the "flexible price supports in the Senate
bill," with a "no comment. . . . I will comment on it when it comes up
to me for signature."[54]

The Gore-Anderson bill, a political compromise that made concessions to nearly everyone, emerged from this conference. It contained
the principle of flexible supports but delayed their implementation
even further, and, because of southern influence, the bill allowed for
much higher support levels than Anderson initially suggested. The
Agricultural Act of 1949 (often called the "Anderson Act") "was, in
the main," according to Murray R. Benedict, "a victory for those who
favored high mandatory price supports and was, primarily, a product
of the thinking of the Southern Democrat bloc rather than of those
whose views were expressed in the proposals made by Secretary Brannan." It was the "handiwork," explained Edward Schapsmeier and
Frederick Schapsmeier, "of Southern Democrats and Midwestern
Republicans, [who] once more delayed implementation of flexibility."
Anderson himself later admitted that his flexible supports had been
seriously weakened by compromises, and that the sentiment for 90
percent parity was so strong that all they were really able to do was
move toward flexibility.[55]

The principle of flexibility as contained in the 1948 act was retained,
and provision was made for a sliding scale to determine the level of
support depending on production. It ranged from 90 to 75 percent

54. Truman, *Public Papers of the Presidents, 1949,* 511. Anderson's remarks
quoted in the *New York Times,* October 8, 1949, 2. The October 11 meeting was
attended by Brannan, Lucas, Thomas, Anderson, Pace, Cooley, Rayburn, McCormack, and the vice president (see *Congressional Digest* 29 [March 1950]: 79; file
memo, October 11, 1949, OF, Truman Papers; *CR,* 81st Cong., 1st sess., Senate,
October 12, 1949, 95, pt. 11: 14324). Actually, the Senate took up H.R. 5345
(Gore bill) on October 7 and then voted to substitute the Anderson bill (S. 2522)
for everything after the enacting clause. From this point on it went by the House
bill number.
55. Benedict, *Farm Policies of the United States,* 481; Schapsmeier and
Schapsmeier, "Farm Policy from FDR to Eisenhower," 367; Forsythe, "Clinton P.
Anderson," 629. See also Saloutos, "Agricultural Organizations and Farm Policy,"
391–92; Anderson, *Outsider in the Senate,* 98; Estabrook, "Bogey in the Brannan
Plan," 76.

of parity for basic commodities. This only set the minimum level of support, however, and the scale was to be phased in over a two-year period. Cooperating producers were to receive "not less than 90 per centum of the parity price for the 1950 crop of any basic agricultural commodity" and "not less than 80 per centum" for their 1951 crop.[56] Most nonbasic commodities were to be supported, at the discretion of the secretary of agriculture, between 90 percent and 75 percent of parity. "Thus," concluded Benedict,

> for virtually all commodities except the "basic" crops there was provision for adjusting price supports to the realities. But it was in the "basic" crop segment that high mandatory price supports were most likely to give trouble. These were the ones involving large volume and high cost. They were also the ones with fewest alternatives and the greatest tendency to chronic overproduction. Hence, it was in respect to these crops that the political and economic repercussions were most significant.[57]

Many other provisions were carried over from the 1948 act, such as the retention of the 50 percent minimum parity price support for basic crops if marketing quotas had been disapproved. But the new legislation placed less emphasis on keeping down supply as a condition for receiving high supports. Wages paid to hired labor were also to be included in determining the costs of what farmers bought; therefore the levels of support prices would be raised. The new act also reflected the continued attachment to the old parity and its original base period (1909–1914). "Notwithstanding the foregoing provisions of this section," the act read, "the parity price for any basic agricultural commodity, as of any date during the four-year period beginning January 1, 1950, shall not be less than its parity price computed in the manner used prior to the enactment of the Agricultural Act of 1949."[58] The new formula would be used, therefore, only where it would bring the producers of basic commodities higher prices. Efforts to begin a readjustment in American agriculture, contemplated in the 1948 act,

56. Rasmussen, ed., *Agriculture in the United States,* 4:2960; "An Act to Stabilize Prices of Agricultural Commodities," *U.S. Statutes At Large* (October 31, 1949), Public Law 439, Chapter 792, 1051.
57. Benedict, *Farm Policies of the United States,* 482–83.
58. Rasmussen, ed., *Agriculture in the United States,* 4:2965.

with an emphasis on livestock production over the traditional field crops, were thus further postponed.

Although hailed by Senator Lucas as permanent farm legislation, *The Nation* doubted that the new law would "prove anything of the sort." It was a result of "trading between pressure groups," and the paper editorialized that "in general this compromise bill seems thoroughly unsatisfactory." There were some calls for a presidential veto and, once again, serious objections were voiced within the administration. The most notable protest came from the Bureau of the Budget, which, after detailed study, concluded, "In comparison with the Aiken Act, the enrolled bill is clearly inferior, except to the extent that the higher levels of support are considered desirable." The BOB believed that the "reduced flexibility and high support levels on basic crops" were a disadvantage that would lead to increased expenditures. Bureau officials also criticized the Anderson bill's failure to provide for production payments and the fact that it would make necessary production adjustments even more difficult. In the report that he personally delivered to the White House on October 28, Director Frank Pace warned the president about the serious surplus (storage) problems facing the CCC and clearly stated the BOB's preference for the Aiken Act that "would provide a better framework for a workable, long-range farm support program than would the present bill."[59]

The USDA also found much to criticize in the Anderson bill, but the department had previously decided to support the Gore-Anderson compromise as a stopgap measure.[60] In his report to Director Pace, Brannan admitted that this bill had many defects. The secretary's list of deficiencies included: the absence of a "realistic income standard" as the basis for price supports; the failure to provide for "mandatory minimum level support" on livestock and poultry products; and the general inadequacy in the "methods of support" provided by the proposed legislation—it did not allow the use of Brannan's preferred production payment approach and the minimum support levels for

59. Report to "Director," October 26, 1949, Agricultural Adjustment Act of 1949, Office of the Secretary of Agriculture, RG 16, NA; *The Nation* 169 (October 29, 1949): 406.

60. Charles Rohrer, national committeeman, Indiana Progressive party, to Matt Connelly, October 8, 1949, OF, Truman Papers; McCune to Connelly, October 14, Farm Program 6, Office of the Secretary of Agriculture, RG 16, NA.

basic commodities were "still too low." "The new parity formula established in this bill" was better in light of "recent experience" than the "existing formula," the secretary wrote, but its provision for allowing a choice between the old and the new (depending on which was higher) "until 1954 on the basic commodities" would "undoubtedly open the parity concept and the price support program to attack."

Brannan cited only one specific example of where the Anderson bill was "more desirable" than "the legislation [Aiken bill] that will go into effect on January 1, 1950, if this Bill does not become law." This was "with respect to levels of price support and commodity coverage." Nevertheless, the secretary believed support levels were pegged too low, largely because of the provision for a gradual shift toward a sliding scale of price supports, and he raised several objections with regard to the commodities that were given priority status. "I have not yet been convinced," Brannan wrote, for example, "that there is any sound justification for including tung nuts, honey and mohair among the commodities that will be given first call on available funds." Despite these and other objectionable features, included on four full pages of the secretary's eight-page report, the department had been given sufficient funds to administer the program for the current fiscal year, and "it is recommended that the President approve it."[61]

The third major opinion generated from within the administration came from the president's Council of Economic Advisors. In a letter to Director Pace, Vice Chairman Leon H. Keyserling, speaking for himself and for John D. Clark, informed the BOB that they were recommending that the president sign the measure primarily because it "settle[d] the price support program for 1950 before the agricultural year" commenced.[62] Keyserling's stated position paralleled that of the USDA. As he saw it, "the enrolled bill possesses certain distinct

61. Brannan to Pace, October 25, 1949, Bill file/H.R. 5345, Bureau of the Budget, Truman Papers; same report, Agricultural Adjustment Act of 1949, Bureau of the Budget, RG 51, NA.

62. Keyserling to Pace, October 27, 1949, Agricultural Adjustment Act of 1949, Bureau of the Budget, RG 51, NA. See also Flash, *Economic Advice and Presidential Leadership,* 20–28; Donald K. Pickens, "Truman's Council of Economic Advisers and the Legacy of New Deal Liberalism," in Levantrosser, ed., *Harry S. Truman: The Man from Independence,* 249; Truman, *Public Papers of the Presidents, 1949,* 523–24. Clark was the third member of the three-member council. Chairman Nourse's break with the administration on many policy choices,

and important advantages over the current law: conspicuously, that it raises the minimum level of mandatory supports for basic commodities to 75 per cent, provides extension to dairy products, and graduates over a three-year period the now contemplated downward adjustment of supports." With regard to the latter point, the delay would "afford opportunity for more study and better conclusions with respect to basic agricultural policy." The bill had "substantial defects," however, the most important of which was "its elimination of certain production payments and its concentration solely upon keeping prices high instead of upon stimulating distribution and consumption.... In short, it omits certain creative features of existing legislation and recently discussed agricultural plans which should not summarily be dismissed."[63]

President Truman signed the Agricultural Act of 1949 on October 31, 1949, "because it provides better protection against declining farm prices and income than did the legislation of the 80th Congress which this Act replaces." He was not particularly enthused about the new law, but at least the Democratic Congress had "decided as a matter of national policy that we cannot afford to allow farm prices and income to go down out of relationship with the balance of our economy. I am confident," the president concluded, "that next year the Congress will consider with equal foresight the policy questions which are left undecided."[64] Thus, Truman managed publicly to applaud the Eighty-first Congress for its efforts in the area of agricultural policy. But the president, who had condemned the Democratic Seventy-ninth Congress, privately admitted that the new Democratic Eighty-first Congress had proven only slightly more receptive to

including this one, had become more public. He had already turned in his resignation and was succeeded by Keyserling—first as acting chairman, and finally chairman in 1950.

63. Keyserling to Pace, October 27, 1949, Agricultural Adjustment Act of 1949, Bureau of the Budget, RG 51, NA. Keyserling closed with the following: "Mr. Nourse has requested that we note that he has at this time refrained from joining Mr. Clark and me in considering and expressing the Council's views on this enrolled bill."

64. Statement issued by Truman on signing H.R. 5345, Bill file/H.R. 5345, Bureau of the Budget, Truman Papers; Brannan to Pace, October 25, 1949 (including a copy of statement), Public Relations 10–2, Office of the Secretary of Agriculture, RG 16, NA.

In December 1949, Congressman Clifford R. Hope, who represented southwest Kansas in the U.S. House of Representative for thirty years (1927–1957), met with members of the Lane County Farm Bureau at Dighton, no doubt to discuss the provisions of the recently passed Agricultural Act of 1949. Courtesy of the Kansas State Historical Society.

his legislative program than had the "Do-nothing Republican 80th Congress."[65]

Brannan's support for the modified Anderson bill hinged on the fact that it continued high price supports and effectively delayed the implementation of the sliding scale for several years. Although in August he had said that he believed "it would be tragic if we were left saddled with the restrictive provisions of H.R. 5617 [Gore bill], with a mandatory 90 percent support level and inadequate program operating authority," Brannan supported the Gore-Anderson compromise in October.[66] Almost everyone agreed that Title II of the

65. Ferrell, ed., *Off the Record,* 168; Ferrell, ed., *Dear Bess: The Letters from Harry to Bess Truman, 1910–1959,* 526.

66. Brannan to Senator Elmer Thomas, August 6, 1949, Farm Program 6, Office of the Secretary of Agriculture, RG 16, NA. This lengthy letter dealt primarily with the egg support program that was quickly becoming for 1949 what

Agricultural Act of 1948, previously scheduled to take effect January 1, 1950, contained many more of the Brannan principles than did the Anderson bill. Politics, and his commitment to the NFU position that the bottom line was at least 90 percent of parity for 1950, must be taken as the primary reasons for the Brannan action.[67]

The secretary remained intransigent on this issue. He would not compromise his opposition to the implementation of a flexible price support system for storable commodities such as wheat and cotton even though it would have given him the production payments tool for perishables. Production payments were no panacea, of course, but they were a logical approach to the support of perishable or non-storable commodities such as eggs and potatoes, and they were allowed under the Aiken part of the Agricultural Act of 1948 (Hope-Aiken Law). Compromise here might have been a first step toward the eventual adoption of a production payment option for the major storable commodities as well.

The capping of production that was eligible for support payments would also have been logical, and, perhaps, it would have been possible had compromise been the order of the season. The eighteen hundred-unit limitation probably would have had little immediate impact, but a new and potentially significant principle would have been established had this feature of the Brannan plan been preserved. Facing the political realities of 1949, Brannan was quick to abandon that aspect of his proposal, but he insisted that he remained committed to it for the long haul.[68]

---

the potato problem had been in 1946 and 1947; in December 1949, only 25 percent of Americans polled approved of the egg program, while 30 percent favored supports for potatoes (Gallup, *Gallup Poll,* 2:872). See also Ralph Baker, "What to Do about ... Egg Price Props?" 15.

67. Brannan, of course, had no corner on political motivation ("Farm Facts in the 81st Congress," 74; Black to Brannan, July 29, 1949, Farm Program 6, Office of the Secretary of Agriculture, RG 16, NA). See also Pace, *CR,* 81st Cong., 1st sess., Senate, July 20, 1949, 95, pt. 7: 9855.

68. Congressman Hugh B. Mitchell to Brannan, June 30, and Brannan to Mitchell, July 12, 1949, Farm Program 6; W. N. Thompson to Wesley McCune, March 14, 1950; McCune to Thompson, March 21, 1950; and Brannan to Clarence Poe, *Progressive Farmer,* May 25, 1950, Farm Program 6–1, Office of the Secretary of Agriculture, RG 16, NA.

Interestingly, in discussing the defeat of the Brannan plan in his 1956 *Memoirs,* Truman placed considerable emphasis on the unit-limitation feature of the proposal. Under the old plan, according to the former president, too much money was being paid out to very large, commercial farms.

> There is probably a place in our economy for this kind of farm operation, but it is not as vital to the life and welfare of the nation as the work of the millions of families who—often literally—'toil in the sweat of their brow'....
>
> Secretary Brannan warned me that this recommendation in favor of what we called the family-sized farmer would be attacked as containing political implications....
>
> Interestingly enough, the unit limitation was hardly criticized at all, and the reason for this, I believe, was that the critics of the plan saw the irrefutable reasoning on which the limitation policy was based.[69]

Truman's memory was obviously quite selective on this point. Generally speaking, the reasoning was "irrefutable," but criticism of the "limitation policy" was relatively short-lived because the principle was abandoned before the fight had hardly begun. Even though one could and some did argue that the limitation was too low—by Brannan's own estimate only a portion of the production on about 2 percent of the nation's farms would have been excluded—this was an inherently just policy that simply did not have political legs at this point in time.[70]

Unbeknownst to the administration, 1949 had been the first and last chance for the Brannan plan, and three years of inability to significantly influence long-range agriculture policy followed. Truman and Brannan were geared for a renewed battle for the secretary's plan in 1950 and hoped to make it a major issue in that year's congressional campaigns. In light of the continued problems in agriculture, especially

69. Truman, *Memoirs,* vol. 2, 266–67.
70. According to Congressman Hope, Brannan's "apparent definition of a family-sized farm is considerably more than 160 acres.... On the basis of present prices this would mean about $26,000 worth of production which is a fairly good sized farm" (Hope to Clayton E. Kline, April 16, 1949, FF, Hope Papers). For Brannan's estimate, see House Committee, *General Farm Program* (pt. 2), 152.

the surplus problem that plagued several supported commodities, Brannan had every reason to be optimistic. Unfortunately, other events in 1950 were to attract far more public attention and make another change in farm policy appear unwise. Brannan carried on the fight, but by midyear Truman was fully occupied in other areas. The battle against communism at home and abroad and the increased demand for farm products stimulated by the Korean conflict, once again postponed the day of reckoning for the high price support policy.

8

THE BRANNAN PLAN IN 1950

Truman felt somewhat beleaguered at the end of the 1949 session of Congress. On November 1, the day after he signed the Agricultural Act of 1949, Truman wrote, "I have another hell of a day." "Trying to make the 81st Congress perform is and has been worse than cussing the 80th.... I've kissed and petted more consarned S.O.B. so-called Democrats and left wing Republicans than all the Presidents put together. I have very few people fighting my battle in Congress as I fought F.D.R.'s."[1] The Fair Deal had not fared well in 1949, but publicly Truman exuded confidence for the future. In an address at St. Paul, Minnesota's "Truman Day" celebration, the president renewed his campaign against the "calamity of the 80th Congress" and told his audience that the Democratic Congress had "reversed the backward trend and has made substantial progress in many fields. Moreover, I am confident that the 81st Congress will accomplish a good deal more next year in its second session."[2] Unfortunately for the administration of Harry S. Truman, this did not prove to be the case. The last session of what Republicans dubbed the "Eighty-worst" Congress did not treat Truman's domestic program any better than did the first session, and the Brannan plan was one of the casualties.

Although the farm policy debate of 1949 was disquieting, it was hardly the only problem facing Truman during his first year as president

---

1. Diary entry for November 1, 1949, in Monte M. Poen, ed., *Strictly Personal and Confidential: The Letters Harry Truman Never Mailed*, 62–63. See also Arthur Krock, "An Interview with Truman," in Krock, *In the Nation, 1932–1966*, 149–50.
2. Truman, *Public Papers of the Presidents, 1949*, 553. See Ferrell, ed., *Off the Record*, 201; Sitkoff, "Years of the Locust," 96.

in his own right. In January 1949, the president believed he had received a mandate for his domestic program. But it soon became obvious that the change of balance in Congress was not going to significantly affect relations between the White House and Capitol Hill. The conflict between Democrats who supported administration policy and Democrats who opposed various aspect of the Fair Deal made party control of Congress, regained in November 1948, of little value. The result was a dismal domestic record for the administration, which was rebuffed on civil rights, price controls, health insurance, and the Brannan farm plan. The only major piece of social legislation that the administration saw enacted, the National Housing Act of 1949, which provided programs for slum clearance, low-rent public housing, and farm-housing grants and loans, was a victory for conservative Republican senator Robert A. Taft as well as for the administration.[3]

In addition to these vital domestic issues, the administration was being challenged on other fronts. According to Congressman Richard M. Nixon of California, who had previously announced his candidacy for the U.S. Senate, "Freedom versus state socialism" was a central issue in America, as was the domestic security question, which was destined to become even more troublesome for the Truman administration during the forthcoming election year.[4] Tack on the Soviet detonation of an atomic bomb and the fall of Nationalist China, and there emerges an ominous catalog of critical issues and crises confronting the president at the end of 1949.

Through it all, Truman had not fared too badly in the public eye. "The pattern that emerged was one of favorable but not intense feelings," observed Elmo Roper. "Those who were critical of him rarely expressed fear or hatred toward him. Those who were friendly toward him were rarely strongly enthusiastic about him." In late 1949, the majority of Americans had come to respect Truman for his pugnacity and frankness. Although some expressed a lack of confidence, overall, "The man whom everybody had counted out in 1948 was

3. Barton J. Bernstein, ed., *Politics and Policies of the Truman Administration,* 14; Donovan, *Tumultuous Years,* 118–25, 127; David B. Truman, *The Congressional Party: A Case Study,* 20; *Newsweek* 34 (October 24, 1949): 21–23; Richard O. Davies, *Housing Reform during the Truman Administration,* 102.

4. Nixon, *Memoirs of Richard M. Nixon,* 73; Stephen E. Ambrose, *Nixon: The Education of a Politician, 1913–1962,* 197–212.

now a popular President in his own right." Near the end of the first session of the Eighty-first Congress, George Gallup found the president enjoying a 51 percent approval rating—not bad after a four and a half year struggle with America's postwar problems.[5]

Truman had more than survived this difficult year and was in a reasonably good position to launch another campaign for his Fair Deal program. The Democrat Eighty-first Congress's shortfall in the area of farm policy opened the door for a new Truman-Brannan offensive in 1950. "The indications are," the *Congressional Digest* editorialized, "that a drive to put across the Brannan Plan will become a part of the Administration's political campaigns next year." In a friendly article in the *New Republic,* Avrahm G. Mezerik predicted that Brannan's plan to provide reasonable consumer prices and sustained farm income "constitute the makings of a political coalition, the beginnings of which can already be seen in some states." He insisted that the plan was becoming a major national issue even though some had already written it off, and that its grassroots support in both parties was growing.[6] Disciples also were encouraged by what they considered significant signs of defection within the ranks of the major farm organizations, in particular the protest vote for the Brannan plan that had surfaced at the annual convention of the National Grange.[7]

Confident that things would only get better, the USDA wasted no

5. Roper, *You and Your Leaders: Their Actions and Your Reactions, 1936–1956,* 142–44; Gallup, *The Gallup Poll,* 2:860, 890, 903. Thirty-one percent of those polled disapproved, and 18 percent had no opinion. Interestingly, Truman did not score as well among farmers: 45 percent approved; 40 percent disapproved; and 15 percent had no opinion. By the first week of January 1950, the president's overall approval rating reflected what it had been among farmers during the previous fall; in three months, it had fallen still further to 37 percent approval and 44 percent disapproval.

6. "Highlights on 'The Hill,'" *Congressional Digest* 28 (November 1949): 259; Mezerik, "The Brannan Plan," 11. The coalition about which Mezerik wrote was the long sought after alliance between farmers and workers, a primary objective of the NFU. See also James Patton to Wesley McCune, October 11, 1949, Publications 1, General Correspondence, 1949, Office of the Secretary of Agriculture, RG 16, NA.

7. McCune to Robert T. Elson, editor of *Time* magazine, December 7, 1949 and January 3, 1950; Brannan to Joseph Fichter, master, Ohio State Grange, January 16, 1950, Public Relations 2; and Rudolph Johnson, secretary, Colorado State Grange, to Brannan, December 30, 1949, Farm Program 6–1, Office of the Secretary of Agriculture, RG 16, NA.

time in kicking off its 1950 campaign. Indeed, the day after the signing of the agricultural act, Secretary Brannan sent a reply to the president's "letter of September 26 requesting suggestions for inclusion
in the State of the Union message and your Economic Report to the
Congress." "The most urgent matter" was "improving our price support legislation," Brannan emphasized. He suggested that Truman
comment "as favorably as possible" on the signing of "the Agricultural Act of 1949," but that his remarks should be "followed by a call
for changes in this important legislation along the lines of the Administration's proposals." Brannan propounded that "special attention"
in the economic report "be given to the need for maintaining and
increasing consumption of food and other agricultural products....
This would naturally lead into, and strengthen, the need for using
production payments as a means of supporting prices of perishable
agricultural commodities and for broad scale efforts to raise the
incomes of low income consumers generally."[8]

To underscore the need for congressional action, the secretary also
supplied some information on the "essential current trends in the
farm situation." Farm production, according to the secretary's statistics, was 35 percent above prewar levels, but prices received for agricultural goods were down—21 percent below the postwar peak and
about 12 percent under levels for the fall of 1948. At the same time,
prices paid by farmers for goods were down only 5 percent and 3.5
percent respectively. But perhaps the most significant finding was that
the farmer's net income had dropped precipitously to about 15 percent
below 1948, and that projections indicated it might be a third less in
1950 than 1947. Two months later, Brannan reiterated many of the
same points and added an additional warning about the expected
further decline in the 1950 export market. Farm commodity exports
had peaked in 1947 and were down considerably during the last six
months of 1949. More than half of these exports, he said, were "being
paid for by ECA [Economic Cooperation Administration] and mili-
tary appropriations."[9]

8. Brannan to Truman, November 1, 1949, Public Relations 10–2, Office of
the Secretary of Agriculture, RG 16, NA.
9. Brannan to Truman, December 27, 1949, PSF, Truman Papers.

Thus, well before the end of 1949, the campaign of 1950 had begun. Secretary Brannan's commitment to the Agricultural Act of 1949 had been born of expediency and political necessity. He had no intention of waiting around for what he thought was its inevitable failure. According to Mezerik, the secretary had "been given the green light." Brannan traveled widely, and the USDA intensified its efforts to educate Americans about the merits of the department's preferred approach to farm policy. "Meanwhile, the Farm Bureau, *Life* magazine, the *Wall Street Journal,* the U.S. Chamber of Commerce, the metropolitan press and the radio will continue to smother news of the Brannan plan." Mezerik predicted that "in 1950 and 1952, the Brannan plan will be the great issue in the doubtful states."[10]

In December 1949, the administration had reason for some optimism in the farm policy area, but in certain respects the battle was as intense as ever. Republicans had launched their drive for a farm program for the 1950 campaign at a Sioux City, Iowa, rally in late September 1949. Although billed as a nonpartisan conference, which did include representatives from the opposition camp, the political implications were clear. Participants sought a GOP alternative to the "Brannan or Bust" farm plan but insisted that the farm problem "should not become the football of partisan politics." Republicans, proclaimed National Committee Chairman Guy George Gabrielson, "do not come with something wrapped in rolls of red tape, with the admonition that you must accept it because it has been worked out by all-wise supermen in Washington."[11] Clifford Hope repeated the charge that the Brannan program was actually the plan of organized labor. and asked, that being the case, why it was not tried on labor first. "If high incomes and low prices are a good thing for the farmer, why aren't high incomes and low wages a good thing for working people?" The consumer would benefit in many ways if government would adopt a "low wage policy," and "if the Brannan plan advocates are right, workers wouldn't lose because the Government would give

10. Mezerik, "The Brannan Plan," 13. Regarding the educational campaign, see C. A. Thaxton to Brannan, December 9, 1949, and Brannan to Thaxton, December 23, 1949, Farm Program 5, Office of the Secretary of Agriculture, RG 16, NA.
11. *New York Times,* September 24, 1949, 8.

Looking on as President Truman signed the rural telephone bill on October 28, 1949, are Secretary of Agriculture Charles F. Brannan (third from left), REA administrator Claude R. Wickard (third from right), a former USDA secretary, and several other labor and farm organization representatives. U.S. Department of Agriculture, courtesy of the Harry S. Truman Library.

them a check every so often to make up the difference between actual wages and a fair wage rate to be determined by the Government."[12]

In addition to the challenge presented by a Republican Party determined not to be bushwhacked again on the farm policy front, the Truman administration labored under heavy pressure from the biggest obstacle to the Brannan plan, the American Farm Bureau Federation.

12. Sioux City Republican Farm Conference, September 23, 1949, Speech file, Hope Papers; National Farm Conference of the Republican National Committee, September 23–24, 1949, Sioux City, IA, addresses and statements, Farm Bill Material, Aiken Papers; *New York Times,* September 24, 1949, 8; Hope to Benton J. Stong, September 29, 1949, and to Richard P. White, October 21, 1949, FF, Hope Papers. For a similar Democrat argument, see "Address by Congressman Albert Gore," February 14, 1950, Public Relations 10, Office of the Secretary of Agriculture, RG 16, NA.

After he was snubbed by bureau officials—he was not invited to speak at the federation's annual meeting—the secretary shot off a blunt epistle to the organization's pugnacious president, Allan Kline. Released to the press "in the interest of adding to their [AFBF members] information," Brannan's reprimand conveyed his "regret" that convention delegates would "not have the opportunity to hear more than one point of view during their deliberations on agricultural price supports." He appealed to Kline "to bring to the attention of your members several points of great importance to a full discussion of price supports and the vital postwar adjustments in agriculture." First was the serious decline in farm prices. "It should be remembered," he argued, "that support prices based either on parity or on the income standard I have proposed would go down if nonfarm prices went down and that a sliding scale merely permits farm prices to fall faster in relation to nonfarm prices." The second point was that the sliding scale would "not work to adjust production." And the third was the need to "find a workable method to support the price of perishable commodities, including livestock." Brannan insisted that his "production payment method" was "only one suggestion" and that he had "repeatedly invited others." All I ask," he wrote, "is that the criticism be objective and constructive." He closed with an appeal "to put aside any personal differences which might deprive the farmers of this country of the information necessary for wise decisions. Progress, in a democracy, depends on full and free discussion."[13]

Kline's almost vindictive reply can be seen as the harbinger of a deteriorating relationship that regrettably would detract from a serious search for long-range agricultural policy in the year ahead. He scolded Brannan for implying "that a group of free American citizens cannot objectively discuss both sides of questions of policy unless the discussion is guided by some Federal appointee." The AFBF, Kline continued, "is a free democratic organization of farmers," who "are remarkably well-informed on public policy matters." They were "particularly well-informed" about the Brannan plan, which had "been thoroughly discussed at local, county, and state Farm Bureau meetings." With

13. Brannan to Kline, December 10, 1949; Brannan to A. Threlkeld, December 1, 1949; and Mitchell Gresser to Brannan, December 7, 1949, Farm Program 6, Office of the Secretary of Agriculture, RG 16, NA. A copy of the Kline letter is also in Political Campaigns folder, Brannan Papers.

regard to the secretary's suggestion that there was "something personal about this matter," Kline insisted that "nothing could be further
from the truth. Through a life-time of work in agriculture and in Farm
Bureau, it has been an unfaltering rule of mine to discuss issues on
their merit and to leave personalities out of the discussion."[14]

The next day Brannan heard from at least one local bureau official
who did not "feel . . . gagged and muzzled" and resented the secretary's
"unjust criticism of the leaders of a very fine Farm Organization."
Brannan's reply was courteous but direct.

> Your national president attacked my suggestions immediately
> after I gave them without bothering to ascertain the beliefs of
> the members of his organization. He attacked on the grounds of
> "politico-economic philosophy," which as nearly as I can under-
> stand means that he does not like my politics. The feeling is mu-
> tual—I don't like his either—and I wonder if the membership
> has given him a mandate to make the American Farm Bureau
> Federation the agricultural wing of the Republican Party.[15]

Although Secretary Brannan considered Kline "public enemy number one," the bureau president and his organization were by no means
the only obstacles to general acceptance of the administration's farm
plan. At best, professional economists also remained skeptical. Theodore Schultz's continued critical commentary again came to the attention of Jim Patton in December 1949. Reacting to remarks the economist delivered to the Missouri agricultural extension agents, Patton
wrote Schultz that "on the whole it was a very good speech," but he
wished Schultz had been a bit less "sarcastic" with regard to such
things as the proposed application of production payments and income support standards. "In any event," he continued, "I wish that
you . . . would be more generous and less petty in your relationships
with Brannan, and go and have a visit with him once in awhile." Patton

14. Kline to Brannan, December 12, 1949, Farm Program 6, Office of the
Secretary of Agriculture, RG 16, NA. For Kline's media assault on the Brannan
plan, see *New York Times,* December 14, 1949; *Denver Post,* December 13, 1949.

15. Brannan to Irvin Durbin, December 29, 1949, Farm Program 6, Office
of the Secretary of Agriculture, RG 16, NA. For another objection to the Kline/
AFBF attitude, see Alexander Nunn, managing editor, *Progressive Farmer,* to
Brannan, January 6, 1950, Farm Program—Correspondence, Brannan Papers.

insisted that the secretary was "sincere" and was not playing "politics any more than anyone else is." Personally, the NFU president "welcome[d] the opportunity for a full fledged, far flung debate. I think it is much better to have that kind of a debate and have it a campaign issue than it is to have the kind of log-rolling which brought forth the Anderson bill."[16]

In thanking Patton "for the copy of your letter to Ted Schultz," the secretary wrote: "Apparently Ted took your advice in part, for he called by here a few days ago for a short visit. We must both remember that Ted has for a long time been very close to Allan Kline and that he considers Roger Fleming one of his outstanding graduate students. This whole situation probably puts him in a difficult fix."[17] Brannan had a hard time admitting that there could be legitimate objections to his plan. In reality, however, all could not be blamed on the AFBF.

Schultz's criticism continued, and early in 1950 he focused on a point that was anything but a Farm Bureau argument. In a *Farm Policy Forum* article entitled "That Turbulent Brannan Plan," Schultz reiterated a shortcoming in the Brannan proposal that he had been discussing since the outset of the debate. The Brannan plan, he wrote, "has made it crystal clear that no one—at least no major political group— is seriously concerned about the problem of the 1 or 2 million farm families who are really poor." Southern Democrats, for the most part, wrote Schultz, had long opposed "measures to reduce poverty in agriculture," and "the Republicans have in the main been indifferent. Now Mr. Brannan also has chosen to bypass the poor. His plan is designed to help those who are already well-situated within agriculture."[18] Schultz gave short shrift to opposition claims that Brannan's payment proposal "would put the farmers at the mercy of government appropriations" and continued to defend the use of production

16. Patton to Schultz, December 28, 1949, Farm Program 6–1, Office of the Secretary of Agriculture, RG 16, NA.

17. Brannan to Patton, January 3, 1950, Farm Program 6–1, Office of the Secretary of Agriculture, RG 16, NA. It is doubtful that Patton's "advice" had any bearing on the Schultz visit.

18. Schultz, "That Turbulent Brannan Plan," 5–6. Lauren Soth's *Des Moines Register* and *Des Moines Tribune* editorials expressed a similar point of view and attracted the attention of USDA officials (Soth to Wesley McCune, June 3, 1950, Farm Program 6, Office of the Secretary of Agriculture, RG 16, NA).

payments. "Open subsidies," he argued, "certainly are preferable to concealed subsidies of the type the Commodity Credit Corporation now uses in its loan and storage operation to support the so-called basic commodities and the other support operations of our government." One was "fully as 'socialistic'" as the other. But Schultz believed Brannan's income standard "would put farm price supports altogether too high" and thus "seriously over-value farm products." This was the "one basic weakness" in the administration plan, but since he believed the Agricultural Act of 1949 was "unworkable," he was optimistic that the Brannan plan could, and would, be made "workable."[19]

Despite their disagreements, the Brannan-Schultz dialogue was generally a constructive one. The same can be said with regard to the USDA's relationship with other agricultural economists, many of whom continued to engage in critical analysis of the department's policy.[20] It was the Brannan-Kline exchange of December 1949, however, that set the tone for the debate of 1950 in agriculture. As bitter as this relationship was at the end of 1949, it got progressively worse, erupting in a virtual war in September and October of 1950.

In his January 4 State of the Union address, President Truman tried to set a positive and progressive tone for the overall administration effort, a renewed liberal offensive. He called for the maintenance of a strong national defense, continued support to free nations resisting communism, repeal of the Taft-Hartley Act, enactment of civil rights programs, and extension of rent controls. He issued his strongest appeal to date for the passage of the Brannan plan. Although improved during the last session of Congress, Truman said the nation's farm legislation was "still not adequate." There were "serious shortcomings in the methods" available for carrying out the price support program, and many major commodities were left uncovered by the system. He then specifically recommended that Congress authorize a "system of production payments." Truman insisted that this was the best

19. Schultz, "That Turbulent Brannan Plan," 7–8. The Schultz article attracted much attention and was widely circulated; see Brannan to R. E. Elmquist, March 22, 1950, Farm Program 6–1, Office of the Secretary of Agriculture, RG 16, NA.

20. Brannan to Schultz, May 19, 1950, Farm Program 6–1, Office of the Secretary of Agriculture, RG 16, NA.

method for dealing with the surplus problem, and that it would "allow consumers to obtain the full benefit of our abundant agricultural production."[21]

According to Richard E. Neustadt, a noted presidential scholar and a former Truman staff member, this was "the occasion for Truman's first formal use of the magic words connoting 'Brannan Plan.' There he first attached the adjective 'mandatory' to price supports, first urged 'a system of production payments,' first declared, 'as a matter of national policy,' that 'safeguards must be maintained against slumps in farm prices,' in order to support 'farm income at fair levels.'" "To the uninitiated," explained Neustadt,

> these words may look very little different from their counterparts in prior presidential messages. But in the language of farm bureaucrats and organizations, these were magic words indeed, fighting words, emphasizing finally and officially, a sharp turn in Truman's agricultural policy—a turn which had begun in 1948, progressively distinguishing Democratic from Republican farm programs, and bringing the administration now to ground where the Republicans in Congress—not to speak of many Democrats—could not or would not follow.[22]

By January 1950, "Brannan plan" already had come into use as a scare tactic, but Truman, to the delight of his liberal backers, saw it as a way to cement his 1948 farm belt support. His January 4 address served as a fitting kick off for the new administration offensive for the Brannan farm plan.

Farm policy was not the only bone of contention highlighted in the president's annual address. Truman also asked for a moderate tax increase, something neither Democrats nor Republicans were eager to support during an election year. Conservatives in both parties already were convinced that federal expenditures were too high, and the projected four billion dollar plus deficit submitted by Truman in his budget on January 9 added more fuel to the fire. Any hopes Truman may have had that 1950 would offer more cooperation from the

21. Truman, *Public Papers of the Presidents, 1950,* 8, and the January 6 "Economic Report," 27, 31.
22. Neustadt, "Congress and the Fair Deal; A Legislative Balance Sheet," in Hamby, ed., *Harry S. Truman and the Fair Deal,* 31–32.

so-called Democrats were quickly dashed when Senator Harry F. Byrd took the lead in efforts to economize. According to *New York Times* correspondent Anthony Leviero, the Virginia Democrat made "the heaviest counter-attack to date on Truman's views." On January 18, the senator lamented the country's steady march down "this primrose path" and predicted that America would be "irrevocably committed to socialism" if the Congress passed the president's program of "socialized medicine, British brand; [and] socialized agriculture, called the Brannan plan."[23]

These budgetary concerns were bad news for supporters of the administration's farm program. It had frequently been attacked not only because it meant "state socialism" for agriculture, but also because it was a potential budget buster. Nevertheless, supporters of the Brannan plan were happy with the president's address and confident of success. The secretary and members of his staff continued their seemingly tireless promotional efforts. During the late winter and spring, with potato and egg surpluses again casting serious doubt on the viability of the new farm law, things were looking up. Political commentators and observers, according to Brannan, were still predicting that most of his plan would be adopted; and, just as encouraging, "No polls have appeared that indicate a majority of farmers opposed to the Administration's proposals."[24]

Despite this general optimism, the formidable opposition force in Congress, made up primarily of Republicans and southern Democrats, remained steadfast in its objections, which did not rest solely on scare tactics. There were fundamental philosophical differences between the camps, which, in retrospect, appear to have been uncompromisable. The USDA's "Suggestions for the Agricultural State of the Union

23. *New York Times,* January 9, 1950, 1, and *New York Times,* January 18, 1950, 13.

24. Brannan to Joseph Lucas, February 16, 1950, Farm Program 6–1; Congressman Andrew J. Biemiller (D-WI) to Brannan, February 9, 1950, Publications 1; Wesley McCune to Gordon Roth, February 15, 1950, Publications 1; Robert W. Chandler, *Denver Post,* to Brannan, February 3, 1950; J. S. Russell, *Des Moines Register* and *Des Moines Tribune,* to McCune, February 9, 1950, Farm Program 6–1, Office of the Secretary of Agriculture, RG 16, NA; Brannan to Donald R. Murphy, editor, *Wallaces' Farmer,* January 30, 1950, and to North Carolina governor W. Kerr Scott, January 30, 1950, Farm Program—Correspondence, Brannan Papers.

Message" for 1950, much of which was incorporated in the actual address, included a clear statement of its commitment to the economy of abundance philosophy. This philosophy was fully embraced by the new chairman of the CEA, Leon Keyserling, and the majority of Truman's other liberal backers. With the USDA, they believed, "If everyone in this country can have enough food, clothing and shelter, and if a fair level of world trade is maintained, farm surpluses will not become burdensome. On the contrary, agriculture will prosper and help the whole nation to become more prosperous and secure."[25]

These developments, however, would not occur on their own; positive government action was needed, according to the department, "to keep our economy growing." The statement admitted that agriculture was producing more than was being consumed, and that "the trend toward surplus production represents a grave problem which must be met." Unlike most of the nation's agricultural economists, Brannan and his colleagues believed consumption could be adequately increased with proper policies. The situation had been helped by the actions of the Eighty-first Congress in passing the International Wheat Agreement and the Reciprocal Trade Agreements Act and in restoring the authority of the CCC. Further action, especially the implementation of the production payments method of supporting farm income, was needed.

> In agricultural as in other legislation, let us remember that prosperity and poverty are not divisible. Encourage business to produce in abundance, and you lessen the farmer's need for price supports. Help labor to keep steady employment at good wages, and you reduce the possibility of farm surpluses. Provide the farmer with opportunity to earn good returns from his production, and you help assure the businessman of markets and the laboring men and women of jobs. Expand the total economy and everybody gains. Cut it back and nobody gains but the enemies of democracy.[26]

25. Brannan to Truman, November 1, 1949, Public Relations 10–2; Brannan, "The Extra Bushel," speech, National Farm Institute, Des Moines, IA, February 18, 1950, Public Relations 10–3, Office of the Secretary of Agriculture, RG 16, NA; Leon H. Keyserling, "Harry S. Truman: The Man and the President," in Levantrosser, ed., *Harry S. Truman: The Man from Independence,* 241.

26. Brannan to Truman, November 1, 1949, Public Relations 10–2, Office of the Secretary of Agriculture, RG 16, NA.

The department recognized the issue economists referred to as "elasticity in demand" for food, but administration officials had much more confidence in the potential consumptive capacity of the lower income groups, especially if the USDA was given the production payments tool. Critical to their argument was the necessity for, and possibility of, America's highly integrated economy remaining in a constant state of expansion.[27]

Reflected frequently in the "cheap food" comments of Clifford Hope and other Republicans, the opposition's rejection of this basic philosophy as it applied to agriculture was clearly enunciated in a February 14 address delivered by Democratic Representative Albert Gore. Although recognizing the sincerity in Brannan's efforts to sell what he believed was the best solution to the farm problem, the Tennessee congressman warned the Fourteenth Annual North Carolina Farm Bureau Convention that consumers were being "misinformed about and prejudiced against what farmers consider a sound and fair farm price support program." Unfortunately, USDA officials, including the secretary himself, were propagating some of this misinformation, "calculated to foster and encourage a prejudiced and dangerous attitude toward the farmer and toward a farm price support program." According to Gore, even if one accepted the idea that food prices were too high, this had little or no relationship to the prices received by farmers. The farmer did not expect the "perpetuation of the peak price he enjoyed during the period of unprecedented demand" that followed World War II. "What the farmer does want, and expects, and feels entitled to," the congressman explained, "is a stabilization of prices, not at war or post war peaks but at a reasonable and fair parity relationship. This was the goal of the 1949 Agricultural Act."

27. In this particular debate, one can clearly see Fair Deal farm policy as a reflection of an emerging postwar or "vital-center" liberalism. Brannan, like Leon Keyserling, who was now in control of the CEA, and other administration liberals, "used the concept of abundance as an intellectual foundation"—a "politico-economic strategy" that clearly distinguished the Fair from the New Deal (Hamby, "The Vital Center," in Hamby, ed. *Harry S. Truman and the Fair Deal,* 149; Allen J. Matusow, *The Unraveling of America: A History of Liberalism in the 1960s,* especially chap. 1, which provides the late 1940s and 1950s context).

Gore reminded his audience of the "two philosophies, or schools of thought on the farm problem and a farm program." One, he explained,

> supported by the American Farm Bureau Federation, by the National Grange, by just about all of the commodity organization groups, and the platforms of both the Democratic and Republican Parties, proposes a system of price supports by which, through loans and purchases and adjusting supply to within reasonable proximity of demand, the prices of farm commodities are supported in the market place. . . .
>
> The other . . . , supported by the Farmers Union, by powerful organizations of groups primarily consumer in character, by Secretary of Agriculture, Charles F. Brannan in part, if not in whole, and by the 1948 platform of the Progressive Party, proposes to let farm prices fall to whatever levels they will in an unsupported market and that the difference between what the farmer gets in the market place and what a Secretary of Agriculture or a Congress thinks he should get be made up to him by subsidy payments out of the Treasury of the United States.

According to Congressman Gore, "supplies in mountanious [sic] volumes would be encouraged . . . under the Brannan Plan school of thought—the so-called philosophy of abundance." He also insisted that even in the case of potatoes, which had admittedly been a problem under the old system, "the Brannan Plan would be three or four times as costly." Gore also "emphatically" denied that the philosophy for which he was arguing was one of "scarcity." It was "a program of balanced abundance."[28]

Not surprisingly, Secretary Brannan took strong exception to the congressman's characterization of his proposals and to his remarks charging USDA officials with intentionally trying to discredit the farm support program by blaming the farmer for the high cost of food.[29]

28. "Address by Congressman Albert Gore," February 14, 1950, and Gore to Brannan, February 20, 1950, Public Relations 10, Office of the Secretary of Agriculture, RG 16, NA.

29. Brannan to Gore, February 15, 1950, and unsent letter prepared in response to Gore's letter of February 20, 1950, Public Relations 10, Office of the Secretary of Agriculture, RG 16, NA.

More and more, however, Brannan's offensive for the administration's farm plan, and the philosophy of abundance, focused on Allan Kline and the AFBF. The secretary also recognized the "two entirely different" philosophies, but his interpretation was a striking contrast with that discussed by Congressman Gore. "One group, of which the present Administration is a part," Brannan instructed the National Farm Institute, "believes it is in the best interest of the entire Nation to use price support as a means for providing agriculture the opportunity to earn a fair income." The other group "preach[ed] that the only role of price supports is to protect the farmer against bankruptcy." In a sixteen-page speech devoted almost equally to promoting the administration's proposal and castigating Kline, the secretary singled out the "Farm Bureau's present national leadership" as a champion of the latter philosophy. "On the one hand," he elaborated,

> we have those with determination to maintain a full, expanding economy; to live in prosperity with the abundance we can produce by properly utilizing it to raise the living standards of all.
>
> On the other hand, we have the stop-lossers, the temporizers, those who are willing to gamble on getting by themselves regardless of what happens to the other fellow. They are willing to risk the entire Nation's welfare on their own stubborn lack of vision and foresight....
>
> They are bound by the fallacious assumption that downward sliding prices provide an acceptable way to adjust production, they are willing to starve farmers into compliance if necessary to obtain that adjustment, instead of doing it the more humane way—by the incentive of fair rewards. They are willing to sacrifice small farmers under the brutal survival-of-the-fittest concept even if it means large numbers of farms and farmers forced out of business at a heavy loss. That's what they mean by so-called "natural adjustments".[30]

Obviously, the Brannan plan's antagonists had no corner on the use of scare tactics.

The administration's campaign for the Brannan plan continued, featuring such creative efforts as a radio program broadcast by ABC

30. Brannan, "The Extra Bushel," speech, National Farm Institute, Des Moines, IA, February 18, 1950, Public Relations 10–3, Office of the Secretary of Agriculture, RG 16, NA. Brannan appeared on a program that included Allan Kline, James Patton, and Theodore Schultz.

on February 24, 1950—*On Trial.* The subject of the litigation: "Do the scales of American justice have an answer to the question, 'Should Congress pass the Brannan Plan?'" The program starred "Mr. Clark M. Clifford, as counsel for the Brannan plan" and "Mr. William D. Embrie, an eminent New York attorney" as "counsel for the negative." The secretary of agriculture was, not surprisingly, the star (and only) witness.[31] Unfortunately, this production and those that followed were already being upstaged by other national media events.

On January 21, a real court proceeding came to an end with the announcement of a verdict in the trial of Alger Hiss. The jury found the former State Department official guilty on the charge of perjury stemming from House Un-American Activities Committee investigations, casting a shadow of treasonous activity within the administration. A few days later, Secretary of State Dean Acheson made the politically unfortunate statement that regardless of the "outcome of any appeal... I do not intend to turn my back on Alger Hiss." Arthur Krock of the *New York Times* declared the Hiss case a "burning political issue in which may be consumed the influence of important officials and vital national policies."[32]

Then, on February 9, at Wheeling, West Virginia, Senator Joseph McCarthy delivered the now infamous speech in which he claimed to have irrefutable evidence proving that the State Department was infested with communists and communist sympathizers. Before the end of the month, he had repeated these charges on the Senate floor, and a subcommittee was authorized to investigate, and presumably discredit, the flimsy accusations. "The investigation," according to journalist and Truman biographer Robert Donovan, "produced one of the greatest backfires Washington has ever known." The action figured prominently, to say the least, in the fall congressional campaign; try as he might, the president could not discredit this "pathological liar" enough to avoid irreparable damage to his administration.[33] The

31. "Should Congress Pass the Brannan Plan," *On Trial,* transcript of American Broadcasting Company radio program, February 24, 1950, OF, Truman Papers.

32. Krock, *In the Nation,* 145; Herbert Agar, *The Price of Power: America since 1945,* 100–106; Eric F. Goldman, *The Crucial Decade—and after; America, 1945–1960,* 135; Donovan, *Tumultuous Years,* 134.

33. Donovan, *Tumultuous Years,* 165; Truman to Nellie Noland, March 31, 1950, in Ferrell, ed., *Off the Record, 176.*

outbreak of war in Korea in late June only added intensity to the charges that the administration was following a misguided policy that, in the opinion of some, proved even more conclusively that the government was teeming with "communists and fellow travelers."

Meanwhile, the Brannan plan continued to look like a viable alternative to the troubled farm program and, just as important, a pivotal issue during the upcoming congressional campaigns. Key to President Truman's election year strategy, motivated by his desire for a Fair Deal majority in Congress, was his ability to hold the Midwest farm vote. Thus, Truman and Brannan decided to make the early Iowa senatorial primary a battleground against the Farm Bureau and for the Brannan plan. Although the Iowa Democratic Party was not entirely convinced of the wisdom of "staking so much on the Secretary's farm program," in March the administration threw its considerable influence behind the senatorial candidacy of Under Secretary of Agriculture Albert J. Loveland who ultimately won the opportunity to challenge incumbent Republican Bourke B. Hickenlooper.[34]

The administration's strategy might have been successful had 1950 been a more typical election year, but, as *Newsweek* reported, "somehow the Brannan plan never set the Midwest prairies afire the way the Democrats thought it would." During the late winter and spring, the secretary's mail continued to reflected a divided electorate, even among small farmers. In February, Gallup released a poll that indicated that in the Midwest only 29 percent of the people had followed the discussions of the plan, and of those only 9 percent approved of it. In April, all regions of the country mentioned unemployment as the nation's number one problem, and in May national opinion ranked the threat of war, general economic problems (cost of living, inflation, and taxes), unemployment, and communism as the most important problems "facing the entire country today." The farm problem did not make the list.[35]

34. "Test for Brannan Plan," 26. Loveland formally resigned his position at USDA on March 27, 1950 (Loveland to Truman, OF, Truman Papers).

35. "Test for Brannan Plan," 25; Gallup, *The Gallup Poll,* 2:889, 905, 907. Brannan specifically questioned the results of Gallup's April poll, suggesting that his questions might have been "loaded against the Plan." These comments came in response to an advance copy of a Gallup article that was to appear in *Look*'s April 25 issue— "Voters Split on Truman Program" (Brannan to William

To the chagrin of many farm leaders, all too often when the public did comment on the farm policy debate, it focused on high grocery prices. Secretary Brannan frequently tried to use these complaints to his advantage and often blamed the Congress. "Price support programs as they now stand," wrote the secretary, "have been pricing certain supported articles 'off the table.'"[36] Just as frequently, his congressional opponents blamed the administration, which they accused of trying to sabotage the existing program to improve the chances of the Brannan plan. On April 11, 1950, Senator Aiken, who had charged Brannan with politically abusing his and the department's position in 1949, accused the secretary of attending a PMA meeting at St. Paul for the purpose of lobbying for his program and delivering a political speech while the government was paying his expenses. Aiken accused Brannan of using federal funds to influence legislation.[37]

Secretary Brannan, however, was confident, and President Truman remained optimistic and pleased with the efforts to promote the administration's farm program. From the vantage point of his "nonpolitical" western tour, he wrote his agriculture secretary that "we have the opposition so badly scared [I think] we are going to get some action."[38]

Houseman, April 12, 1950, Public Relations 2, Office of the Secretary of Agriculture, RG 16, NA).

36. Brannan to Mrs. Ethel Anderson, March 31, 1950, Farm Program 6–1, Office of the Secretary of Agriculture, RG 16, NA. Specifically, Brannan claimed that production payment authority would have solved the problems with eggs, potatoes, and butter.

37. "Brannan Hired Audience," *Better Farms,* June 1950, clipping in Farm Bill—Brannan Plan, 1950, Aiken Papers; Drew Pearson, "The Washington Merry-Go-Round," in the *Montpelier Evening Argus,* May 5, 1950; Rich, *U.S. Agricultural Policy in the Postwar Years,* 30. On October 24, 1950, the Democratic majority on the House Select Committee on Lobbying Activities concluded that Brannan had done nothing wrong. Liberals had established the so-called Buchanan Committee (Frank Buchanan [D-PA]) in 1949 to investigate and expose forces that were blocking reform legislation. Public hearings began in April 1950 and, obviously, did not always have the desired focus. The committee also investigated Oscar Ewing, and eventually, "under pressure from Republicans," liberal groups such as the NFU and the ADA (Hamby, *Beyond the New Deal,* 325; Christenson, *The Brannan Plan,* 114–42).

38. Truman to Brannan, May 10, 1950, PSF, Truman Papers. With regard to the nonpolitical characterization of Truman's May 1950 trip, see Truman, *Public Papers of the Presidents, 1950,* 254–55; *New York Times,* April 14 (sec. 4, 17), April 16 (sec. 4, 7), and May 7, 1950 (sec. 4, 1–8).

Two days before, on his sixty-sixth birthday, May 8, 1950, the president had delivered the first major address on his journey to the state of Washington to dedicate the Grand Coulee Dam. It was a farm speech at Lincoln, Nebraska.[39] Truman reminded a rain soaked crowd of the resistance faced by the farm policy recommendations during the debates of the 1930s.

> It was the same kind of mudslinging, name-calling opposition that you hear now every time we bring up a new proposal for the benefit of the whole people.
>
> I remember when I first went to the Senate, an important farm bill was being debated which became the foundation of our present agricultural conservation program. Over in the House of Representatives, one Congressman said this legislation was "an attempt to enslave the farmer," and that it was "communistic." Another Congressman said that under this legislation farmers would be "dominated and regimented for all time"—they would "no longer...be free men." ...
>
> When you think how miserably wrong they have proved to be in the past, you can see just how little truth there is in the wild charges they are throwing around now.

Rather than leading to enslavement and communism, "These laws led to freedom and prosperity. They were, and are, strong bulwarks for our free and democratic society. Remember that fact when you hear people today croaking the old charges of 'socialism' and 'regimentation' about every new proposal for progress." The old programs had "served us well" but "there are defects in the present system which require correction." Truman then proceeded to defend, explain, and call for the enactment of the recommendations made by his secretary of agriculture the previous year, which had been designed to accomplish four major goals: abundant production of commodities desired by American consumers; efficient support of perishable products with a system of production payments; encouragement of good soil and water conservation practice; and adequate assistance "to the family-size farm."[40]

39. Hechler, *Working with Truman,* 140; Truman, *Public Papers of the Presidents, 1950,* 309.
40. Truman, *Public Papers of the Presidents, 1950,* 310–14.

Although no substantive action had been taken in Congress, the campaign for and against the Brannan plan accelerated during May and June. In addition to various appearances by the secretary and other administration officials, the Democratic National Committee was producing an abundance of campaign material on the farm program, including a comic book presentation—"John and Mary Blake and the Brannan Plan."[41] The opposition also kept busy with speaking engagements and, whenever possible, argued its case in print. By this time, it appeared that the contestants would be fighting it out primarily on the campaign trail and not in the halls of Congress. The House had tentatively scheduled long-range farm program hearings for June 12, but no one, according to Congressman Hope, "thinks there is a possibility of legislation at this session."[42]

By the end of June, the Commodity Credit Corporation's inventories were reaching critical levels. According to the Secretary Brannan, the CCC had in its possession "approximately one pound of butter, two and a half pounds of dried milk, almost a half pound of cheese and 2 dozen shell eggs (in dried form) for every man, woman and child in the United States."[43] But as was the case in 1940 and 1941, international events had already intervened. On June 25, 1950, North Korean forces crossed the 38th parallel and, in a matter of days, the United States, under United Nations auspices, was fighting a land, sea, and air war to defend the Republic of South Korea. This new

41. In this eight-page broadside, John and Mary, who operate a small Missouri farm, learn that under the Brannan plan they will see a 45 percent increase in their net income. The stories villains are "the lobby-dominated Eightieth Congress" and its Hope-Aiken Act and a cigar-smoking dandy from Wall Street ("John and Mary Blake and the Brannan Plan," Democratic National Committee, copy in Farm Bill—Brannan Plan, 1950, Aiken Papers; "Brannan Plan Sees Double," *Washington News,* June 7, 1950; "Comic Book Tells Story of Brannan Farm Plan," *Washington Post,* April 30, 1950; Brannan to T. K. Wolfe, May 26, 1950, Farm Program 6–1, Office of the Secretary of Agriculture, RG 16, NA). See also "Misconceptions—And Facts about the Administration Farm Program," Farm Program, Brannan Papers.

42. Hope to H. W. Clutter, June 1, 1950, General Correspondence, Hope Papers; Kline, "Government and Agriculture," 78; George Price to Brannan, May 11, 1950; Brannan to Price, July 20, 1950; Brannan to Hope, August 11, 1950, Farm Program 6–1, Office of the Secretary of Agriculture, RG 16, NA.

43. Brannan to Allen J. Ellender Sr., acting chairman, Senate Committee on Agriculture and Forestry, June 30, 1950, Farm Program 6, Office of the Secretary of Agriculture, RG 16, NA.

war forced the administration to change its emphasis in agriculture. With demand soaring, farm prices would be on the rise, and, for the most part, large commodity inventories became a national asset.[44]

Initially, this was not the case for perishables, and Brannan took the opportunity to further plug his production payments approach for this group of farm commodities.[45] Congress did not respond, but this late July testimony gave rise to the most heated exchange yet between the secretary of agriculture and the president of the AFBF— characterized by some at the time, as an "open war." In its usual opportunistic fashion, the Farm Bureau, in this case represented by Roger Fleming, seized the occasion to announce that the Brannan plan would have "dissipated the reserves of corn, cotton and wheat and other storables." Ironically, the plan, which had frequently come under fire because opponents believed it would encourage over-production and worsen the surplus problem, was now being attacked as a threat to safe reserves that most saw as a real asset in wartime.

The secretary had every reason to be disturbed by this blatant mis-representation of his well-known positions. Brannan was outraged and, in a public letter to President Kline, vented all his hostility toward the leadership of the organization that he continued to blame for the legislative failure of his farm program.[46] The pent-up emotions, re-leased in this September 23 letter, had reached an intense level even before the Korean conflict began.

Responding to remarks made by Senator Aiken to the effect that the hostility between Congress and the USDA was the country's major farm problem, Brannan denied the existence of such "bitterness": "Perhaps what you meant to say is that there is a deep bitterness on the part of the national leadership of the American Farm Bureau toward me which those leaders are vigorously attempting to inject

44. Brannan to John R. Steelman, assistant to the president, July 13, 1950; enclosed "Report on Agricultural Production Potentials: Current Situation and Prospects," Agriculture/ Confidential file; "Confidential" memo, Brannan to Truman, July 19, 1950, PSF, Truman Papers.
45. House Committee on Agriculture, *Disposal of Surplus Perishable Agricultural Commodities,* 81st Cong., 2nd sess., July 24, 1950, 127–28; Brannan to Kline, September 15, 1950, OF, Truman Papers.
46. Brannan to Kline, September 23, 1950, Farm Program 6, Office of the Secretary of Agriculture, RG 16, NA.

into the acts and conduct of some members of the Congress." Senator Aiken insisted that he held no personal "ill will" toward Brannan, but they could not "ignore the fact that dissension is present and has been growing since April 7, 1949." The senator was disappointed "that during the 81st Congress there has not been the cooperative effort between the Department of Agriculture and the Senate which existed during the 80th Congress and I hope the time will come when we can again work together in the interest of American agriculture and the country in an atmosphere free from suspicion and politics." Insisting that it was only because he liked "Charlie" personally that he wrote so frankly, Aiken added that many members of Congress felt that the secretary was "constantly trying to force [his] own desires on the Congress."[47]

The secretary's September 23 letter to Kline was released to the press and mailed to several hundred individuals and organizations two days later. It opened with Brannan expressing regret that "the Korean situation" had not caused Kline to redirect his "own energies and those of your immediate staff away from the vicious personal attacks you have leveled against me and the Department of Agriculture and toward the things that must be done by, for, and with the American farmers in the months ahead." Brannan closed by saying that "in lack of truth and in obvious intent to mislead, your attack is grossly unfair. I am sure you would not retract merely to be fair to me. But if you feel any responsibility to the public and to the members who pay dues which you are using to attack and discredit those who refuse to subjugate their views and actions to yours, you will see to it that a correction is sent to all who received the false information."[48]

The secretary's epistle brought immediate praise from expected

47. Brannan to Aiken, June 23, 1950, and Aiken to Brannan, July 3, 1950, Public Relations 10, Office of the Secretary of Agriculture, RG 16, NA. See also Farm Bill—Brannan Plan, 1950, Aiken Papers. Aiken added, "The Congress is very jealous of its Constitutional prerogative as the lawmaking body."

48. Brannan to Kline, September 23, 1950, and mailing lists, Farm Program 6, Office of the Secretary of Agriculture, RG 16, NA. The secretary's mailing list included: the major farm organizations, congressional agricultural committee members and more than one hundred other members of Congress, and college and university presidents. It was released to the press on September 25 (Brannan to Hope, September 25, 1950, General Correspondence, Hope Papers).

quarters, including the NFU's Jim Patton who thought it was "an excellent" letter.[49] Support also arrived from unforeseen sources, such as Edward F. Holter, the master of the Maryland State Grange and lecturer for the national organization, who thought Brannan was "fully justified in objecting to being mis-quoted." Kline, however, was unrepentant, and the AFBF assault only intensified. On September 29, he told the secretary "your statement that I continue 'vicious personal attacks' on you is truly remarkable." Kline insisted that he had been discussing many critical issues, and "so far as I can remember, I haven't discussed you or, as a matter of fact, even mentioned you in a single one of these speeches."[50]

In the final analysis, the exchange added nothing constructive to the debate. In fact, it probably hurt the secretary much more than it did his adversary. The Massachusetts Farm Bureau went so far as to call for Brannan's resignation, which it said would actually be "an act of patriotism" in light of the current crisis. Most did not go this far, but many seemed to agree with the sentiments of the president of the South Carolina Farm Bureau who wrote: "I deplore the fact that the American Farm Bureau Federation and the United States Department of Agriculture, particularly President Kline and Secretary Brannan, have failed to disagree without sometimes getting rather personal and maybe obnoxious about it. I think that the cause of agriculture and the prospect for a sensible and sound and workable farm program is being jeopardized because of this feud." Curiously, at the same time the department was being criticized for threatening the nation's stockpiles, Brannan was, during the last weeks of the campaign, receiving complaints about high food prices and fielding charges that the administration was "hording food."[51]

49. Patton to Brannan, September 27, 1950, Farm Program 6, Office of the Secretary of Agriculture, RG 16, NA. Brannan also received support from several state Farmers Unions and a number of Democratic congressman including Milton Young, Stephen Pace, Eugene McCarthy, and John W. McCormack.

50. Kline to Brannan, September 28, 1950, and Holter to Brannan, October 4, 1950, Farm Program 6, Office of the Secretary of Agriculture, RG 16, NA.

51. S. L. Davenport and Carleton I. Pickett to Brannan, October 2, 1950, and E. H. Agnew, South Carolina Farm Bureau, to Brannan, September 28, 1950, Farm Program 6, Office of the Secretary of Agriculture, RG 16, NA. With regard to hording, see Brannan to Mike Mansfield, October 25, 1950, Farm Program 6, Office of the Secretary of Agriculture, RG 16, NA.

Secretary Brannan continued working for his proposals and the Democratic Party during the fall campaign, but in the face of the immediate emergency, serious consideration and interest in the controversial Brannan plan waned, as it did with other efforts to change significantly the nation's farm policy.[52] Heightened agricultural demand after the beginning of Korean conflict ended the Brannan plan's appeal and effectively removed one of the key players from the game. Forced to "play the role of war leader," Truman took himself out of the political fight, and despite his earlier plans for active participation, he delivered only one partisan speech thereafter, on the eve of the November election.[53]

Korea and McCarthyism became the dominant issues in the fall campaign. Under wartime conditions, Fair Deal issues had less appeal generally, and the Brannan plan played only a peripheral role. In Iowa, where the administration had essentially sponsored the candidacy of Albert Loveland, the conservative incumbent Bourke Hickenlooper won handily. Loveland had won the primary while strongly endorsing the Brannan plan, but, like many Democratic candidates, he shied away from many of the more controversial Truman programs during the fall campaign. As the campaign wore on Loveland began to back away from his "soft peddling" approach to the Brannan plan; but Hickenlooper refused to let the issue fade and took advantage of "the issues of the Korean War, communism, taxes and other domestic subjects."[54]

Loveland was not the only Democrat who sought to play down the Brannan plan and its author. The secretary who had played a pivotal role in the campaign of 1948 was conspicuously less occupied

52. Hope to Joe Berkely, July 22, 1950, General Correspondence, Hope Papers.

53. Neustadt, "Congress and the Fair Deal," 33–40; Hamby, "The Vital Center," both in Hamby, ed., *Harry S. Truman and the Fair Deal*, 155–56. For Truman's speech, see Truman, *Public Papers of the Presidents, 1950*, 697–703.

54. *New York Times*, November 1, 1950, 32, and *New York Times*, November 9, 1950, 37; Norman MacKenzie, "After the U.S. Polls," 450; Brannan to Loveland, September 13, 1950, Correspondence, Brannan Papers; Hamby, "The Vital Center," in Hamby, ed., *Harry S. Truman and the Fair Deal*, 160; Hamby, *Beyond the New Deal*, 419; Joseph LaPalombara, "Pressure, Propaganda, and Political Action in the Election of 1950," 323; Dean, "Farm Policy Debate of 1949–1950," 33.

politically during the fall of 1950. Senator Clinton Anderson who served as vice chairman of the Democratic National Committee (DNC) was reportedly responsible for this sharply reduced campaign schedule. In addition, while Brannan was engaged in battle with Allan Kline, Vice President Alben Barkley cast some doubt on the paternity of the secretary's farm plan. Barkley was quoted as having said, "The Brannan plan is controversial." "It is entitled to be studied, but I am not committed to it and the party is not committed to it." By the end of October, it was even rumored that Brannan could be out of a job if the Democratic Party lost the farm vote in November.[55]

Facing a different political climate during the fall campaign, Secretary Brannan had begun to change his tune slightly. He did not waver in his commitment to the principles, but in a letter to Senator Herbert Lehman (D-NY), the secretary wrote: "As you may know, we were not attempting to formulate a 'plan' in the usual sense of the word" but simply recommending amendments to the current farm legislation. "It has not been due to any intention or desire on my part that the recommendations I advocate have come to be known as the 'Brannan Plan.' "[56] Although Brannan and his staff had made the first point on previous occasions, if it seemed like the prudent course, for the first time in nearly a year and a half Brannan was issuing a disclaimer with the latter remark. Early on, the department had often modified the commonly used epithet with *so-called*. But this had been dropped, and the entire administration frequently used the title "Brannan plan." Now, however, the department realized that the label itself had become an issue, and that it was a political liability.[57]

As for the president, he had little opportunity to become involved in the fray and made few comments on the farm policy question after hostilities commenced in Korea. On November 4, 1950, in his only real campaign speech of the political season, Truman singled out his

55. Milton Gordon to Brannan, October 23, 1950 (and enclosed newspaper clipping; article by Fulton Lewis), Aubrey Williams to Brannan, October 12, 1950, Farm Program 6–1, Office of the Secretary of Agriculture, RG 16, NA; *New York Times,* November 9, 1950, 37.

56. Brannan to Lehman, September 8, 1950, Farm Program 6–1, Office of the Secretary of Agriculture, RG 16, NA.

57. Wesley McCune to Kenneth Julian, December 5, 1950, Farm Program 6–1, Office of the Secretary of Agriculture, RG 16, NA.

vice president for his role in the campaign and, as he had in 1948, tried to make "that Republican no-good, do-nothing 80th Congress" the central issue. With regard to agriculture, he confined his remarks to a repetition of Republican sins and Democratic accomplishments. Not surprisingly, he made no reference to the Eighty-first Congress's failure to pass the administration's farm program, about which he said nothing.[58] Despite the president's last minute appeal for a Democratic victory, the election returns were bad news for the administration. The Democrats remained the majority party in Congress, but the GOP made some significant gains, and the administration had failed to gain "actual control of the Eighty-second Congress." Although Kenneth Hechler maintained that the administration continued to draw a significant farm vote in the Midwest, "for all practical purpose," wrote Hamby, "the returns from the corn belt spelled an end to the Brannan strategy of constructing a farm-labor coalition."[59]

In the wake of the election, with no prospects for renewed legislative consideration of the Brannan plan in sight, the secretary turned his attention to international and family farm issues. The department's suggestions for the 1951 State of the Union message emphasized the "ability of agriculture to gear its production to increased but changing requirements in the interest of national defense and the stemming of inflation" and "the basic strength of agriculture as an element in the ideological struggle between democracy and totalitarianism." There were specific calls for an improved price support program "to help insure needed increases in production" and programs to protect and defend the family farm but no explicit recommendations.[60]

Truman followed the department's lead and said nothing definite

58. Truman, *Public Papers of the Presidents, 1950,* 699; *New York Times,* November 5, 1950, 1.

59. Hamby, *Beyond the New Deal,* 421; Hechler, *Working with Truman,* 163; William A. Glaser, "Hindsight and Significance," in William N. McPhee and William A. Glaser, eds., *Public Opinion and Congressional Elections,* 279; Krock, "In the Nation," *New York Times,* October 19, 1950, 30, and *New York Times,* November 10, 1950, 26; James Reston, *New York Times,* November 8, 1950, 4.

60. Information for the President's State of the Union Message and Economic Report, November 30, 1950, Public Relations 10–2, and McCune to Francis Kutish, November 15, 1950, Public Relations 2, Office of the Secretary of Agriculture, RG 16, NA; Under Secretary McCormick, "Strengthening the Family Farm," speech, December 12, 1950, OF, Truman Papers.

about agricultural legislation in his 1951 State of the Union address, and he was vague on specifics in 1952. With regard to the Fair Deal, the war effectively took Truman out of the fight. In the final analysis, as Hamby explained, although the president had considerable success gaining extension of New Deal programs in 1949 and early 1950, and took significant executive actions, "The heart of the Fair Deal ... — repeal of the Taft-Hartley Act, civil rights legislation, aid to education, national medical insurance, and the Brannan Plan—failed in Congress."[61]

Truman had failed to hold the midwestern farm vote in 1950 that had been so critical to the success of the administration's agricultural program, and farmers returned to the Republican Party. Curiously, in a Gallup poll released on November 28, 1951, midwestern farmers continued to indicate their belief that the Democratic Party best served their interests, but they also cited the GOP as their party of preference—48 to 30 percent.[62] Secretary Brannan continued to believe that there was grassroots support for his proposal. In the wake of his defeat in 1949, and especially after 1950, however, he "was very, very disappointed. I would have liked the chance to continue working on it," he said in a 1985 interview, but, in retrospect, he concluded that the Brannan plan's chances were never very good. "The vested interest in the status quo was a little bit too strong," he continued, and basically the same situation had continued to the present.[63]

61. Hamby, "The Vital Center," 155, and Neustadt, "Congress and the Fair Deal," 33–40, in Hamby, ed., *Harry S. Truman and the Fair Deal*; Bernstein, ed., *Politics and Policies of the Truman Administration,* 11.

62. Survey of midwestern farmers only: Which party was best when it came to farm interests? 39 percent, Democrats; 33 percent, Republicans; 19 percent, no difference; and 9 percent had no opinion. On party preference: 48 percent considered themselves Republican, 30 percent said Democrat, and 22 percent were Independent (Gallup, *The Gallup Poll,* 2:1024).

63. Brannan, interview. Brannan likened his 1949–1950 situation to that of the mid-1980s; farmers continued to support the Republican Party and President Ronald Reagan, despite the harm done them by Reagan administration policies.

9

CONCLUSION

Before the flexible schedule of the Agricultural Act of 1949 could take effect, war intervened and price stabilization became the focus of attention. The new support schedule was applied only to one basic commodity in 1951—peanuts, and it was raised to 90 percent of parity in 1952. With the outbreak of war in Korea, the concern became sufficient production, not surplus. Facing a new crisis, President Truman again received divided counsel. The Bureau of the Budget opposed the postponement of the flexible schedule "under the guise of stimulating needed agricultural production," while the USDA seized on any opportunity to block sliding scales. Truman sided with the department and signed H.R. 8122 on July 18, 1952. The new law set aside the sliding scale, extending the period of mandatory price support at 90 percent of parity to 1954, and delayed the shift to a single parity formula for basic commodities.[1] In 1953, southern and western congressmen again joined forces; this time to amend the Defense Production Act so as to extend high mandatory price supports for basic commodities through 1954.[2] The post-World War II search for a long-range policy for agriculture had failed, and the nation continued to operate under the old system that, with relatively minor modifications, had been enacted to address the emergency of the Great Depression.

1. Rasmussen, Baker, and Ward, *Short History of Agricultural Adjustment,* 12; Brannan to Harold Cooley, February 14, 1952; BOB Report, May 9, 1952, General Legislation, H.R. 6582; Statement by Truman on Signing H.R. 8122, July 18, 1952; and other documents, General Legislation, Bureau of the Budget, RG 51, NA.
2. Saloutos, "Agricultural Organizations and Farm Policy," 393; Schapsmeier and Schapsmeier, "Farm Policy from FDR to Eisenhower," 367.

Interest in farm policy revision remained during the Korean conflict, but, as Secretary Brannan wrote, "the production of adequate supplies of food and fiber is one of the most essential defense activities facing us," and all other programs were geared to meet this challenge. Conservation attracted more and more attention, but the emphasis was on "increasing the productive capacity of our farm lands" as "a vital part of the defense effort."[3] The secretary and his department continued to advocate the basic principles of the Brannan plan through the election of 1952, but the focus of attention had changed, and, after the election of 1950, they entertained only faint hopes of its enactment.[4]

Despite signs that the Democratic National Committee had ostracized him during the 1950 campaign and rumors that he might be forced out of the USDA, Secretary Brannan survived and remained a tireless champion of the administration's cause.[5] At nearly every turn, however, he continued to face unrelenting opposition from the American Farm Bureau Federation. Whether it was in the day-to-day operation of the support program, the application of wartime price controls, or the USDA's Family Farm Policy Review, Truman and Brannan agreed that Allan Kline did everything he could "to embarrass the administration."[6]

3. Brannan to Senator Lyndon Johnson, May 23, 1951, Farm Program 2, General Correspondence, 1951, Office of the Secretary of Agriculture, RG 16, NA. Interest in the proposed Agricultural Conservation Program intensified in the wake of the devastating floods in the Missouri River Basin during the summer of 1951 (see, for example, James Patton to Brannan, August 6, 1951; K. T. Hutchinson, acting secretary of agriculture, to Stanley Matzke, November 26, 1951, Farm Program 2, General Correspondence, 1951, Office of the Secretary of Agriculture, RG 16, NA; "Agricultural Conservation Program," Clarence J. McCormick Papers, Harry S. Truman Library [hereafter cited as McCormick Papers]).

4. For example McCormick to Senator Thomas C. Hennings, June 2, 1952; Wesley McCune to Bert Gross, July 29, 1952; and McCune to Earl Schmidt, December 16, 1952, Farm Program 5–1, Office of the Secretary of Agriculture, RG 16, NA.

5. Brannan, "The Big Truth versus the Big Doubt," Jefferson-Jackson Day speech, Cheyenne, WY, May 26, 1951, OF, Truman Papers; Brannan to Wilson Wyatt, September 24, 1952, and to Murray D. Lincoln, September 23, 1952, PSF, Truman Papers. There is no indication that Brannan ever actually felt threatened with ouster or that Truman ever entertained such thoughts. He always believed Brannan to be "the finest of fine people" (Diary entry, June 24, 1955, in Ferrell, ed., *Off the Record,* 316; Brannan, interview).

6. Truman to Brannan, March 30, 1951, PSF, Truman Papers.

The Family Farm Policy Review initiative had commenced imme-diately after the 1950 election with the creation of a committee chaired by Under Secretary Clarence J. McCormick. According to Secretary Brannan, who introduced the idea, its objectives were,

> first, to develop and put into operation such changes as are pos-sible under existing legislation in the Department's policies, pro-grams, and procedures that would result in improving our ser-vices to family farms and farm families; and second, to develop and have available for the consideration of the Congress a com-prehensive set of recommendations for changes in existing legis-lation that would allow the Department of Agriculture to improve still further its services to family farms and farm families.[7]

McCormick's committee included representatives from many depart-ment agencies, farm organizations, and other groups such as the National Council of Churches and the National Catholic Rural Life Conference.

Despite USDA protests that it was not trying to "sell" any particular idea but rather gathering a wide spectrum of opinion on "how well the existing farm programs are serving family farmers and how they can be improved," the AFBF smelled the Brannan plan and quickly withheld its support.[8] In September 1951, the Chamber of Com-merce of the United States, focusing specifically on the Family Farm Policy Review, charged "that government agencies are invading the province of the Congress and the people by formulating policy in Washington and seeking support for it through country-wide gather-ings steered by federal employees." According to Walter B. Garver, secretary of the chamber's agricultural committee, the suggestions outlined in the USDA committee's statement "set the tone for a pro-gram that implies complete paternalism over American agriculture."[9]

7. Quoted in Herbert J. Waters, assistant to the under secretary, to Congress-man William G. Bray, October 19, 1951, "Land Reform-Family Farm-General, 1950–52," McCormick Papers.

8. Ibid.; "Summary of the Family Farm Policy Review," September 11, 1952, Miscellaneous Press Releases—USDA, 1952; McCormick to Kline, May 25, 1951, McCormick Papers; Hardin, *Politics of Agriculture,* 36; Matusow, *Farm Policies and Politics,* 239.

9. Chamber of Commerce news release, September 25, 1951, McCormick Papers.

By this time, administration opponents saw politics in everything in which Brannan had a hand. Many Republicans agreed with former senator Arthur Capper who insisted that it was "time to give the USDA back to farmers"; "The USDA should be divorced from politics. It should be directed and administered by a scientist, rather than a politician of the stripe of Charles Brannan."[10] Although many of these charges were unwarranted, the president and his secretary of agriculture had, for more than three years, greatly contributed to this type of opposition. Politics was not the only reason for the defeat of the Brannan plan and the administration's other agricultural initiatives, but it was a major contributor.

The Truman administration had been unable to implement liberal reforms in agriculture and thereby bring policy in line with the new conditions resulting from the "second agricultural revolution." Thus, in 1953 the task fell to the conservative Eisenhower administration. Secretary of Agriculture Ezra Taft Benson sought to reform New Deal agricultural programs to adapt them to the free market and the new technologies that were being continually developed and adopted for use on the farm. To rectify the problems that it believed had resulted from 90 percent price supports—huge surpluses that depressed domestic prices and cost millions of dollars in storage, the loss of world markets, and production patterns that were unresponsive to consumer demand—the Eisenhower administration, according to the Edward L. Schapsmeier and Frederick H. Schapsmeier, "requested Congress to enact a farm bill that would restore flexible price supports, modernize parity, stimulate foreign trade, and promote agricultural research (in consumer and industrial use)."[11]

The result was the passage of the Agricultural Act of 1954 that, Republican control of the Congress notwithstanding, did not move nearly as close to the free market as Eisenhower had hoped. The Dixiecrat-Republican coalition, which had blocked many of Truman's efforts in this and other areas, continued to function, and it forced a

10. Capper to R. J. McGuinnis, November 6, 1951, Agricultural Correspondence, Capper Papers; Capper, "It Is Time to Give the USDA Back to Farmers," 3.

11. Schapsmeier and Schapsmeier, "Farm Policy from FDR to Eisenhower," 367.

compromise. Although a flexible schedule was introduced, again it was to be phased in gradually. The sliding scale was set at 82.5 to 90 percent of parity for the first year, with the minimum eventually reaching 75 percent. An exception, however, was made for tobacco, and the "provision for transition to modern parity was so temporized that it would take years to achieve."[12]

The implementation of the Soil Bank in 1956 took some land out of production, but high price supports and increased technology continued to push total output to higher levels. In 1957, Secretary Benson championed legislation to allow the flexible schedule to work between 65 and 90 percent of parity. Congress took little heed of Benson's warning that action was needed in light of the "technological explosion" and did not act until 1958, when southern Democrats, in tandem with some "wheat belt" Republicans, postponed flexible supports for another three years. By that time, the Democrats had returned to the White House and proceeded to launch yet another high price support program. The farm policy problem, however, continued to elude solution.[13]

America had witnessed three decades of dramatic change in the nature of its agricultural industry but surprisingly little change in the nation's farm policy. Labor productivity had increased dramatically— farm policy hardly at all.[14] More important than labor productivity during the decades following World War I, however, was land productivity that rose 1.4 percent per year between 1925 and 1950 and 2.5

12. Ibid., 368. See also Rasmussen, ed., *Agriculture in the United States,* 4: 2989; Edward L. Schapsmeier and Frederick H. Schapsmeier, *Ezra Taft Benson and the Politics of Agriculture: The Eisenhower Years, 1953–1961,* passim; Chester J. Pach Jr. and Elmo Richardson, *The Presidency of Dwight D. Eisenhower, Revised Edition,* 55, 125, 177; Albert B. Genung, *The Fight for 'Flexible' Farm Aid: An Account of the Effort of the Eisenhower Administration to Bring about a Retreat from Former Policies of High, Fixed Price Supports,* 9; Stephen E. Ambrose, *Eisenhower: The President,* 159–60, 299–300.

13. Schapsmeier and Schapsmeier, "Farm Policy from FDR to Eisenhower," 370; Rich, *U.S. Agricultural Policy in the Postwar Years,* 1; Ambrose, *Eisenhower: The President,* 460–61.

14. Rasmussen, "The Impact of Technological Change," 590; Luther G. Tweeten, "Commodity Programs for Agriculture," in Ruttan, Waldo, and Houck, eds., *Agricultural Policy in an Affluent Society,* 107; Wilcox, Cochrane, and Herdt, *Economics of American Agriculture,* 5.

percent between 1950 and 1964.[15] Despite this revolutionary change, agricultural policy continued to be based on New Deal legislation adopted before the "second agricultural revolution flowered." Farm economists of the 1940s recognized that fundamental changes had affected price relationships and that this fact should be reflected in farm policy; many policy makers also were cognizant of the new situation's potential impact. Unfortunately, they were unable or unwilling to devise new policies, which would have recognized "the impact of the technological revolution."[16]

Although there was an obvious need for a significant overhaul of national farm policy during the post-World War II era, the basic ideas for the program, which emerged in the 1920s and were implemented during the depression of the 1930s, were continued. In retrospect it is safe to conclude, as did Willard Cochrane, that the more things changed the more they stayed the same.

> The design and operation of the programs by individual commodities has never changed. Price support and deficiency payments have always been, and continue to be, effectuated on a per unit basis of the commodity; thus the more units of a commodity that a farmer produces, the more he benefits from the programs. The nonrecourse loan concept was forged in the 1930s and remains in 1985 the principal mechanism for supporting the price of storable commodities. Production control from 1933 to the present day has been effectuated through voluntary acreage restrictions—a weak form of production control that renders the control features of the commodity program ineffective and inefficient.[17]

The "great restructuring" of American agriculture, which featured the concentration of productive resources "into a relatively few very large farms," accelerated after World War II.[18] Throughout this period,

15. Vernon W. Ruttan, "Agricultural Policy in an Affluent Society," in Ruttan, Waldo, and Houck, eds., *Agricultural Policy in an Affluent Society*, 5.

16. Rasmussen, "The Impact of Technological Change," 591; Cochrane, "Need to Rethink Agricultural Policy," 1002.

17. Cochrane, "Need to Rethink Agricultural Policy," 1004.

18. Ibid., 1002; Ruttan, "Agricultural Policy in an Affluent Society," in Ruttan, Waldo, and Houck, eds., *Agricultural Policy in an Affluent Society*, 10.

the American farmer has been caught on what Cochrane, for the first time in 1958, called the "agricultural treadmill." "In the pure theory of the treadmill," he explained,

> the early-bird adopter of an important new and improved technology reaps a profit for his innovative act, since his cost structure falls as the result of that act but the price of the commodity does not. As more and more farmers adopt that technology, the supplies of that commodity begin to increase and the price begins to decline. After a widespread adoption of that new technology, a new equilibrium solution is reached with adopters back in a no-profit situation and the price of the commodity is at a new, lower level.[19]

Government policy has impacted upon the theory in that price-supporting mechanisms intervene to keep prices at or above predetermined levels. The incentive is to overproduce, and the "early and aggressive adopters . . . seek to expand their operations." They apply greater technology and expand their operations through the acquisition of more land, by necessity from those who are in financial difficulty. "A point is reached when the competition for the scarce input, land, forces the price of land to rise." The "early-bird" benefits because the price of his land holdings increases, and "the level of price and income support must be raised again" to "help farmers whose costs structures have risen to a level that makes their operations unprofitable." The farmers being helped, however, are those in the least need because the "laggard farmer" is being forced out in this ongoing process.[20] Therefore the government, through its commodity based programs, actually encourages the concentration of agricultural resources and hurts the "moderate-sized family farmer" who it intended to "save" and is unresponsive to the needs of the rural poor.

Since the late 1940s, the struggle over farm policy had been fought

19. Cochrane, "Need to Rethink Agricultural Policy," 1005; Cochrane, *Farm Prices: Myth and Reality.*

20. Cochrane, "Need to Rethink Agricultural Policy," 1005. A useful collection of Cochrane's policy analyses over the years that brings his thinking into the twenty-first century is Willard W. Cochrane, *The Curse of American Agricultural Abundance: A Sustainable Solution.* See also Richard A. Levins, *Willard Cochrane and the American Family Farm.*

chiefly by two loosely knit alliances. One coalition, represented by most Republicans, southern Democrats, and conservative farm organizations, had sought to hold farm prices up with production controls and supply management. The other, the cohorts of Secretary of Agriculture Charles F. Brannan (the "vital center" liberals), wanted to let commodities find their own levels in the market place with income support being provided through direct (production or, later deficiency) payments. Subsequently, these positions were compromised with the passage of the Food and Agricultural Act of 1965.[21] Price and income supports were both incorporated and, as was feared by many during the post-World War II debate, farm incomes came to depend more on the generosity of the federal treasury. Americans finally came to accept income payments as a more satisfactory way to support farmers than price supports. Some of Secretary Brannan's ideas were adopted but never the whole package.

It is not the purpose of this study to suggest an alternative approach for national agricultural policy; that is a task that falls outside the province of this writer. Many highly qualified scholars, especially those in the field of agricultural economics, have entered this conversation, and the result has been the emergence of an impressive literature, most of it based on highly sophisticated statistical analyses.[22] These studies of what the country's agricultural policies should have or could have been, or should be, call for a new approach and for programs that will seriously consider and bring into balance the social costs with the benefits for the larger society. Most have come to agree with Bruce Gardner, who concluded "that our policies do not promote

21. Willard W. Cochrane, *Development of American Agriculture*, 287–89.

22. The dean of this group of writers is, unquestionably, Theodore W. Schultz, whose work *Agriculture in an Unstable Economy*, was discussed earlier in this volume. Among many works that have contributed substantially to the ongoing postwar debate are Johnson, "High Level Support Prices and Corn Belt Agriculture," 509; Collins, "Agricultural Policy and the General Economy," 191; Theodore W. Schultz, *The Economic Organization of Agriculture;* Cochrane, *Farm Prices: Myth and Reality* and *Curse of American Agricultural Abundance;* Charles M. Hardin, *Agricultural Policy, Politics, and Public Interest;* Johnson, *Farm Commodity Programs*; Gardner, *Governing of Agriculture,* and *Economics of Agricultural Policies;* Day, ed., *Economic Analysis and Agricultural Policy;* Browne et al., *Sacred Cows and Hot Potatoes;* Cochrane and Runge, *Reforming Farm Policy.*

the public interest as well as they should and that the principal route to improvement is through less intervention in the commodity markets."[23]

For the most part, these scholars do not lament the defeat of the Brannan plan, which veered only slightly from the old farm policy course and would have pegged prices too high and cost too much and resulted in even more government intervention in the agricultural economy. They do, however, mourn the opportunity lost. Charles Brannan recognized some of the hazards that lay ahead and sought to chart a new course, but his basic proposals respecting price support policy, like those with more political viability during his day, failed to adequately address the postwar farm problem. A real change of direction was needed; the Brannan plan was not it.

The principle objective of this volume has been to examine this failed policy initiative, and secondarily to review the early history of farm policy (especially the commodity price support programs that have tended to dominate the debate) as we know it today. The debate of 1948–1950 is particularly important because it marked the first postwar effort to break the political stalemate and redirect agricultural programs to confront the mid-twentieth century farm crisis. The Truman administration and many of the more farsighted members of the U.S. Congress recognized the need, but they were unable to find (or agree on) the solution.

In spite of the seemingly endless debate and tireless effort expended by lawmakers and the USDA, the farm policy that emerged was warmed-over New Deal. No consensus could be reached "for a thoroughgoing and permanent policy either of a free market or a sharply managed farm economy." In fact, as Spencer Rich explained, when the support system was tested after Korea, "it proved unable to achieve the ends for which it was constructed." The compromise farm program continued to work to the benefit of the efficient farmer who learned

---

23. Gardner, *Governing of Agriculture,* xi; Johnson, *Farm Commodity Programs,* 2–5. Johnson found that the major farm commodity programs "impose substantially greater costs upon taxpayers and consumers than the benefits realized by farm families" and concluded that most of the benefits have gone to farmers with better than average incomes, while "almost none has gone to low-income farm families, whether farm operators or hired farm workers. . . . In sum, a new approach is needed because outmoded programs have imposed higher and higher costs and provided fewer and fewer benefits" (2–5).

to take advantage of the system; it did not save the marginal producers. The result was the "paradox of the 1950s: despite lower prices and shrinking profit margins which reinforced the squeeze on small farmers to abandon farming, production on the remaining farms was rising and surpluses were increasing."[24]

Subsequent developments underscore the significance of the failed effort in the late 1940s and raise several interrelated questions. In light of political realities of the times, was a good compromise farm program a possibility in 1949? Why did the postwar search for a long-range policy for agriculture fail at a time when most agreed some change in the basic law was essential? Why was this seemingly great opportunity lost? There can be, of course, no definitive answer to these questions, but some speculation is warranted.

Most likely, the answer lies first in the nature of the American political system. Members of the national government are given the responsibility for making policy for the entire nation, but they are accountable to only a fraction of that nation's electorate. To make policy, they must be elected, and too often to be elected they must be solicitous of relatively narrow parochial interests. In the case of agriculture, which is characterized by vast differences between commodities, this means that each representative and senator is invariably driven by what seems best for his or her particular region; politically, it becomes difficult, if not impossible, to keep the big picture in focus.[25] If this were not trouble enough, farm policy formulation is also plagued by

---

24. Rich, *U.S. Agricultural Policy in the Postwar Years,* 2.

25. For more on the agricultural lobby and the legislative process, see William P. Browne, *Private Interests, Public Policy, and American Agriculture.* Browne argued that from the 1920s and "into the 1950s, [agricultural] insiders included a small cadre of farm state legislators, ranking USDA officials, and representatives of the Farm Bureau, the NFU, and the Grange. At times, and on such major issues as the Brannan plan, widespread partisan conflict between the Republican-oriented Farm Bureau and the Democratic-allied Farmers Union [the voice of the smaller-scale farmer] broke out." (41) In more recent times, because of the many dimensions and complexity of agricultural legislation, "distinctions between agricultural insiders and outsiders have lost much of their policy relevance" (41–42). See also John Mark Hansen, who examined "interest group access" over time and found a significant redistribution taking place in the late 1950s and 1960s: "agricultural commodity groups" gained access to lawmakers at the expense of the general farm organizations, most notably the AFBF (*Gaining Access,* 120–21).

the existence of special interests not directly involved in the production of agricultural commodities, in particular processors and consumers. Each has a vested interest in agricultural programs affecting supplies, marketing and prices, and often, through their own organizations, they exert considerable influence in the formulation of policy.

A second explanation for this legislative morass can be found in the specific political circumstances of the period from 1947 to 1949. When the Republican Party took over Congress in 1947 for the first time in a decade and a half, it recognized that one of its responsibilities and opportunities lay in the area of farm policy. Months of hearings and hours of debate, however, failed to forge a consensus, and the resulting Hope Aiken Act did not even satisfy the principal authors. Indeed, Congressman Clifford Hope adopted the unusual strategy of advocating its passage while promising revision in the next Congress. Although the Agricultural Act of 1948 was not as mongrelized as its harshest critics maintained, there was no doubt that the Republican Eightieth Congress had botched its opportunity to provided truly effective long-range policy. The electorate did not give it a second chance.

With its shortfall in agriculture and other policy areas, the GOP invited partisan exploitation. Harry Truman was not one to turn down such an invitation. In a fight for their political lives, the president and his party seized a golden opportunity in a no-holds-barred campaign to castigate the "Do-Nothing 80th Congress." As is often the case, extreme partisanship was the rule during the election of 1948, and agriculture was not exempt. Truman won a stunning presidential victory, and his party regained majority control of the House of Representatives and the Senate, but this was not, as it turned out, a Fair Deal Congress. The antiadministration coalition was as formidable as ever, and, at least partially because of the bitterness engendered by the past campaign, the president was unable to build an alternative coalition in support of his domestic initiatives.

It would be easy to contend that a farm policy compromise was unattainable in 1949. There is no denying the existence of some fundamental philosophical differences between the various parties involved, and it is likely that some powerful factions would never have come around. Certain provisions of the Brannan plan, which treated agricultural policy as part of a whole and integrate it into an overall economic policy for the nation, were totally unacceptable to key groups within agriculture's diverse constituency.

These differences notwithstanding, the basis for an executive-legislative coalition on farm policy seems to have existed. Senator George Aiken and Representative Hope, two highly respected Republican leaders, were potential allies lost as a result of USDA intransigence. It goes without saying that both sides were in part politically motivated. Agriculture had been a political football for many years, and Republicans were hardly above the use of scare tactics in an effort to gain political advantage. The administration, however, must shoulder the major responsibility for making farm policy so intensely partisan in 1948, and again in 1949. What was needed was some creative and positive domestic diplomacy, a commodity that was in short supply at the White House, the USDA, and in both houses of Congress.

For its part, the administration had decided, probably as a result of a misreading of the 1948 farm vote, that high-level supports, by far the most significant roadblock in the path of compromise, were desirable and would ensure further Democratic inroads into the farm belt in 1950. Thus, President Truman, who was so effective in working his foreign policy coalition, and Secretary Brannan were willing to await a favorable election (anticipated in 1950) so they could obtain a whole loaf rather than half. In this instance, however, half may actually have been better policy. Brannan was committed to his constituency and believed he was pursuing a worthy goal, but he seems to have lost sight of political realities. Blinded by the conviction that it was only the Farm Bureau that blocked his road to success, he failed to heed much sound advice—counsel that came from inside and outside the administration. For their part, Republicans (including Aiken and Hope) and their allies were convinced that the administration was motivated solely by political considerations. They lashed out at the Brannan plan, thus contributing to the degeneration of the debate and the ultimate failure of the legislative process where agriculture was concerned.

Nevertheless, the great debates on postwar farm policy, occurring primarily in 1948 and 1949, are of historical significance. Certainly, one cannot begin to comprehend the subsequent dialectic on these complex issues without first looking at this episode. It was here that the arguments, which would dominate agricultural debate for years to come, first crystallized. As was the case in so many domestic policy areas—civil rights, federal housing, national health care, and aid to education—the Fair Deal's success was not in actual legislation but in the introduction of concepts that would eventually gain currency or at least grudging acceptance. In addition, the debate was permanently refocused: not on whether the federal government had a role in agriculture but on what its role and specific policy should be. Members of Congress and the American public might still object philosophically to government largess, but they expected it, at least where their special interests were concerned, and accepted the accompanying increases in the size and power of the national government.[26] This was as true for America's farmers as it was for the elderly and the unemployed, for workers, and for business people.

26. McCoy, *Presidency of Harry S. Truman,* 311; Dean, "Farm Policy Debate of 1949–1950," 33.

BIBLIOGRAPHY

Primary Sources

Manuscript Collections

Harry S. Truman Library, Independence, Missouri
    Clinton P. Anderson Papers
    Charles F. Brannan Papers
    Clarence J. McCormick Papers
    J. Howard McGrath Papers
    Edwin G. Nourse Papers, Microfilm Copy
    Harry S. Truman Papers
Kansas State Historical Society, Topeka, Kansas
    Arthur Capper Papers
    Clifford Hope Papers
University of Vermont, Burlington, Vermont
    George D. Aiken Papers

Government Archives

National Archives and Records Administration, Washington, D.C.
    Records of the Bureau of the Budget, Record Group 51
    Records of the Office of the Secretary of Agriculture, Record
    Group 16

Published Government Documents

Bureau of the Census. *Historical Abstracts of the United States, Colonial Times to 1970, Bicentennial Edition, Parts 1 and 2.* Washington, D.C.: U.S. Government Printing Office, 1975.

Committee on the Economic Report. *January 1949 Economic Report of the President.* Hearings before the Joint Committee on the Economic Report. 81st Cong., 1st sess., February 8–18, 1949.

Congressional Record.

House of Representatives. Committee on Agriculture. *Long-Range Agricultural Policy. Hearings before the Committee on Agriculture.* 80th Cong., 1st sess., April 21-May 29, 1947.

———. Committee on Agriculture. *General Farm Program: Hearings before a Special Subcommittee.* 81st Cong., 1st sess., pt. 1, March 22–28, 1949.

———. Committee on Agriculture. *General Farm Program, including Joint Hearings with the Senate Committee on Agriculture and Forestry.* 81st Cong., 1st sess., pt. 2, April 7-May 19, 1949.

Senate. Committee on Agricultural and Forestry. *Long-Range Agricultural Policy and Program.* 80th Cong., 1st sess., October 6–November 10, 1947.

———. Committee on Agricultural and Forestry. *Agricultural Act of 1948.* 80th Cong., 2nd sess., April 12–24, 1948.

———. Committee on Agriculture and Forestry. *Hearings before the Subcommittee on the Agricultural Adjustment Act of 1949.* 81st Cong., 1st sess., July 7–19, 1949.

———. Committee on Agricultural and Forestry. *Price Support for Hogs: Hearings before a Special Subcommittee on S. 1721.* 81st Cong., 1st sess., June 17–18, July 6, 1949.

U.S. Statutes at Large.

Published Sources

Ferrell, Robert H., ed. *Dear Bess: The Letters from Harry to Bess Truman, 1910–1959.* New York: W. W. Norton, 1983.

———, ed. *Off the Record: The Private Papers of Harry S. Truman.* New York: Harper and Row, 1980.

————, ed. *Truman in the White House: The Diary of Eben A. Ayers.* Columbia: University of Missouri Press, 1991.

Gallup, George H. *The Gallup Poll: Public Opinion 1935–1971.* Vols. 1–2. New York: American Institute of Public Opinion, 1972.

Poen, Monte M. *Strictly Personal and Confidential: The Letters Harry Truman Never Mailed.* Boston: Little, Brown, 1982.

Porter, Kirk H., and Donald Bruce Johnson, comps. *National Party Platforms, 1840–1964.* Urbana: University of Illinois Press, 1966.

Rasmussen, Wayne D., ed. *Agriculture in the United States: A Documentary History.* 4 vols. New York: Random House, 1975.

Roper, Elmo. *You and Your Leaders: Their Actions and Your Reactions, 1936–1956.* New York: William Morrow, 1957.

Truman, Harry S. *Public Papers of the Presidents of the United States: Harry S. Truman, 1945–1950.* Washington, D.C.: U.S. Government Printing Office, 1961–1965.

Secondary Sources

Abels, Jules. *Out of the Jaws of Victory.* New York: Henry Holt, 1959.

Agar, Herbert. *The Price of Power: America since 1945.* Chicago: University of Chicago Press, 1957.

Albertson, Dean. *Roosevelt's Farmer: Claude R. Wickard in the New Deal.* New York: Columbia University Press, 1961.

Ambrose, Stephen E. *Eisenhower: The President.* New York: Simon and Schuster, 1984.

————. *Nixon: The Education of a Politician, 1913–1962.* New York: Simon and Schuster, 1987.

Anderson, Clifford B. "The Metamorphosis of Agrarian Idealism in the 1920s and 1930s." *Agricultural History* 35 (October 1961): 182–88.

Anderson, Clinton P. "Is the Farmer Heading for Trouble Again?" *Saturday Evening Post* 213 (December 22, 1945): 18–19, 94–96.

————. *Outsider in the Senate: Senator Clinton Anderson's Memoirs.* New York: World Publishing, 1970.

————. "'Work Conquers All Things': Full Employment First Requisite for Farm Prosperity." *Vital Speeches of the Day* 11 (August 15, 1945): 661–64.

Anderson, Patrick. *The President's Men: White House Assistants of Franklin D. Roosevelt, Harry S. Truman, Dwight D. Eisenhower, John F. Kennedy, and Lyndon B. Johnson.* Garden City, N.Y.: Doubleday, 1968.

Baker, Gladys L., Wayne D. Rasmussen, Vivian Wiser, and Jane M. Porter. *Century of Service: The First 100 Years of the United States Department of Agriculture.* Washington, D.C.: Centennial Committee, U.S. Department of Agriculture, 1963.

Baker, Ralph. "What to Do about . . . Egg Price Props?" *Farm Policy Forum* 3 (January 1950): 15–18.

Bendiner, Robert. "Has the American Voter Swung Right? The Midterm Election in Perspective." *Commentary* 11 (January 1951): 27–35.

Benedict, Murray R. *Can We Solve the Farm Problem? An Analysis of Federal Aid to Agriculture.* New York: Twentieth Century Fund, 1955.

———. *Farm Policies of the United States, 1790–1950: A Study of Their Origins and Developments.* New York: Twentieth Century Fund, 1953.

Benedict, Murray R., and Oscar C. Stine. *The Agricultural Commodity Programs: Two Decades of Experience.* New York: Twentieth Century Fund, 1956.

Berger, Samuel R. *Dollar Harvest: The Story of the Farm Bureau.* Lexington, Mass.: D. C. Heath, 1971.

Bernstein, Barton J. "Clash of Interests: Postwar Battle between the Office of Price Administration and the Department of Agriculture." *Agricultural History* 41 (January 1967): 45–57.

———, ed. *Politics and Policies of the Truman Administration.* Chicago: Quadrangle Books, 1970.

———. "The Postwar Famine and Price Control, 1946." *Agricultural History* 38 (October 1964): 235–40.

Bernstein, Barton J., and Allen J. Matusow, eds. *The Truman Administration: A Documentary History.* New York: Harper and Row, 1966.

Black, John D. "Farm Problems: II. Agricultural Price Support. Discussion." *American Economic Review* 41 (May 1951): 747–54.

———. *Parity, Parity, Parity.* Cambridge: Harvard Committee on Research in the Social Sciences, 1942.

Block, William J. *The Separation of the Farm Bureau and the Extension Service.* Urbana: University of Illinois Press, 1960.

Bowers, Douglas E. "The Research and Marketing Act of 1946 and Its Effects on Agricultural Marketing Research." *Agricultural History* 56 (January 1982): 249–63.

Brannan, Charles F. "Agricultural Abundance, for Better or Worse?" *Vital Speeches of the Day* 15 (October 1, 1949): 764–67.

Branyan, Robert L., and A. Theodore Brown, eds. *The Paradox of Plenty: Readings on the Agricultural Surplus since World War I.* Dubuque, Iowa: William C. Brown, 1968.

Browne, William P. *Private Interests, Public Policy, and American Agriculture.* Lawrence: University Press of Kansas, 1988.

Browne, William P., et al. *Sacred Cows and Hot Potatoes: Agrarian Myths in Agricultural Policy.* Boulder: Westview Press, 1992.

Burns, James MacGregor. *The Deadlock of Democracy.* Englewood Cliffs, N.J.: Prentice-Hall, 1963.

Cady, Darrell. "The Truman Administration's Reconversion Policies, 1945–1947." Ph.D. diss., University of Kansas, 1974.

Campbell, Christiana McFadyen. *The Farm Bureau and the New Deal: A Study of the Making of National Farm Policy, 1933–1940.* Urbana: University of Illinois, 1962.

Capper, Arthur. *The Agricultural Bloc.* New York: Harcourt, Brace, 1922.

———. "American Farmers Revolt: Economic Causes." *Current History, a Monthly Magazine* 24 (May 1926): 189–91.

———. "It Is Time to Give the USDA Back to Farmers." *Capper's Farmer* 62 (November 1951): 3.

Case, H. C. M. "The Agricultural Act of 1948." *Journal of Farm Economics* 31 (February 1949): 227–36.

Christenson, Reo M. *The Brannan Plan: Farm Politics and Policies.* Ann Arbor: University of Michigan Press, 1959.

Clemens, Cyril, ed. *Truman Speaks.* New York: Kraus Reprint, 1969.

Clifford, Clark. *Counsel to the President: A Memoir.* New York: Random House, 1991.

Cochrane, Bert. *Harry Truman and the Crisis Presidency.* New York: Funk and Wagnalls, 1973.

Cochrane, Willard W. *The Curse of American Agricultural Abundance:*

A Sustainable Solution. Lincoln: University of Nebraska Press, 2003.

———. *The Development of American Agriculture: A Historical Analysis.* Minneapolis: University of Minnesota Press, 1979.

———. *Farm Prices: Myth and Reality.* Minneapolis: University of Minnesota Press, 1958.

———. "Farm Problems: II. Agricultural Price Support. Discussion." *American Economic Review* 41 (May 1951): 754–57.

———. "Income Payments as a Substitute for Support Prices." *Journal of Farm Economics* 28 (November 1946): 1024–29.

———. "The Need to Rethink Agricultural Policy in General and to Perform Some Radical Surgery on Commodity Programs in Particular." *American Journal of Agricultural Economics* 67 (December 1985): 1002–1009.

Cochrane, Willard W., and C. Ford Runge. *Reforming Farm Policy: Toward a National Agenda.* Ames: Iowa State University Press, 1992.

Cochrane, Willard W., and Mary E. Ryan. *American Farm Policy, 1948–1973.* Minneapolis: University of Minnesota Press, 1976.

Collins, Geoffrey P. "Agricultural Policy and the General Economy." *Southwestern Social Science Quarterly* 31 (December 1950): 191–96.

"Congress Explores the Brannan Plan." *Congressional Digest* 29 (March 1950): 69–70.

"Contradiction in Price Policy." *U.S. News* 21 (February 28, 1947): 24–25.

Counts, Tim. "Editorial Influence on GOP Vote in 1948 Presidential Election." *Journalism Quarterly* 66 (Spring 1989): 177–81.

Crampton, John A. *The National Farmers Union: Ideology of a Pressure Group.* Lincoln: University of Nebraska Press, 1965.

Current Biography. New York: H. W. Wilson, 1940–1954.

Davies, Richard O. *Housing Reform during the Truman Administration.* Columbia: University of Missouri Press, 1966.

Davis, Chester C. "The Development of Agricultural Policy since the End of the World War." In *Farmers in a Changing World, Yearbook of Agriculture 1940,* U.S. Department of Agriculture. Washington, D.C.: U.S. Government Printing Office, 1940.

Day, Richard H., ed. *Economic Analysis and Agricultural Policy.* Ames: Iowa State University Press, 1982.

Dean, Virgil W. "Charles F. Brannan and the Rise and Fall of Truman's 'Fair Deal' for Farmers." *Agricultural History* 69 (Winter 1995): 28–53.

———. "Farm Policy and Truman's 1948 Campaign." *The Historian* 55 (Spring 1993): 501–16.

———. "The Farm Policy Debate of 1949–1950: Plains State Reaction to the Brannan Plan." *Great Plains Quarterly* 13 (Winter 1993): 33–46.

———. "Why Not the Brannan Plan." *Agricultural History* 70 (Spring 1996): 268–82.

"Defeat of the Farm Plan." *New Republic: A Journal of Opinion* 121 (September 12, 1949): 7–8.

Divine, Robert A. "The Cold War and the Election of 1948." *Journal of American History* 59 (June 1972): 90–109.

Donaldson, Gary A. "Who Wrote the Clifford Memo? The Origins of Campaign Strategy in the Truman Administration." *Presidential Studies Quarterly* 23 (Fall 1993): 747–54.

Donovan, Robert J. *Conflict and Crisis: The Presidency of Harry S Truman, 1945–1949.* New York: W. W. Norton, 1977.

———. *Tumultuous Years: The Presidency of Harry S Truman, 1949–1953.* New York: W. W. Norton, 1982.

Eisenhower, Milton S. *The President Is Calling.* Garden City, N.Y.: Doubleday, 1974.

"The Elusive Cost Factor." *Congressional Digest* 29 (March 1950): 78.

Estabrook, Robert H. "The Bogey in the Brannan Plan." *Antioch Review* 10 (Spring 1950): 73–77.

"Farm Acts in the 81st Congress." *Congressional Digest* 29 (March 1950): 74–75.

Fenno, Richard F. *The President's Cabinet: An Analysis in the Period from Wilson to Eisenhower.* Cambridge: Harvard University Press, 1959.

Ferrell, Robert H. *Harry S. Truman: A Life.* Columbia: University of Missouri Press, 1994.

———. *Harry S. Truman and the Modern American Presidency.* Boston: Little, Brown, 1983.

Field, Bruce E. *Harvest of Dissent: The National Farmers Union and the Early Cold War.* Lawrence: University Press of Kansas, 1998.

Finegold, Kenneth. "From Agrarianism to Adjustment: The Political Origins of New Deal Agricultural Policy." *Politics and Society* 11, no. 1 (1982): 1–27.

Fite, Gilbert C. *American Agriculture and Farm Policy since 1900.* American Historical Association, Service for Teachers of History Publication No. 59. New York: Macmillan, 1964.

———. *American Farmers: The New Minority.* Bloomington: Indiana University Press, 1981.

———. *Cotton Fields No More: Southern Agriculture, 1865–1980.* Lexington: University Press of Kentucky, 1984.

———. "Farmer Opinion and the Agricultural Adjustment Act, 1933." *Mississippi Valley Historical Review* 48 (March 1962): 656–73.

———. *George N. Peek and the Fight for Farm Parity.* Norman: University of Oklahoma Press, 1954.

Flamm, Michael W. "The National Farmers Union and the Evolution of Agrarian Liberalism, 1937–1946." *Agricultural History* 68 (Summer 1994): 54–80.

Flash, Edward S., Jr. *Economic Advice and Presidential Leadership: The Council of Economic Advisers.* New York: Columbia University Press, 1965.

Formisano, Ronald, and William Shady. "The Concept of Agrarian Radicalism." *Mid-America: A Historical Review* 52 (January 1970): 3–30.

Forsythe, James L. "Clifford Hope of Kansas: Practical Congressman and Agrarian Idealist." *Agricultural History* 51 (April 1977): 406–20.

———. "Clinton P. Anderson: Politician and Businessman as Truman's Secretary of Agriculture." Ph.D. diss., University of New Mexico, 1970.

———. "Postmortem on the Election of 1948: An Evaluation of Cong. Clifford R. Hope's Views." *Kansas Historical Quarterly* 38 (Autumn 1972): 338–59.

Gardner, Bruce L. *The Economics of Agricultural Policies.* New York: Macmillan, 1987.

———. *The Governing of Agriculture.* Lawrence: Regents Press of Kansas, 1981.

Garraty, John A., and Mark C. Carnes, eds. *American National Biography.* New York: Oxford University Press, 1999.

Genung, Albert. *Farm Aid Programs: A Brief Survey of Thirty-Five Years of Government Aid to Agriculture Beginning in 1920.* Ithaca: Northeast Farm Foundation, 1955.

———. *The Fight for 'Flexible' Farm Aid: An Account of the Effort of the Eisenhower Administration to Bring about a Retreat from Former Policies of High, Fixed Price Supports.* Ithaca: Northeast Farm Foundation, 1957.

Gilpatrick, Thomas, V. "Price Support Policy and the Midwest Farm Vote." *Midwest Journal of Political Science* 3 (November 1959): 319–35.

Gosnell, Harold F. *Truman's Crises: A Political Biography of Harry S. Truman.* Westport, Conn.: Greenwood Press, 1980.

"G.O.P. Rebels' Key Position: Four Who Could Prevent Overriding of Vetoes on Labor and Taxes." *U.S. News* 22 (May 16, 1947): 20–23.

Graham, Otis L., Jr., and Meghan Robinson Wander, eds. *Franklin D. Roosevelt: His Life and Times, an Encyclopedic View.* Boston: G. K. Hall, 1985.

Grant, Michael J. "'Food Will Win the War and Write the Peace': The Federal Government and Kansas Farmers during World War II." *Kansas History* 20 (Winter 1997–1998): 242–57.

Halcrow, Harold G. *Agricultural Policy of the United States.* New York: Prentice-Hall, 1953.

Halcrow, Harold G., and Roy E. Huffman. "Great Plains Agriculture and Brannan's Farm Program." *Journal of Farm Economics* 31 (August 1949): 497–508.

Hall, Tom. "The Aiken Bill, Price Supports, and the Wheat Farmer in 1948." *North Dakota History* 39 (Winter 1972): 13–22, 47.

Hamby, Alonzo L. *Beyond the New Deal: Harry S. Truman and American Liberalism.* New York: Columbia University Press, 1973.

———, ed. *Harry S. Truman and the Fair Deal.* Lexington, Mass.: D. C. Heath, 1974.

———. "The Liberals, Truman, and FDR as Symbol and Myth." *Journal of American History* 56 (March 1970): 859–67.

———. *Man of the People: A Life of Harry S. Truman.* New York: Oxford University Press, 1995.

Hamilton, David E. *From New Day to New Deal: American Farm Policy from Hoover to Roosevelt, 1928–1933.* Chapel Hill: University of North Carolina Press, 1991.

Hansen, John Mark. *Gaining Access: Congress and the Farm Lobby, 1919–1981.* Chicago: University of Chicago Press, 1991.

Hardin, Charles M. *Agricultural Policy, Politics, and Public Interest.* Philadelphia: American Academy of Political and Social Science, 1960.

———. "The Politics of Agriculture in the United States." *Journal of Farm Economics* 32 (November 1950): 571–83.

———. *The Politics of Agriculture: Soil Conservation and the Struggle for Power in Rural America.* Glencoe, Ill.: Free Press, 1952.

Harris, Joseph P., ed. "The 1950 Election in the West." *Western Political Quarterly* 4 (March 1951): 67–96.

Hathaway, Dale E. *Government and Agriculture: Public Policy in a Democratic Society.* New York: Macmillan, 1963.

Heady, Earl O. *A Primer on Food, Agriculture, and Public Policy.* New York: Random House, 1967.

Hechler, Ken. *Working with Truman: A Personal Memoir of the White House Years.* New York: G. P. Putnam's Sons, 1982.

Heller, Francis H., ed. *The Truman White House: The Administration of the Presidency, 1945–1953.* Lawrence: Regents Press of Kansas, 1980.

Hendrix, W. E. "The Brannan Plan and Farm Adjustment Opportunities in the Cotton South." *Journal of Farm Economics* 31 (August 1949): 487–96.

Hirsch, Julius, and Edith Hirsch. "Uncle Sam's Indigestion." *Nation's Business* 37 (July 1949): 25–26, 72–73.

Hope, Clifford R. "Views on the Brannan Plan." *Congressional Digest* 29 (March 1950): 83–85.

Hope, Clifford R., Jr. *Quiet Courage: Kansas Congressman Clifford R. Hope.* Manhattan, Kans.: Sunflower University Press, 1997.

Hurt, R. Douglas. *American Agriculture: A Brief History.* Ames: Iowa State University Press, 1994.

———. "Prices, Payments, and Production: Kansas Wheat Farmers and the Agricultural Adjustment Administration, 1933–1939." *Kansas History* 23 (Spring/Summer 2000): 72–87.

Jesness, O. B. "What Do We Expect from a Farm Program." *Farm Policy Forum* 3 (January 1950): 5.

Johnson, D. Gale. "Agricultural Price Policy—1948 Style." *Farm Policy Forum* 2 (January 1949): 18–21.

————. *Farm Commodity Programs: An Opportunity for Change.* Washington, D.C.: American Enterprise Institute for Public Policy Research, 1973.

————. "High Level Support Prices and Corn Belt Agriculture." *Journal of Farm Economics* 31 (August 1949): 509–19.

Johnson, Glenn L. *Forward Prices for Agriculture.* Chicago: University of Chicago Press, 1947.

Johnson, Glenn L., and C. Leroy Quance, eds. *The Overproduction Trap in U.S. Agriculture: A Study of Resource Allocation from World War I to the Late 1960s.* Baltimore: Johns Hopkins University Pres, 1972.

Johnson, Stewart, and George Brincgar. "What about the Brannan Plan? Some Suggestions on How the Brannan Plan Could Be Improved." *Farm Policy Forum* 2 (October 1949): 9–12.

Johnson, William R. "National Farm Organizations and the Reshaping of Agricultural Policy in 1932." *Agricultural History* 37 (January 1963): 35–42.

Jones, William O. "Current Farm Price-Support Proposals in the United States." *Journal of Politics* 13 (May 1951): 253–68.

Kelley, Darwin N. "The McNary-Haugen Bills, 1924–1928: An Attempt to Make the Tariff Effective for Farm Products." *Agricultural History* 14 (October 1940): 170–80.

Key, V. O., Jr. *Southern Politics in State and Nation.* New York: Alfred A. Knopf, 1949.

————. "A Theory of Critical Elections." *Journal of Politics* 17 (February 1955): 3–17.

Kile, Orville M. *Farm Bureau through Three Decades.* Baltimore: Waverly Press, 1948.

Kirkendall, Richard S. "Harry S. Truman: A Missouri Farmer in the Golden Age." *Agricultural History* 48 (October 1974): 467–83.

————, ed. *The Harry S. Truman Encyclopedia.* Boston: G. K. Hall, 1989.

————. *Social Scientists and Farm Politics in the Age of Roosevelt.* Columbia: University of Missouri Press, 1966.

Kline, Allan B. "Government and Agriculture." A Series of Addresses and Papers Presented at the Semiannual Meeting of the Academy of Political Science, April 26, 1950. *Proceedings of the Academy of Political Science* 24 (May 1950): 78–87.

Koenig, Louis W., ed. *The Truman Administration: Its Principles and Practices.* New York: New York University Press, 1956.

Kramer, Randall A. "Federal Crop Insurance, 1938–1982." *Agricultural History* 57 (April 1983): 181–200.

Krock, Arthur. *In the Nation, 1932–1966.* New York: McGraw-Hill, 1966.

LaPalombara, Joseph G. "Pressure, Propaganda, and Political Action in the Election of 1950." *Journal of Politics* 14 (March 1952): 300–325.

Lee, R. Alton. *Truman and Taft-Hartley: A Question of Mandate.* Lexington: University of Kentucky Press, 1966.

————. "The Turnip Session of the Do-Nothing Congress: Presidential Campaign Strategy." *Southwestern Social Science Quarterly* 44 (December 1963): 256–67.

Leuchtenburg, William E. *In the Shadow of FDR: From Harry Truman to Ronald Reagan.* Ithaca: Cornell University Press, 1983.

Levantrosser, William F., ed. *Harry S. Truman: The Man from Independence.* New York: Greenwood Press, 1986.

Levins, Richard A. *Willard Cochrane and the American Family Farm.* Lincoln: University of Nebraska Press, 2000.

Low, W. Augustus, and Virgil A. Clift, eds. *Encyclopedia of Black America.* New York: McGraw-Hill, 1981.

Lubell, Samuel. *Future of American Politics.* New York: Harper and Brothers, 1952.

————. "Who Really Elected Truman?" *Saturday Evening Post* 221 (January 22, 1949): 15–17, 54–64.

MacKenzie, Norman. "After the U.S. Polls." *New Statesman and Nation* 40 (November 18, 1950): 450–51.

Marcus, Maeva. *Truman and the Steel Seizure Case: The Limits of Presidential Power.* New York: Columbia University Press, 1977.

Markowitz, Norman D. *The Rise and Fall of the People's Century: Henry A. Wallace and American Liberalism, 1941–1948.* New York: Free Press, 1973.

Matusow, Allen J. *Farm Policies and Politics in the Truman Years.* Cambridge: Harvard University Press, 1967.

————. *The Unraveling of America: A History of Liberalism in the 1960s.* New York: Harper and Row, 1984.

McConnell, Grant. *The Decline of Agrarian Democracy.* Los Angeles: University of California Press, 1953.

McCoy, Donald R. *Calvin Coolidge: The Quiet President.* Lawrence: University Press of Kansas, 1988.

——. *Coming of Age: The United States during the 1920s and 1930s.* New York: Penguin Books, 1973.

——. *The Presidency of Harry S. Truman.* Lawrence: University Press of Kansas, 1984.

McCoy, Donald R., and Richard T. Ruetten. *Quest and Response: Minority Rights and the Truman Administration.* Lawrence: University of Kansas Press, 1973.

McCullough, David. *Truman.* New York: Simon and Schuster, 1992.

McCune, Wesley. *The Farm Bloc.* Garden City, N.Y.: Doubleday, Doran, 1943.

——. *Who's Behind Our Farm Policy?* New York: Frederick A. Praeger, 1956.

McDean, Harry C. "Professionalism, Policy, and Farm Economists in the Early Bureau of Agricultural Economics." *Agricultural History* 57 (January 1983): 64–82.

McDonald, Angus. "Anderson's Program." *New Republic: A Journal of Opinion* 117 (November 10, 1947): 30–32.

——. "Toward a New Plan." *New Republic: A Journal of Opinion* 117 (August 18, 1947): 31.

McPhee, William N., and William A. Glaser, eds. *Public Opinion and Congressional Elections.* Glencoe, Ill.: Free Press, 1962.

Mehren, George. "Farm Problems: II. Agricultural Price Supports. Comparative Costs of Agricultural Price Support in 1949." *American Economic Review* 41 (May 1951): 717–46.

Mezerik, A. G. "The Brannan Plan." *New Republic: A Journal of Opinion* 121 (November 28, 1949): 11–13.

Miller, Merle. *Plain Speaking: An Oral Biography of Harry S. Truman.* New York: Berkley Medallion, 1974.

Mitchell, Broadus. *Depression Decade: From New Era through New Deal, 1929–1941.* Vol. 9. The Economic History of the United States. New York: Rinehart, 1947.

Neal, Steve. *The Eisenhowers.* Lawrence: University Press of Kansas, 1978.

Neustadt, Richard. *Presidential Power: The Politics of Leadership.* New York: John Wiley and Sons, 1960.

"New Aid Ahead for Farmers." *U.S. News* 21 (January 10, 1947): 44–45.

"New Farm Plan Needed." *The Nation* 168 (June 11, 1949): 649–50.

"New Farm Program Is in 'Blueprint Stage.'" *Saturday Evening Post* 219 (June 21, 1947): 160.

Nixon, Richard M. *Memoirs of Richard M. Nixon.* New York: Gossett and Dunlap, 1978.

Nordin, Dennis S., and Roy V. Scott. *From Prairie Farmer to Entrepreneur: The Transformation of Midwestern Agriculture.* Bloomington: Indiana University Press, 2005.

Norris, George W. "The Farmers' Situation, a National Danger." *Current History, a Monthly Magazine* 24 (April 1926): 9–12.

Nourse, Edwin G. "Agriculture in a Stabilized Economy." *Journal of Farm Economics* 31 (February 1949): 201–12.

Nye, Russell B. *Midwestern Progressive Politics: A Historical Study of Its Origins, 1870–1950.* East Lansing, Mich.: Mid State College Press, 1951.

Pach, Chester J., Jr., and Elmo Richardson. *The Presidency of Dwight D. Eisenhower. Revised Edition.* Lawrence: University Press of Kansas, 1991.

Parmet, Herbert S. *The Democrats: The Years after FDR.* New York: Oxford University Press, 1976.

Patterson, James T. *Mr. Republican: A Biography of Robert A. Taft.* Boston: Houghton Mifflin, 1972.

Pemberton, William E. *Bureaucratic Politics: Executive Reorganization during the Truman Administration.* Columbia: University of Missouri Press, 1979.

———. *Harry S. Truman: Fair Dealer and Cold Warrior.* Boston: Twayne Publishers, 1989.

Perkins, Van L. "The AAA and the Politics of Agriculture: Agricultural Policy Formulation in the Fall of 1933." *Agricultural History* 39 (October 1965): 220–29.

Phillips, Cabell. *The Truman Presidency: The History of a Triumphant Succession.* New York: Macmillan, 1966.

Pratt, William C. "The Farmers Union and the 1948 Henry Wallace Campaign." *Annals of Iowa* 49 (Summer 1988): 349–70.

Rasmussen, Wayne D. "The Impact of Technological Change on American Agriculture, 1862–1962." *Journal of Economic History* 22 (December 1962): 578–91.

Rasmussen, Wayne D., and Gladys L. Baker. *The Department of Agriculture.* New York: Praeger Publishers, 1972.

Rasmussen, Wayne D., Gladys L. Baker, and James G. Ward. *A Short History of Agricultural Adjustment, 1933–1975.* Washington, D.C.: Economic Research Service, U.S. Department of Agriculture, 1976.

"Record of the 81st Congress." *Congressional Digest* 30 (January 1951): 15–21.

Rich, Spencer A. *U.S. Agricultural Policy in the Postwar Years, 1945–1963: The Development of U.S. Farm Problems; an Eighteen-Year Legislative Review.* Washington, D.C.: Congressional Quarterly Service, 1963.

Riddick, Floyd M. "The Eighty-First Congress: First and Second Sessions." *Western Political Quarterly* 4 (March 1951): 48–66.

———. "The Eighty-Second Congress: First Session." *Western Political Quarterly* 5 (March 1952): 94–108.

Rohrer, Wayne C., and Louis H. Douglas. *The Agrarian Transition in America: Dualism and Change.* Indianapolis: Bobbs-Merrill, 1969.

Rose, John Kerr. *The Brannan Plan: A Proposed Farm Program.* Washington, D.C.: Public Affairs Bulletin no. 78, April 1950.

Rosenof, Theodore. "The Economic Ideas of Henry A. Wallace, 1933–1948." *Agricultural History* 41 (April 1967): 143–53.

Ross, Irwin. *The Loneliest Campaign: The Truman Victory of 1948.* New York: New American Library, 1968.

Rothstein, Morton. "Farmers Movements and Organizations: Numbers, Gains, Losses." *Agricultural History* 62 (Summer 1988): 161–81.

Rushay, Samuel W. "The Farm Fair Dealer: Charles F. Brannan and American Liberalism." Ph.D. diss., Ohio University, 2000.

Ruttan, Vernon W., Arley D. Waldo, and James P. Houck, eds. *Agricultural Policy in an Affluent Society.* New York: W. W. Norton, 1969.

Ryan, Thomas G. "Farm Prices and the Farm Vote in 1948." *Agricultural History* 54 (July 1980): 387–401.

Salmond, John. *A Southern Rebel: The Life and Times of Aubrey Willis Williams, 1890–1965.* Chapel Hill: University of North Carolina Press, 1983.

Saloutos, Theodore. "Agricultural Organizations and Farm Policy in the South after World War II." *Agricultural History* 53 (January 1979): 377–404.

———. *The American Farmer and the New Deal.* Ames: Iowa State University Press, 1982.

———. "New Deal Agricultural Policy: An Evaluation." *Journal of American History* 61 (September 1974): 394–416.

———. "The New Deal and Farm Policy in the Great Plains." *Agricultural History* 43 (July 1969): 345–55.

Saloutos, Theodore, and John D. Hicks. *Agricultural Discontent in the Middle West, 1900–1939.* Madison: University of Wisconsin Press, 1951.

Scammon, Richard M., comp. and ed. *America Votes: A Handbook of Contemporary American Election Statistics.* New York: Macmillan, 1956.

Schapsmeier, Edward L., and Frederick H. Schapsmeier. *Encyclopedia of American Agricultural History.* Westport, Conn.: Greenwood Press, 1975.

———. *Ezra Taft Benson and the Politics of Agriculture: The Eisenhower Years, 1953–1961.* Danville, Ill.: Interstate Printing and Publishers, 1975.

———. "Farm Policy from FDR to Eisenhower: Southern Democrats and the Politics of Agriculture." *Agricultural History* 53 (January 1979): 352–71.

———. *Henry A. Wallace of Iowa: The Agrarian Years, 1910–1940.* Ames: Iowa State University Press, 1968.

———. *Prophet in Politics: Henry A. Wallace and the War Years, 1940–1965.* Ames: Iowa State University Press, 1970.

Schlebecker, John T. *Cattle Raising on the Plains, 1900–1961.* Lincoln: University of Nebraska Press, 1963.

———. *Whereby We Thrive: A History of American Farming, 1607–1972.* Ames: Iowa State University Press, 1975.

Schlesinger, Arthur M., Jr. *The Age of Roosevelt: The Coming of the New Deal.* Boston: Houghton Mifflin, 1959.

———, ed. *History of U.S. Political Parties: Volume IV, 1945–1972, the Politics of Change.* New York: Chelsea House, 1973.

———. *The Vital Center: The Politics of Freedom.* Boston: Houghton Mifflin, 1949.

Schoenebaum, Eleanora W., ed. *Political Profiles: The Truman Years.* New York: Facts on File, 1978.

Schultz, Theodore W. *Agriculture in an Unstable Economy.* New York: McGraw-Hill, 1945.

————. "Agricultural Price Policy." *Proceedings of the Academy of Political Science* 23 (January 1949): 108–17.

————. *The Economic Organization of Agriculture.* New York: McGraw-Hill, 1953.

————. *Production and Welfare of Agriculture.* New York: Macmillan, 1949.

————. "That Turbulent Brannan Plan." *Farm Policy Forum* 3 (February 1950): 5–8.

Schuyler, Michael W. *The Dread of Plenty: Agricultural Relief Activities of the Federal Government in the Middle West, 1933–1939.* Manhattan, Kans.: Sunflower University Press, 1989.

Shepherd, Geoffrey S. *Agricultural Price Policy.* Ames: Iowa State College Press, 1947.

————."Sizing Up the New Farm Price Law." *Farm Policy Forum* 2 (January 1949): 61–64.

Shideler, James H. *Farm Crisis, 1919–1923.* Los Angeles: University of California Press, 1957.

Shover, John L. "Populism in the Nineteen-Thirties: The Battle for the AAA." *Agricultural History* 39 (January 1965): 17–24.

Sitkoff, Harvard. "Years of the Locust, Interpretations of the Truman Presidency since 1965." In *The Truman Period as a Research Field: A Reappraisal, 1972,* edited by Richard S. Kirkendall. Columbia: University of Missouri Press, 1974.

Slichter, Gertrude Almy. "Franklin D. Roosevelt and the Farm Problem, 1929–1932." *Mississippi Valley Historical Review* 43 (September 1956): 238–58.

Smith, Richard Norton. *Thomas E. Dewey and His Times.* New York: Simon and Schuster, 1982.

Smith, Russell. "The Brannan Plan: Counterattack in Favor." *Antioch Review* 10 (Spring 1950): 62–83.

Socolofsky, Homer E. *Arthur Capper: Publisher, Politician, and Philanthropist.* Lawrence: University of Kansas Press, 1962.

Soth, Lauren. "Conflicts in Farm-Price Policy." *Antioch Review* 9 (Spring 1949): 60–66.

————. *The Farm Policy Game Play by Play.* Ames: Iowa State University Press, 1989.

————. *Farm Troubles.* Princeton: Princeton University Press, 1957.

Soule, George. *Prosperity Decade: From War to Depression: 1917–1929.* Vol. 8. The Economic History of the United States. New York: Rinehart, 1947.

"Test for the Brannan Plan." *Newsweek* 35 (March 20, 1950): 25–26.

Tontz, Robert L. "Membership of General Farmers' Organizations, United States, 1874–1960." *Agricultural History* 38 (July 1964): 143–56.

Truman, David B. *The Congressional Party: A Case Study.* New York: John Wiley and Sons, 1959.

Truman, Harry S. "Capitalism on Trial: Responsibilities Rest on Business, Labor, Farmer, and Government." *Vital Speeches of the Day* 13 (May 1, 1947): 423–25.

————. *Memoirs by Harry S. Truman: Year of Decisions.* Vol. 1. Garden City, N.Y.: Doubleday, 1955.

————. *Memoirs by Harry S. Truman: Years of Trial and Hope.* Vol. 2. Garden City, N.Y.: Doubleday, 1956.

————. *Mr. Citizen.* New York: Bernard Geis Associates, 1953.

Tucker, William P. "Populism Up-to-Date." *Agricultural History* 21 (July 1947): 198

Tweeten, Luther. *Foundations of Farm Policy.* 2nd ed. Lincoln: University of Nebraska Press, 1979.

Underhill, Robert. *The Truman Persuasions.* Ames: Iowa State University Press, 1981.

Vogeler, Ingolf. *The Myth of the Family Farm: Agribusiness Dominance of U.S. Agriculture.* Boulder: Westview Press, 1981.

Wallace, Henry C. *Our Debt and Duty to the Farmer.* New York: Century Company, 1925.

"Why Farmers Swung to Truman." *U.S. News* 25 (November 19, 1948): 23–24.

Wilcox, Walter W. *The Farmer in the Second World War.* Ames: Iowa State College Press, 1947.

Wilcox, Walter W., and Willard W. Cochrane. *Economics of American Agriculture.* 2nd ed. Englewood Cliffs, N.J.: Prentice-Hall, 1974.

Wilcox, Walter W., Willard W. Cochrane, and Robert W. Herdt. *Eco-*

nomics of American Agriculture. 3rd ed. Englewood Cliffs, N.J.: Prentice-Hall, 1974.

Williams, Herbert Lee. *The Newspaperman's President: Harry S Truman.* Chicago: Nelson-Hall, 1984.

Winsberg, Morton D. "Agricultural Specialization in the United States since World War II." *Agricultural History* 56 (October 1982): 692–701.

Wood, Junius B. "Seed Beds of Socialism: No. 3: Department of Agriculture." *Nation's Business* 38 (December 1950): 54–60.

"Would the 'Brannan Plan' be a Sound National Farm Policy?" *Congressional Digest* 29 (March 1950): 82–96.

Yarnell, Allen. *Democrats and Progressives: The 1948 Presidential Election as a Test of Postwar Liberalism.* Berkeley: University of California Press, 1974.

INDEX

Page references for photographs are in bold.